FROM THE SHADOWS

FROM THE SHADOWS

THE ARCHITECTURE AND AFTERLIFE OF NICHOLAS HAWKSMOOR

OWEN HOPKINS

REAKTION BOOKS

To admirers of Hawksmoor's architecture – past, present and future

Published by Reaktion Books Ltd
Unit 32, Waterside
44–48 Wharf Road
London N1 7UX, UK
www.reaktionbooks.co.uk

First published 2015
Copyright © Owen Hopkins 2015

Printed and bound in China by 1010 Printing International Ltd

A catalogue record for this book is available from the British Library

ISBN 978 1 78023 515 8

CONTENTS

INTRODUCTION
THE MAN AND THE MYTH

GETTING OFF THE TRAIN at Radlett, we see little that suggests any connection with one of Britain's greatest architects. Despite the town's location on the important Roman road of Watling Street, and in particular on the stretch linking London to the major settlement of Verulamium (now St Albans), Radlett is largely a nineteenth-century creation. Like many Hertfordshire towns its history is inextricably tied to the advent of the railways. And this is confirmed by the size of its station: far larger than a village of this size would seem to need and, indeed, for the few passengers who alight with us.

We wheel our bikes through the station, pause briefly to check the map and then set off towards the rather ominous sounding Shenley Hill. Sure enough, it proves too steep for our city bikes to handle and we end up pushing them up the final third. At the top, amid a group of late twentieth-century houses and an adjacent golf course, the low undulating hills of the surrounding countryside come into view. This is a strange part of the country, just a few miles north of where London abruptly ends and the Green Belt begins. But London's magnetic attraction is still in full force here, with many local people spending their mornings and evenings commuting to jobs in the nearby metropolis.

The other side of Shenley Hill proves longer and less steep, and after about a mile or so of easy riding we come to Shenley itself. There is hardly anyone about, even the supermarket car park we pass is near-deserted. Shenley's history stretches further back than

Hawksmoor's bust at All Souls College, Oxford.

Radlett's and the village is actually mentioned in the Domesday Book. Today Shenley mainly consists of streets of unremarkable houses laid out around the old country estate of Porters Park, where, it is said, Hawksmoor lived for a short time towards the end of his life. The much altered mansion and outbuildings are now houses and flats. We skirt around the village and head north towards our destination of Shenleybury. The suffix 'bury' (or borough) on a place name is a corruption of the Old English word 'burh', meaning a fortified site. No sign of any fortifications remain though, and today Shenleybury is barely even a hamlet.

Peter Buttle by Hawksmoor's grave in St Botolph's churchyard, Shenleybury.

Descending the hill from Shenley quite rapidly, we slam on our brakes as a churchyard appears on our right. Upon crossing the road, we see a large church emerge from behind the trees. We are greeted by Maureen Buttle, who is mowing the lawn – 'the first chance this year', she says – while her two Labradors look on inquisitively. Maureen and her husband, Peter, live in the former parish church of St Botolph. Dating originally from the early fifteenth century, the church has been altered many times over its history, and especially during the nineteenth century. Despite its Victorian embellishments, we still get a sense of the original simple grandeur of the nave in which Maureen and Peter live.

Soon Peter appears and takes us through the garden to the church's east end. 'Well, that's it', he says, sensing we might perhaps be a little underwhelmed by what we have come to see. Lying before us is a large rectangular slab of black marble flecked with the piercing red berries of a nearby yew tree. The gravestone is dark, grubby and covered with lichen, but there is a name, barely legible, though unmistakable: HAWKSMOOR.

We crouch down to try to read the full inscription, but are hampered by a large crack that runs diagonally across the centre of the slab, which has been filled by what, alas, looks very much like concrete. It seems likely this fissure was caused by the roots of the yew tree – which Peter reports to have 'recently taken care of' – gradually undermining the slab that originally probably sat flat on the ground.[1] Now, though, it is raised on a three-brick-high base and, as one of the few graves in what is now Maureen and Peter's garden, receives far better care than at probably any time in its history – at least before St Botolph's conversion into a house in the mid-1970s.

Little can be done, however, to reverse nearly three centuries of erosion and we have to trace the Latin inscription with our fingers:

P M S

L

Hic J[acet]

NICHOLAUS HAWKSMOOR Amr

ARCHITECTUS

obijt vicesimo quin[t]o die [Martii]

Annon Domini 1736

Ætatis 75

'Here lies Nicholas Hawksmoor Esq., Architect, died on the 20th day of March, 1736, aged 75'. Kerry Downes, writer of a pioneering monograph on Hawksmoor, suggests that P M S L might stand for *Piae memoriae sacer locus*, which roughly translates as 'A sacred place of pious memory'.[2] It is a brief and seemingly unremarkable inscription, but one that accords with the simple, yet exactly wrought, grandeur of the slab.

Unsurprisingly, Hawksmoor's grave receives few visitors. A coach group of slightly bemused Friends of Christ Church, Spitalfields, paid a visit a few years previously, Peter recalls. But most of the few who do visit the churchyard come to pay their respects to Graham Hill, the two-time Formula One World Champion, who was buried there after his death in a plane crash in 1975. Peter remembers that Hill's son, Damon, the 1996 Formula One World Champion, visited a few years back, arriving on a motorbike.

London's pull

Almost a world away from his best-known buildings, Hawksmoor's grave is so off the beaten track that it would be hard to come across it by chance. Yet that is what happened to the poet and Hawksmoor aficionado Iain Sinclair while he was circumnavigating the metropolis for his book *London Orbital* (2002). Sinclair describes how he more or less 'stumbles' across Porters Park, where Hawksmoor had lived – or rather, as he more tantalisingly put it, stumbled across his half-forgotten knowledge that Hawksmoor had lived there.

After making a few enquiries as to this fact, Sinclair was, of course, soon pointed in the direction of Hawksmoor's grave. But judging by his words, it was something of a disappointment: 'as unspectacular as a deepfreeze unit . . . No pyramids, no decorative motifs, no Masonic symbols'.[3] Despite the grave being a far cry – in location and appearance – from the high-flown eclecticism of Hawksmoor's churches that he knew so well, Sinclair was, however, clearly struck by the affecting plainness and magnetism of the site:

> I couldn't disassociate the man from his chain of East London churches, from city and river . . . St Botolph's was certainly a sacred place. Hawksmoor's grave, along with Temple Bar, were the beacons of our walk; heavily freighted memorials that had been allowed to pull away from the centre.[4]

It seems strange that an architect whose work was so closely entwined with London – and at the moment when it emerged as the world's first modern city – came to be buried in the countryside. But in retrospect Hawksmoor's motivations for taking an estate like Porters Park, and his subsequent burial at Shenleybury, are relatively easy to comprehend. For an architect who struggled throughout his career to gain the recognition and positions his talents deserved, a country estate was an important symbol of his hard-earned social and financial achievements. Despite his preoccupation with the city in both theory and practice over his lifetime, Hawksmoor had a deep affinity with the countryside and what it represented. His will made this clear, stipulating that he was to be buried 'in Shenley church yard in the county of Hertford or in some other church yard belonging to some other village'.[5]

Hawksmoor was largely forgotten soon after his death, his architecture overlooked, and his grave passing into the background of an otherwise unremarkable Hertfordshire churchyard. This fate was in stark contrast to that of Hawksmoor's mentor and collaborator, Sir Christopher Wren. After his death in 1723, Wren's remains were interred in the crypt of his great masterwork, St Paul's Cathedral, where they remain to this day. An inscribed plaque makes explicit the link between this great national monument and its architect: *Lector si monumentum requiris circumspice* ('Reader – if you seek his monument – look around you'). Such is St Paul's importance as a symbol of London – and of the nation itself – there remained little chance Wren would be forgotten, even when his architecture fell out of fashion.

Contemplating the return ride to Radlett and the journey back to London, we ponder what might have been – if Hawksmoor had had his own St Paul's would he have been lost to the vagaries of history quite so quickly after his death? We'll never know, of course, but in any case the story of Hawksmoor's descent, and much later rehabilitation, revival and rebirth is rather more complicated.

Just before we leave St Botolph's, Maureen recounts a story of accompanying her son on a school trip to St Paul's. As the trip's guide explained to the children about the building and the important part played by one of Wren's assistants called Nicholas Hawksmoor, Maureen's son suddenly exclaimed, 'He's buried in my garden!' With a wry smile, Maureen then proceeded to explain to a somewhat startled guide that, yes, he actually was.

Shadows

The modesty of Hawksmoor's grave is in some ways a fitting reflection of a man who was modest in life too. Hawksmoor's architectural imagination soared to heights that few others could hope to reach, yet he remained humble, unassuming and even rather reticent when it came to promoting his talents and the politicking required to secure the best positions. Part of this was due to the fact that, unlike Wren or Sir John Vanbrugh, Hawksmoor was a commoner of lowly origin without access to the elevated social circles in which his more famous colleagues moved. Nevertheless, he almost actively avoided the limelight, hoping his designs would, instead, speak for themselves. It was here, in the shadows, that Hawksmoor remained after his death, only to re-emerge in the first few decades of the twentieth century and begin a remarkable ascent to the very summit of British architectural history.

This book charts that story. It explores how and why Hawksmoor came to design some of the most striking buildings of his day and the ways they have haunted generations of observers. The starting point is Hawksmoor's formation as an architect while working in Wren's office. What he learned from Wren, on both a practical and conceptual level, proved invaluable when he came to work with the untrained Vanbrugh, a charming and charismatic figure who helped feed Hawksmoor's powerful architectural imagination. To a greater extent than perhaps any other architect of the period, Hawksmoor's architecture was eclectic and allusive, drawing from sources that ranged across time and place – especially in his six great London churches. For Hawksmoor, the classical language of arches, columns and mouldings that he learned from Wren was just the starting point for a deeper, almost sculptural understanding of architecture, one of raw form and mass and elemental effects of light and shadow.

We might, therefore, understand Hawksmoor's as an architecture literally built from the shadows – and it is this idea that gives this book its title. But in a metaphorical sense, it also suggests how, as a historical personality, Hawksmoor remained hidden for so long, before finally stepping into the spotlight for the first time in the decades following the Second World War. His reputation certainly suffered by not having a prominent monument to his architectural genius in the way that Wren or even Vanbrugh had. And clearly Hawksmoor's social status, personality and retiring character played a part too. But there was little he could do to avoid the fact that even before his death, architectural taste had changed fundamentally. The turn towards Palladian architecture in the 1720s saw some of his buildings under sometimes vociferous attack, even before their completion.

Hawksmoor's achievements were soon forgotten, decisively shaping how he and his buildings were viewed over history – what this book calls his 'afterlife'.

Afterlife

Unlike most studies of an architect or, indeed, any historical figure, this book does not end with its subject's death. Instead, that event stands as the pivotal juncture in the story that gives equal weight to both 'life' and 'afterlife'. With his reputation 'buried' by his Palladian opponents, Hawksmoor barely got a look-in for the remainder of the eighteenth century, while in the nineteenth he fared little better. Hawksmoor's work was noticed by important figures like Sir John Soane and J.M.W. Turner, but he remained peripheral – a 'pupil' of his more famous contemporaries, Wren and Vanbrugh. Few imagined that an architect of such humble origin as Hawksmoor could have been any more than a mere assistant to his more esteemed colleagues, let alone be an architectural genius in his own right.

It was really only in the twentieth century that people began to look seriously at Hawksmoor's work again. The re-emergence of interest in Hawksmoor was played out against the backdrop of changes in architectural taste and, specifically, the concerted attempts to demolish his church of St Mary Woolnoth in the City of London, his most prominently sited building. As attitudes to the past evolved – and to architectural heritage in particular – people began to look anew at Hawksmoor's work. After the Second World War Hawksmoor received serious scholarly attention for the first time, while campaigns were launched to restore some of his best-known buildings. Architects schooled in the modernist tradition but looking to move beyond it – including major figures from Denys Lasdun and Alison and Peter Smithson to Robert Venturi and James Stirling – began to take inspiration from his buildings and also from his example as an architect prepared to trust his own instincts over subservience to taste or fashion.

Hawksmoor's architecture resonated for different people in different ways, and the appeal of his work was not simply confined to architects and enthusiasts. An important part of the story is the way artists, who began to be attracted to London's East End during the 1970s, saw Hawksmoor's churches as powerful markers in a run-down and forgotten cityscape. Several writers became fascinated by the contrast between the churches and their surroundings and delved into the murky histories of the East End in order to forge seductive mythologies around them and their architect. Peter Ackroyd's novel *Hawksmoor* (1985) is the most famous product of this, where the historical figure of Hawksmoor was co-opted into a fantastical tale of devil worship and the occult. The comparative absence of biographical information about Hawksmoor provided a vacuum which Ackroyd and others were able to fill with myth and mysticism. Yet Ackroyd never lost sight of the rare power of Hawksmoor's buildings, in particular the way in which they emerge literally and symbolically from the shadows. In this passage, for example, we hear Nicholas Dyer – Hawksmoor's evil doppelgänger – explaining to his assistant how

> the art of Shaddowes you must know well, Walter . . . It is only the Darknesse that can give trew Forme to our Work and trew Perspective to our Fabrick, for there is no Light without Darknesse and no Substance without Shaddowe.[6]

Reputations

The trajectory of Hawksmoor's reputation in both life and the afterlife reveals how views of an architect and his work are always inherently mutable. What is remarkable about Hawksmoor's story is the extreme contrast: from barely existing as a creative personality at all during the nineteenth century, to his position today as one of the greats of British architectural history. Hawksmoor's renown now extends well beyond the relatively narrow confines of architectural or London history, and thanks in no small way to the mythology that has grown up around him and his work this recognition has crossed over into mainstream public consciousness. If you asked someone walking down the street to name one British architect past or present, chances are they would answer: 'Christopher Wren'. Richard Rogers, Norman Foster and, among a younger generation, possibly

Zaha Hadid, would probably run Wren close, so successful have these architects been in self-promotion. Hawksmoor, however, would not be far behind – and that is an astonishing transformation.

Among the generation of British and American architects trained in the 1950s and 1960s, Hawksmoor is regularly cited as a significant figure; and for some he is even something of an 'architectural hero'. This interest among architects remains unabated. In 2012 the Venice Architecture Biennale included an exhibition of seductive black-and-white photographs of Hawksmoor's churches by the contemporary architectural photographer Hélène Binet.[7] While Binet's photographs were certainly stunning in their formal composition and tonal simplicity, arguably the most remarkable thing for someone already familiar with Hawksmoor's work was the exhibition's very presence at the Biennale.

For an observer with stakes in both the contemporary and historical, the exhibition stood as a powerful reminder of how reputations, taste and opinion are shaped, strengthened and, ultimately, propagated. What was it saying that Binet felt able to turn her lens towards an eighteenth-century British architect and away, if only temporarily, from usual subjects like David Chipperfield and Peter Zumthor? The exhibition's underlying message was that Hawksmoor belonged on the same elevated plane as these contemporary masters – in a crude sense, Hawksmoor was being inducted into a retrospective 'Hall of Fame', standing shoulder to shoulder with other so-called 'starchitects'. The mere presence of the exhibition at this international architecture jamboree, otherwise focused on contemporary practice, was an unambiguous statement that Hawksmoor was an architect to be revered – and one with something to offer the contemporary moment.

The lens effect

What became abundantly clear to me while visiting the exhibition and the rest of the Biennale's vast array of displays and installations was the deceptively simple idea that, whether we realize it or not, we are always viewing an architect and his or her work through multiple lenses. Some of those lenses may be thick and heavily distorting, in

Hélène Binet, *Christ Church, Spitalfields,* 2012.

effect distancing us from a building and its architect. Others may serve in actually focusing our attention on a particular architect or building. Over time these lenses become internalized, and sometimes without us noticing they begin to shape our visual sensibilities. So what we think of as natural proclivities, predisposing us to respond in certain ways to particular styles or materials, are actually socially and culturally constructed. This obviously affects how we see all architecture – and much else besides. But there is scarcely a more fascinating example than that of Hawksmoor to explore how dramatically views of an architect's work can shift in and out of focus over history.

In thinking about this idea of multiple lenses we also need to address the notion of taste – an important theme that runs throughout this book. Taste is, of course, a slippery and contested idea, and chapter Three explores a very particular understanding of taste that was developed in the early eighteenth century. For now, however, we might consider taste as it is popularly conceived: as a predilection towards what is currently in vogue, as the sustaining impulse of fashion.

Though we might see taste and fashion as entirely formed from commercial imperatives, they do sometimes derive from a far wider set of circumstances and phenomena. As the critic Jonathan Meades has commented in a recent television show examining the polarities in taste provoked by Brutalist architecture,

> not all fashions, not all crazes, not all fads, not all tastes, not even all religions, are blatantly mercantile creations. Some, the worthwhile minority, are borne of commonality, of harmonious unison, of a thread of juncture, of a complex combination of circumstance, chance and coincidence.[8]

Perhaps the most obvious example of this, and one which had a particular bearing on how Hawksmoor's work was viewed, was the Victorian taste for Gothic architecture. Though it became highly fashionable in a whole host of contexts, it had complex and contradictory origins. The Gothic Revival, as it is now known, was bound up with ideas of Christian morality, the historical foundations of individual liberty and national identity, anxieties about the social destabilization caused by the Industrial Revolution, as well as the new structural possibilities offered by innovative building technologies and engineering. When Victorians looked at Georgian churches they did so with quite a different set of eyes to those of the churches' builders – and, indeed, people today. To the Victorians, Georgian churches were plain, echoing boxes, little suited to the liturgy they practised; in many ways this begins to explain how and why so many, including several of Hawksmoor's, were often drastically altered.

In exploring the very different ways people have valued Hawksmoor and his work over history – and considering how and why they might have formed particular opinions at particular moments – it becomes obvious that taste and fashion play major roles. But we also need to account, more broadly, for the ways the building types with which Hawksmoor was principally concerned – churches, public buildings, country houses and university buildings – have themselves undergone considerable change. The complex registers of ideas, associations and memories they embody are in constant and, at times, quite obvious states of flux. Meanwhile, the social, political, economic and, of course, urban contexts around Hawksmoor's works have also changed fundamentally. The latter is of particular importance in regard to Hawksmoor's churches, especially Christ Church, Spitalfields, the rebirth of which, begun in the mid-1970s only to be completed in the early 2000s, was closely related to the change in fortunes of its surrounding area.

Despite the close links at this particular moment, even at the nadir of Hawksmoor's reputation, his buildings – Christ Church included – were frequently seen as distinct from their surroundings, physically and symbolically, and evaded stylistic categorization. While the changing lenses of taste and fashion have played an important part in shaping views of Hawksmoor's architecture over time, they are far from the whole story. For those who have ever laid eyes on them, Hawksmoor's buildings retain a strong, often emotional and sometimes overwhelming hold. At no point in their history have they stood as passive structures, with the way people see them shaped solely by external factors of taste, fashion and changing contexts. Arresting in scale, materials and, vitally, design, Hawksmoor's architecture was always intended to stand out and apart, and this has ensured that the buildings themselves have always played an active role in determining how they are seen and thought of.

How we view Hawksmoor's architecture, therefore, derives from the complex interaction between the lens effect and the sheer intensity of his buildings. This interaction has ensured that the story of how Hawksmoor's architecture has been viewed over history is a remarkably vivid one, perhaps more so than for any other architect. This interaction also means, importantly, that the book's two halves of life and afterlife, separated by the juncture of Hawksmoor's death, should not be considered in isolation, but as part of the same continuous story. When we come to Hawksmoor's architecture 'creation' and 'reception' are not mutually exclusive, but reciprocal – this stands as a powerful theme that runs through the whole book. How we view Hawksmoor's buildings is shaped by what we bring with us, but also by their innate ability to intrigue and inspire, perplex and provoke, appear timeless yet very much of their moment. From the vantage point of history, this is how we must try to understand them.

Synchronicity

By exploring both life and afterlife with equal measure, there are some interesting parallels between this book and Ackroyd's *Hawksmoor*, which is set simultaneously in the early eighteenth century and 1985. Central to Ackroyd's book is the idea of synchronicity – the temporal connection between different events that appear to be otherwise unrelated. Ever present across both these time periods are Hawksmoor's churches, which act as magnets for dark deeds whose origins seem, at least on the surface, to be entirely separate. Similarly, in the present book, the buildings themselves act as the constant touchstones for the wide-ranging and otherwise unconnected narratives, stories and people they weave together.

Ackroyd's book was largely shunned by architectural historians, who saw its myth-making as overshadowing the real Hawksmoor and the tangible, architectural qualities of his work. Yet looking back thirty years, Ackroyd's novel is now an inescapable part of Hawksmoor's story, whether we like it or not, playing a part in shaping how he is viewed today. For all its mysticism, however, Ackroyd's book would have been impossible, at least not in the form it took, without the solid historical research undertaken by various scholars from the late 1940s onwards, which has played a key role in Hawksmoor's rise to prominence. Although some gaps remain, as they always do, we now have a good understanding of Hawksmoor's career, the chronology of the design and construction of his buildings, and his interactions with clients and patrons. This is thanks in large part to Kerry Downes's monograph of 1959, with a revised second edition in 1979, as well as his more compact *Hawksmoor*, published in 1969 in Thames & Hudson's World of Art series and still in print. More recently Vaughan

Hart's *Nicholas Hawksmoor: Rebuilding Ancient Wonders* (2002) has provided a detailed exploration of the sources of Hawksmoor's architecture, while Pierre de la Ruffinière du Prey's *Hawksmoor's London Churches*, which appeared two years before, offers a compelling analysis of their theological context.

This book, then, draws in various ways from the insights and discoveries of these earlier studies. But rather than providing a summary, it poses several new interpretations of Hawksmoor's work, while more broadly seeking to trace links between Hawksmoor's career and the trajectory of his posthumous reputation – between 'life' and 'afterlife'. Hawksmoor's death in 1736 provides the natural split in a largely chronological account, though this does not prevent various – we might say – synchronic connections to be drawn out across the book's two halves. We begin with Hawksmoor's development as an architect under the tutelage of Wren and in particular his work as a draughtsman at St Paul's Cathedral. This training in both the practical and more theoretical aspects of architecture paved the way for Hawksmoor's collaboration with Vanbrugh at Castle Howard and subsequently at Blenheim Palace.

All this was brought to bear when, at the height of his powers, Hawksmoor came to design the six London churches for which he is now best remembered. Many theories have been put forward attempting to explain the unique appearance of Hawksmoor's churches. I analyse them in urban terms, relating the way Hawksmoor drew from various aspects of architectural history to the need for his designs to stand out in a context where conventional, classical architecture was relatively widespread. Such grand architectural statements were unlikely to escape comment or, indeed, criticism, and it is here that I begin to chart the decline of Hawksmoor's reputation even before his death amid the rise, during the 1720s, of the more reserved Palladian taste. Afflicted in his later years by frequent bouts of gout, Hawksmoor suffered various professional ignominies as others usurped his positions and his ideas were ignored or passed over. It was, therefore, testament to his sheer force of will, and faith in his own ideas, that during this time he managed to realize the Mausoleum at Castle Howard – one of the great buildings of the eighteenth century.

Standing atop a windswept Yorkshire hill, the Mausoleum is a fitting emblem for Hawksmoor's architectural genius; its lonely position symbolizes the isolation that Hawksmoor's reputation was to face for much of the next two centuries. Picking up this thread with Hawksmoor's death in 1736, the second half of this book, like the first, is arranged in a broadly chronological and episodic manner, examining the history of how people have viewed and responded to Hawksmoor's buildings up to the present day. This study brings to light the many guises under which Hawksmoor has lived: as Wren's less-talented assistant, an idiosyncratic genius, proto-postmodernist or the mysterious occultist. Its method, therefore, is a combinatory one: bringing together literary and urban history, architectural and art history, newspaper clippings and exhibition reviews, political speeches, personal correspondence and several interviews. The story is textured and multilayered, focused on responses to Hawksmoor and his work but also conscious of how they fit into broader cultural trends, such as the new attitudes to architectural heritage and alternatives to mainstream modernist architecture that became important in the 1950s and 1960s.

While this book is about Hawksmoor, its implications run much wider. The way our impressions of buildings derive from their direct effect on our senses and emotions, mediated by taste and fashion, is, of course, not confined to looking at Hawksmoor's architecture. But his powerful example does, however, pose a number of broader and fundamental questions about the ways in which we understand the architecture of the past and what relevance it might hold for us today. So, while the book makes us look again at Hawksmoor, it also invites us to reconsider how we think about architecture and architects as historical personalities, both ones of the living past and those who have been dead for centuries.

Thinking back to our visit to Shenleybury, it was impossible to look at the black marble slab in an anonymous Hertfordshire village without imagining his soaring London churches, the energy of his north quadrangle at All Souls College, Oxford, and the darkly brooding presence of the Mausoleum at Castle Howard. Unlike his modest grave, Hawksmoor's buildings speak for themselves. Their language, though, is not an easy one to comprehend. Visiting the grave not only strengthened my desire to understand it, but to find out about others who have tried: those who castigated Hawksmoor's architecture, were bemused by it, ignored it, rediscovered it, saved it, mythologized it, and, above all, those who have been enraptured by its strange power. This book is that story.

ONE

EMERGENCE

'ARCHITECTURE AIMS AT ETERNITY', wrote Sir Christopher Wren, in what is arguably his most famous remark. Beginning his career as a scientist before turning to architecture, Wren dominated the English architectural scene for almost five decades. It was Hawksmoor's great fortune to come into contact with, to be taken on by and eventually become apprentice to such a towering figure in British architecture. If there was one overriding thing Hawksmoor took from his master, it was his remarkable sense of ambition. Both sought in related, though at times also quite differing, ways to render in stone the glories past – and those yet to come – of their nation and its capital city.

This chapter is about Hawksmoor's emergence as an architect and in particular the influences and ideas that shaped his architectural outlook. Two major figures played a part: Wren, whose tutelage was highly formative for the aspiring Hawksmoor; and Sir John Vanbrugh, the playwright turned architect, whose influence is more difficult to trace, but was arguably no less important. We examine what little is known of Hawksmoor's early life and explore through his involvement at St Paul's Cathedral how he 'came of age' as a designer in Wren's office, one of the most creative working environments of British architectural history.

The freedom that Wren allowed Hawksmoor working in his office was perhaps due to the thoroughness of the training he gave his pupil. Wren imparted in Hawksmoor a deep understanding of the practical and theoretical aspects of architecture; if we want to understand Hawksmoor as an architect, we need, therefore, to get to grips with Wren. Nevertheless, Hawksmoor quickly began to forge his own architectural identity, and his important collaboration and friendship with Vanbrugh would act as a kind of catalyst for Hawksmoor's explorations of the imaginative possibilities of the very essence of architectural form.

The backdrop to both Wren and Hawksmoor's careers was a particularly tumultuous and critical moment in national history; and one cannot separate their architectural achievements from this historical context. Even after the end of the years of Commonwealth with the restoration of the monarchy in 1660, the political and religious turmoil did not abate, continuing well into the eighteenth century. Yet, during this time the bedrock was being laid for Britain's emergence as the world's first modern nation state, which would see it become the great imperial superpower of the eighteenth and nineteenth centuries.

Amid the tumults at the higher echelons of politics and power, dramatic social, economic, cultural and intellectual transformations were moving apace. After the calamity of the Great Fire of 1666, London was rebuilt anew, reaffirming and strengthening its position as a trading powerhouse. Speculative property development became increasingly common, and provided decent, standardized houses for the well-to-do merchant classes. Coffee-houses sprang up and became popular places for debate and discussion among men of a surprisingly wide social standing. One such establishment, Lloyd's Coffee House on Tower Street, began what would become the Lloyd's of London insurance market.

The most significant economic change arose almost by accident. The state's parlous finances in the 1690s led to the incorporation of the Bank of England, which oversaw the centralized issuing of banknotes and the de facto establishment of the national debt. Meanwhile at Gresham College, the Royal Society – the world's first learned society dedicated to the pursuit of scientific understanding – met regularly to discuss pioneering ideas in the realm of natural philosophy (what we would today call natural or physical science). The investigations of figures such as Robert Boyle, Robert Hooke, Isaac Newton and Wren himself sought to establish both theoretical and practical models to understand natural phenomena. Their study of the movement of comets, the possibilities of lenses and magnification, and the properties of tensile bodies, among many other areas of interest, challenged established truths, putting the Royal Society, and London itself, firmly on the map as a centre of intellectual endeavour.

Wren was embedded in this complex and dynamic world. A well-connected gentlemen with impeccable royalist credentials, he was fortunate to have the ear of the monarch at various moments in his career as both scientist and architect. As a leading figure of the Royal Society during much of the second half of the seventeenth century, he was deeply engaged with its methods, discoveries and its members, and formed a close working relationship with his fellow scientist-architect, Robert Hooke. Wren and Hooke led the rebuilding of London's City churches: Wren as commissioner and Hooke as surveyor. This, along with Wren's near 50-year project at St Paul's Cathedral, put him close to the fast-moving world of commerce, one quite distinct from the realm of the court.

Wren's intellect, achievements and social status as a gentleman meant that he overshadowed Hawksmoor, a commoner of lowly origins, in both life and death. Yet, when seeking to consider Hawksmoor as a historical personality in his own right, we cannot ignore Wren's role in the story. It was Wren who plucked Hawksmoor out of obscurity and moulded him as an architect, so that by the mid-1690s he was familiar with all aspects of designing and constructing the most ambitious of buildings, and predisposed to working collaboratively. Hawksmoor was one of the best-trained architects Britain had ever seen.

So in 1699 when Sir John Vanbrugh, the soldier, playwright and then lately-turned architect, came calling for professional assistance for Castle Howard, the stupendous country house commission he had just landed, Hawksmoor was the obvious man. In terms of personality, Vanbrugh was in many ways Hawksmoor's opposite: flamboyant, outgoing, sociable and very well-connected. Despite these differences, the two quickly formed a close and incredibly fruitful working relationship that was to yield Castle Howard and Blenheim Palace. There was considerable crossover in how Hawksmoor and Vanbrugh conceived architecture, though this was often manifested in different ways. While

Wren acted as a more typical 'mentor' for Hawksmoor, Vanbrugh, we will see, was more of a confidant or catalyst, who helped unleash the creative force of Hawksmoor's architectural imagination.

Beginnings

Nicholas Hawksmoor was born, we think, in 1662.[1] The date of his birth is traditionally thought to have been 1661, an assumption based not unreasonably on the inscription carved into his tombstone. Such inscriptions are, however, not always accurate and doubt still remains.

We do, however, know for certain *where* Hawksmoor was born: East Drayton, Nottinghamshire. His father, a husbandman, also called Nicholas, disappears from the records after 1665. His mother, widowed, it seems, not long after the younger Nicholas's birth, later married William Theaker. Little else is known of Hawksmoor's familial circumstances or, indeed, his early life. His obituary, written by his son-in-law, Nathaniel Blackerby, noted that he was 'bred a scholar', and as his career bore out, Hawksmoor was clearly familiar with the classics, French, possibly Italian too, and had an understanding of applied mathematics.[2] In any case, Hawksmoor's early education must have been sufficient enough for him to be useful to the Doncaster justice Samuel Mellish, who took him on as a clerk. From Mellish's charge, Hawksmoor was then employed by the celebrated plasterer Edward Gouge, under whom he went to London as an eighteen-year-old and met Sir Christopher Wren.[3]

By about 1680, Wren was firmly established as the principal figure driving London's rebuilding projects. As Lisa Jardine writes in her excellent biography of the architect,

> Wren's distinction as the King's architect and a combination
> of his personal charisma in the design process, his leader-
> ship of his office and the sheer quantity of work they had
> produced meant that in the public sphere his professional
> identity as an architect was formidable.[4]

Wren had already served as the Surveyor of the King's Works for over a decade, having been appointed following the death of the former incumbent, Sir John Denham, in 1669.[5] Following the Great Fire of London, the City Churches Rebuilding Act of 1670 had put Wren formally in charge of rebuilding the city's churches, ably assisted by Hooke and Edward Woodroffe, and he was officially named the architect for the rebuilding of St Paul's Cathedral when the royal charter was finally issued in 1673.[6] By 1680, St Paul's was beginning to rise, most of London's churches were under way and some were already nearing completion.[7]

London and St Paul's were not the only focuses of Wren's architectural attention at this time or, for that matter, any other. By the early 1680s, he had already completed the chapel at Pembroke College, Cambridge, the Sheldonian Theatre in Oxford and throughout the 1670s was further engaged in Cambridge with the library at Trinity College and designing a new chapel and courtyard range at Emmanuel College.

Despite these already substantial achievements, Wren's private life had been in a state of upheaval. In 1669 he married Faith Coghill, who bore him two sons: Gilbert, named after Archbishop Sheldon, who died in 1674 before reaching the age of two; and Christopher, born in 1675.[8] Shortly after Christopher's birth, Faith succumbed to smallpox.[9] Wren remarried two years later, in 1677. Jane, his second wife, bore Wren two children: Jane, born soon after their marriage; and, two years later, in 1679, William, who suffered from a mental disability throughout his life. Soon after William's birth, Wren's second wife died.

This was the environment – one of professional success yet of personal tragedy – that met Hawksmoor when he joined Wren's household as his personal clerk in 1680. What did Wren see in the young, eighteen-year-old Hawksmoor at this moment? It is impossible to know for sure. Hawksmoor was relatively well educated and already had some experience as a clerk. It is unlikely at this stage that Wren glimpsed – or, indeed, was looking for – any particular architectural skill or talent in whoever he took on. Hawksmoor's early role was administrative. He would have spent most of his time making lists of materials, checking prices, entering figures into ledgers and negotiating with suppliers and workmen – the unseen and often forgotten work required to manage the huge numbers of projects

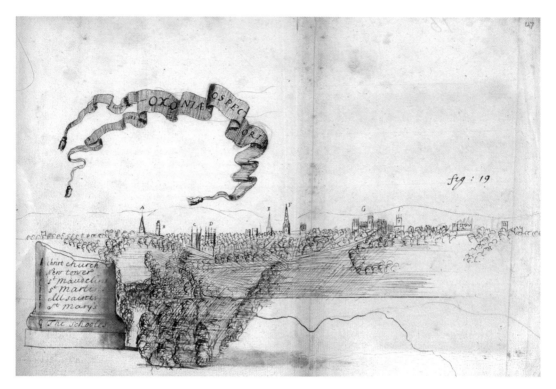

that Wren and his office at Great Scotland Yard were simultaneously engaged with.

Hawksmoor's name first appears in the records as a witness to signatures in 1684 for the City churches office and at Winchester, where Wren was building a later aborted palace for Charles II.[10] In 1685 Hawksmoor is recorded as having been paid at the Office of Works in Whitehall, where Wren had an official residence and Hawksmoor probably lodged. Up to this point, he had probably been paid by his master directly.

Hawksmoor's first big break in his architectural career appears to have occurred in 1683. A draughtsman by the name of Thomas Laine departed Wren's office, leaving a vacancy, which, it seems, Hawksmoor filled.[11] Earlier that year, Hawksmoor had visited several English towns, including Bath, Bristol, Coventry, Northampton, Oxford and Warwick. The trip is recorded in a number of sketches that make up a topographical sketchbook, which resides in the collection of the Royal Institute of British Architects (RIBA). The drawings, which

Hawksmoor's view of Oxford from his topographical sketchbook, *c.* 1683.

include a number of cityscapes and studies of individual buildings, such as Bath Abbey, suggest an aptitude, if not yet any refined skill, for architectural drawing. Perhaps most significantly they suggest an early interest in topography: the way buildings sit in the landscape, and how, in one example, Oxford's soaring spires come together to create a rich and vivid skyline. Viewed in isolation, they are charming but crude, and hardly indicative of a hand that would become one of the greatest that British architectural draughtsmanship has ever seen. Yet with the benefit of hindsight, the almost innate feel they show for architecture as a set of interlinked masses and volumes, defined by light and shadow, does give a hint of what was to come.

In January 1687 Hawksmoor became clerk of the City churches, succeeding Andrew Phillips who had died late the previous year.[12] This was something of a step up for the still young Hawksmoor. He was now responsible for the day-to-day administration of numerous complex construction sites across the City, an experience that would prove invaluable over his career.

Hawksmoor's responsibilities soon began to mount. He became involved in work at Hampton Court and Winchester Palace, and in 1689 he became Clerk of Works at Kensington House, a position secured for him by Wren, perhaps as a reward for being a trusted lieutenant, but also no doubt as a consequence of the potential Wren saw in the young man who was now very much his apprentice. Hawksmoor had begun working at St Paul's as a draughtsman from around 1685, though he was paid in that capacity in the cathedral accounts only from 1691. However, from that moment he became its leading draughtsman for the next decade.[13] It was during these pivotal years that Hawksmoor came of age as an architect, and also as a man, marrying Hester Wells in 1696. St Paul's, therefore, plays a central role in Hawksmoor's career.

St Paul's Cathedral

Even though the city has – literally and symbolically – grown up and around it, St Paul's Cathedral still stands tall and proud over London. In our modern parlance it is truly 'iconic', attracting tourists from all over the world who stream across the Millennium Bridge from Tate

Modern or who slowly trudge up Ludgate Hill and congregate around the statue of Queen Anne which stands outside its west end, before paying the hefty admission charge to gape at its soaring interior. St Paul's is, of course, much more than a mere tourist attraction; it is a building that is inextricably woven into London's identity and those of its inhabitants, with a history dating back to the seventh century. Remarkably, St Paul's remained the tallest building in London until 1962 (when it was finally surpassed by the Post Office Tower). For a structure that is familiar the world over as a symbol of both London and Britain, it is perhaps surprising that the chronology of its design is still being debated.[14]

Hawksmoor never saw Old St Paul's, which was largely destroyed in the Great Fire. Wren, however, knew the building well, though in the curtailed state it was left in after its spire – which for a time had made it the tallest building in the world – was struck by lightning and destroyed in 1561. Before the Great Fire Wren had actually made several drawings for topping the crossing with a dome, not unlike the one that would ultimately rise above the rebuilt cathedral (the main difference externally was the presence of a strange elongated pineapple form that would have extended from the dome's summit). Even though Inigo Jones had carried out numerous restorations during the 1630s the cathedral was in a poor state, having been used for stabling during the Civil War. Some attempt was made to patch up what remained after the Fire, but when this proved impossible, as Wren predicted, he worked up designs for a complete rebuild.[15]

It was during or shortly after this crucial time that Wren wrote the closest thing he ever came to a treatise on architecture. He did not, though, ever publish what he produced and we can only really guess at the purpose of these 'Tracts' on architecture, as Wren called them. They range from investigations of monuments from classical antiquity to detailed specifications for vaulting, rudimentary statics and excursions into rather arcane architectural history.[16] We also do not know for sure whether Hawksmoor even read them, although it is hard to imagine them slipping by such an inquisitive mind. In any case, they are implicit in much of Wren's architecture, and, we might deduce, reflective of how St Paul's was consuming his thoughts at this particular moment.

Tract 1 begins with a now famous statement:

> Architecture has its political Use; publick Buildings being
> the Ornament of a Country; it establishes a Nation, draws
> People and Commerce, makes the People love their native
> Country, which Passion is the Original of all great Actions
> in a Common-wealth.[17]

Wren went on to cite the cities of ancient Greece, Jerusalem and
Rome, arguing that it was their architecture – the very fabric of the
city – that bound their peoples and, indeed, these civilizations
together. 'Modern *Rome*', he continued, 'subsists still, by the Ruins
and Imitation of the *old*'. This observation, made despite having
never visited Rome, prepared the way for Wren's next famous claim:
'Architecture aims at Eternity; and therefore the only Thing uncapable
of Modes and Fashions in its Principals, the *Orders*'. Here, Wren
established himself, first and foremost, as a classical architect: a follower
of the language of architecture established by the ancient Greeks and
Romans in which the Orders are the principal components.

 The five Orders – Tuscan, Doric, Ionic, Corinthian and
Composite – which comprise base, shaft, capital and entablature,
stand as the literal and symbolic building blocks of a classical building, governing its proportional system. Despite their ancient, almost
mythical origin, Wren did not consider the Orders as embodying some
kind of universal ideal, as they are were often held up by others to do,
and in some quarters still are today. For Wren the importance of the
Orders came from their refinement over the ages towards a state of
perfection.

> The *Orders* are not only *Roman* and *Greek*, but *Phoenician*,
> *Hebrew* and *Assyrian;* therefore being founded upon the
> Experience of all Ages, promoted by the vast Treasures of
> all the great Monarchs, and Skill of the greatest Artists
> and Geometricians, every one emulating each other; and
> Experiments in this kind being greatly expenceful, and Errors
> incorrigible, is the Reason that the Principles of Architecture
> are now rather the Study of Antiquity than Fancy.[18]

What is perhaps most interesting about this statement is the way Wren projected his own seventeenth-century outlook onto the past. He saw the Orders as the result and summation of centuries of 'experiments' towards an ultimately refined model – and it is important that he used this particularly scientific word. By arguing for the primacy of the Orders, but in a way that prioritized their 'discovery' through experimentation, Wren was able to justify his adherence to the Orders and to the architecture of antiquity in distinctly modern, rational terms, rather than through unquestioning faith.

As a contrast to this process of rational refinement, Wren used the notion of 'Fancy' – unbridled imagination and originality which, if left unchecked, could, in Wren's view, lead to architectural confection or fantasy.[19] Though Wren cautioned against it, Hawksmoor would go on to sympathize with the role of 'Fancy' in architectural design, and its potentially powerful effects.

The ideas Wren explored in his 'Tracts' were no doubt never far from his mind as he began the long succession of designs that would ultimately yield the cathedral we know today. Prior to the issuing of the royal charter in 1673, Wren's thoughts moved from the relatively modest structure recorded in the 'First Model', through several 'Greek Cross' designs, to the 'Great Model', a design of monumental scale and ambition that was turned into a colossal six-metre-long wooden model. Much to Wren's disappointment, the Great Model was rejected for being both too obviously reminiscent of St Peter's in Rome and, in the eyes of the clergy, impractical for their needs. Thus the design that was signed into law by the royal charter – the so-called 'Warrant Design' – was something of a compromise which attempted to satisfy the triumvirate of interested parties that made this such a politically fraught commission: the crown, clergy and City of London.

Comparing the 'Warrant Design' to the cathedral as built, it is rather obvious that major design changes were made during the 40 years or so of construction. Wren had been granted permission 'to make some Variations, rather ornamental, than essential', though he surely pushed the freedom he was granted to the limit.[20] The chronology of these 'Variations' has been much debated by architectural historians over recent decades. Hawksmoor's arrival in the St Paul's office in 1685 has, therefore, been of considerable interest, especially when it transpired that crucial drawings for the western body of the church appeared to be in his hand.[21] This has in turn led to much research being undertaken into Hawksmoor's drawing techniques, notably by the architectural historians Gordon Higgott and Anthony Geraghty. In particular, Higgott's work on the collections at Sir John Soane's Museum and St Paul's, and Geraghty's cataloguing of the Wren office drawings at All Souls College, Oxford, has shed new light on the importance of drawing in how Hawksmoor conceived his architecture.

Hawksmoor made great progress as an architectural draughtsman during the mid-1680s. From the relative crudeness of his topographical sketchbook he soon developed great skills in technical drawing, becoming accomplished, as Geraghty has identified, in precise, preparatory drawings in pencil as well as presentation drawings.[22] In both of these categories Hawksmoor's debt to Wren was clear. Wren's drawing technique, as Higgott observes, was one of 'great precision and elegance, relying almost entirely on outline to

Presentation drawing by Christopher Wren in brown ink and pencil with grey, blue and yellow washes showing the south elevation of the Warrant Design, *c.* 1675.

convey three-dimensional architectural form'. This exacting technique was in many ways informed by Wren's training as a scientist, which required draughtsmanship of utmost precision in order to record incredibly precise measurements accurately.[23]

This part of Hawksmoor's career culminates with his presentation drawings of the 'revised designs' for St Paul's, which show the first two storeys of the cathedral more or less as built. The dome and west end towers meanwhile appear to be modelled, respectively, on Jules Hardouin-Mansart's church of Les Invalides, Louis xiv's great military hospital in Paris, and Bramante's Tempietto of San Pietro in Montorio in Rome, both the dome and west end towers were at this stage still some distance from the final design. It was Geraghty's dating of this drawing to around 1685–7, and attribution to Hawksmoor, that ultimately paved the way for the reappraisal of the design chronology of the whole cathedral.

Hawksmoor never again aimed for the heights of detail, precision and refinement that he reached in his drawings for the 'revised designs'. This reflected his changing role in the office and, it would seem, the influence and innovations of others working in Wren's office at the time. From the mid-1690s Hawksmoor developed a highly allusive wash technique where he increasingly forewent pen and ink outline to focus almost entirely on expanses of wash shading with pencil underdrawing to express architectural form. Higgott has suggested that Hawksmoor learned this technique working with engravers in the late 1680s, notably the Frenchman Simon Gribelin.[24] But, as Higgott continues, 'It's really his partnership with Grinling Gibbons in the design of the west work of the choir that is the catalyst for the flowering of Hawksmoor's invention as an architectural draughtsman.'[25]

Born in Holland to English parents, Grinling Gibbons was a true virtuoso and the most renowned woodcarver of his day. He rose from relative obscurity to work for successive monarchs, completing major work at Hampton Court, Whitehall and for numerous City churches. So accomplished was the master craftsman that Wren clearly felt comfortable placing Hawksmoor into his care, and entrusting the duo with the design of the choir at the very heart of the cathedral.

South elevation of the 'Definitive' design for St Paul's, drawn by Hawksmoor in grey ink and wash, *c.* 1685–7.

Successive drawings, especially those for the organ case, reveal Hawksmoor moving from the technical delineation of an architectural frame to embrace a method that is all allusion and suggestiveness, picking out and developing the form with the most economical flicks of line and tone. This reaches a climax in his design for the Bishop's Throne at the east end of the choir, in which all aspects of the design – architectural frame and ornament – are depicted in light pencil, and pen and wash. Even though in some areas of the drawing we are offered only the merest hint or suggestion of form, Hawksmoor was still able to lend a degree of firmness to the design, so that if we squint we might readily imagine what he has drawn existing in three dimensions. For Higgott, 'the quality of draughtsmanship [in these drawings] surpassed anything that had been produced in Britain up to that point'.[26]

Hawksmoor's attention at this time was not confined solely to the cathedral's interior. Perhaps the most remarkable drawing is a study for the west towers. The lower part of the drawing, from circa

1685–6, shows the upper stage of the north side of the west end in elevation. By then out of date, the drawing was probably lying around the office and Hawksmoor used it to give a quick, approximate context for his study for the tower. The first level of the tower, a belfry or clock stage, is shown in loose perspective. Above, a lantern is composed of a peristyle of twelve columns, which are rendered in elevation, using grey wash to depict shadow. This is topped, finally, by a small drum and dome drawn in perspective, with the faintest pencil underdrawing picking out successive cornice lines below the grey wash.

By combining the seemingly irreconcilable perspective and elevation, Hawksmoor created an image that appears to break all the rules of architectural draughtsmanship. But in a different light, we might see it actually as a mode of representation that allowed Hawksmoor, in Geraghty's words, to 'pre-empt the experience of looking at (unbuilt) buildings'.[27] Looking at the drawing on the page one can almost get a tangible sense of how the tower, had it been built, would have looked in real life, the sun catching it on one side, plunging the other into shadow. It is an image of startling ingenuity and imagination that takes us to the very heart of how architects of any period conceive and compose their designs. Ideas emerge from the imagination, become tangible through the technical aspects of design and construction, but become intangible again once the building is complete and able to be perceived and experienced. Thus probably the best description of what Hawksmoor was achieving in these drawings actually appears in an unrelated quotation from the great twentieth-century American architect Louis Kahn:

Hawksmoor's study for the canopy of the Bishop's Throne in pen and brown ink over pencil with grey wash, *c.* 1693–4.

A great building . . . must begin with the unmeasurable, must go through measurable means when it is being designed and in the end must be unmeasurable.[28]

Upper north elevation
of the west half of the
western body of St
Paul's, *c.* 1685–6,
extended with a wash
sketch for the clock or
belfry and lantern of
the northwest tower,
c. 1699–1700.

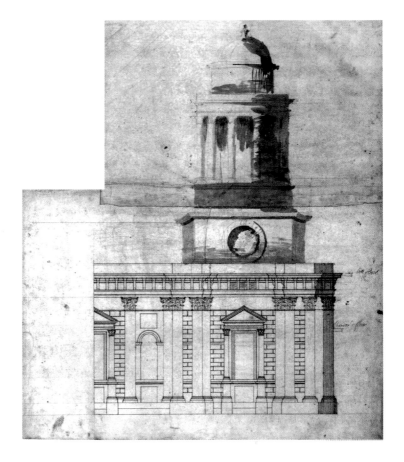

Achieving architectural maturity

The drawings Hawksmoor produced in Wren's office during the 1690s show both his development as an architect under his master's direction and influence, but also the ways in which he was beginning to chart his own course. Wren's office in the 1680s and 1690s was without doubt one of the most exciting centres of architectural activity in the history of British architecture. But a special talent – and, we might add, a dogged mind – was still required just to hold its own in a fast-moving office and make the most of this energy and stream of innovations. Hawksmoor certainly had these qualities. He also had the ability, like his master, to be engaged both conceptually and practically with multiple projects at the same time.

By the time Hawksmoor became clerk of the City churches in 1687 many of the church re-buildings following the Great Fire were nearing completion. The main building accounts were actually closed not long after, in 1693, but the design and construction of the spires continued in earnest.[29] The extent to which Hawksmoor was involved is hard to say. The later tower of St Michael, Cornhill (1718–24), paid for by the Commission for Building Fifty New Churches of 1711, is certainly his, and he claims as much in a letter of 1734–5 to the Dean of Westminster Abbey.[30] St Vedast, Foster Lane, St Andrew, Holborn, and St Margaret Pattens might be attributed to Hawksmoor on stylistic grounds. Their bold massing is seemingly at odds with Wren's earlier spires, although this hypothesis belies the fact that Wren's style clearly evolved over the decades.[31] Nevertheless, it seems reasonable to assume Hawksmoor's involvement at the very least.

Drawings in Hawksmoor's hand for St Augustine, Watling Street (*c.* 1695), employ the same allusive methods and pen and wash technique as the drawings he was then producing at St Paul's. Geraghty argues that 'the design is so wedded to the method of representation that Hawksmoor's authorship seems certain'.[32] The drawings feature a finial of an obelisk with leaf ornament, which also appears at All Hallows, Watling Street, St Mary Somerset and St Margaret Pattens and it seems likely, as Geraghty suggests, that Hawksmoor was at least charged with designing the detail of these spires.[33] Hawksmoor's involvement can also be detected, via drawings, at St Dunstan-in-the-East (begun 1695), St Bride, Fleet Street (1701–4), St Magnus Martyr (1703–6) and St Edmund the King, Lombard Street (1706–7).[34]

Although Hawksmoor's first architectural position had been at Kensington Palace, where he later raised the King's Gallery (1695–6) and the Orangery (1704), both completed under the auspices of Wren's office, the

Hawksmoor's preliminary design for the steeple of St Augustine, Watling Street, in pencil and grey wash, *c.* 1695.

East elevation of the
Writing School for
Christ's Hospital.
Drawn by Hawksmoor
in brown ink over
pencil, *c.* 1692.

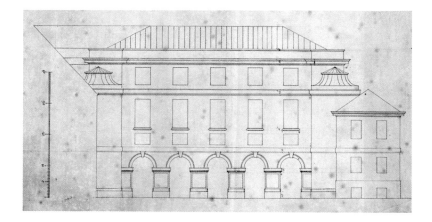

first built architectural work that was wholly his own came a few years earlier, in 1692, with the new Writing School for Christ's Hospital in London.[35] Wren was a governor of the school and in that role it would have generally been assumed that he would take on the project. But given the amount of work in his office at the time, it was no surprise that he handed it over to Hawksmoor. In June 1692 it was noted that,

> Mr Treasurer represented to the Committee the great pains and industry that Mr Hawksmoor Sr Christopher Wrens gentleman hath taken in makeing the draughts of the new intended Writing School and several other matters relating to that affaire, as alsoe what great trouble he is likely to be at in the time of building of it.[36]

Hawksmoor was subsequently paid for his 'troubles', not only in overseeing and executing the building but, importantly, for its design. Several of Hawksmoor's drawings survive and show a reliance on line in their technique for both outline and massing. The design was clearly his, yet on one drawing he endorsed it 'by Sr CW'.[37] This points to the important fact that while it is tempting to view Wren's office as a free space of creative collaboration, akin in many ways to a modern architectural office, it was in fact far more rigidly structured.[38] Duties were delegated and shared around the office, and various ideas explored by individuals within it, but Wren always maintained ultimate control. This remained the case even when he took on another commission that rivalled his great cathedral in scale.

The new Royal Naval Hospital at Greenwich was, after St Paul's, the most significant architectural project of its day. First suggested by Queen Mary as early as 1691, a formal grant of site was eventually made in October 1694. It consisted of an area in Greenwich bounded to the north by the Thames and to the south by the garden of the Queen's House, the Palladian villa commissioned from Inigo Jones in 1616 by Anne of Denmark, queen consort to James I. The site was split, however, by a 115-ft strip or avenue running along the north–south axis that preserved the views from the Queen's House to the river.[39] Part of the site was also occupied by John Webb's King Charles Block (1664–72), one wing of an aborted palace intended to replace the Tudor Greenwich Palace, which remained dilapidated, but still standing, alongside the river.

As Surveyor of the King's Works, the commission came to Wren. His clever solution to the constraints of the site was to replicate the

Greenwich Hospital on a winter's morning, seen from across the Thames.

pre-existing King Charles Block to the east (as Webb himself had intended). The northern fronts of both the original block and its new counterpart to the east were themselves replicated as the over-all plans grew in scale. A central-dome scheme was quickly passed over because it would have blocked the view from the Queen's House. So Wren came up with the idea with which we are familiar today, of the twin domes either side of the avenue, leaving the Queen's House as the arguably slightly puny focus for the whole composition – a situation that Hawksmoor, in particular, was rather unsatisfied with.

Hawksmoor was involved at Greenwich from almost its very beginning in 1696. In 1698 he became Clerk of Works, having already been paid for the previous two years for drawings he pro-duced while working directly for Wren.[40] He held the Clerkship until 1735, while also serving as Deputy Surveyor from 1705 to 1729. Importantly, Hawksmoor played a key role during the pivotal period between 1696 and early 1699, when the overall built scheme was largely settled and then recorded in a wooden model, probably made by James Smallwell, now held by the National Maritime Museum.

The complex design history of the Hospital from 1694 to 1735 can be charted through the drawings at the Soane Museum, thanks mainly to Gordon Higgott, who has meticulously catalogued the collection and grouped it into twelve 'sub-schemes'.[41] These include several plans by Hawksmoor for the addition of a large central chapel and, in the so-called first enlargement plan produced 1698–1700, the creation of a great esplanade and entrance to the hospital from the west. A corresponding drawing shows that Hawksmoor proposed that the chapel would be topped by a 400-ft-high tower to the south, aping in scale and ambition even what Hawksmoor had proposed in his drawings for St Paul's.

Several further schemes for enlargements appeared in 1711, with Hawksmoor no doubt spurred on by the prospect that funds might be available as a consequence of the Act for Building Fifty New Churches that was passed on 6 April that year. A plan for one of these schemes shows the Queen's House again obliterated, this time by a colossal domed church, with a Bernini-esque oval colon-naded court in front of where the Queen's House would have formerly stood.[42] A drawing at the Courtauld Institute shows this

Hawksmoor's elevation for a proposed chapel and 400-ft-high tower for Greenwich Hospital, c. 1698–1700.

Hawksmoor's design for a domed chapel for Greenwich Hospital, *c.* 1711.

chapel in elevation, an astonishing combination of the eternal solidity of Bramante's design for St Peter's in Rome, with the concave and convex interactions of Borromini's Sant'Ivo alla Sapienza.

Standing on the north side of the Thames and looking back at Wren's stunning twin-domed composition with the Royal Observatory on the hill beyond, it is hard to imagine the effect of Hawksmoor's chapel had it been built. The Queen's House is certainly a rather understated centerpiece, yet what Hawksmoor proposed would have bordered on the fantastical – a clash of form and scales that would have been visible for miles around and a true rival to St Paul's.

Although these grand plans ultimately came to nothing, Hawksmoor did see several of his designs realized at Greenwich – for the Queen Anne Block in the northeast corner and the King William Block to the southwest – though, as ever, under Wren's overall control.

While the courtyard and river fronts of the Queen Anne Block had to match the corresponding fronts of Webb's King Charles Block, Hawksmoor was able to produce original frontages for both the internal courtyard and the long east range. As one walks through this extraordinary complex of classical architecture, one is immediately struck by the apparent austerity of Hawksmoor's designs. The ornament is reduced to bold, symbolic gestures, which seem to boil

Queen Anne courtyard at Greenwich.

over in the end loggias of the internal courtyard. To anyone standing in the middle of the courtyard and looking north, with the river visible at high tide through the central arch, the recessed central three bays seem to push the flanking one bay projections forward. The wider central bay, meanwhile, appears to be compressed, while at the same time appearing to be resisting that force. We are left with a dramatic and almost tangible sense of movement from apparently the simplest of forms and compositions.

Heading south, to the King William Block, we see a similar kind of architectural tension reverberating through Hawksmoor's design. Here, though, he achieved it through far more conventionally grand means, as perhaps befitted its more prominent location on the site, looking west towards Greenwich. The two flanking wings of the west front are over-sailed by segmental pediments, with thick Portland stone quoins providing a robust frame for the plain red brick wall surface. The central block is of eleven bays; we might read the nine central bays as projecting forward, or the two either side as recessed – it appears deliberately ambiguous. Either way, a three-bayed portico rises through the centre; its thick Doric pilasters and engaged columns are reminiscent of Wren's Royal Hospital Chelsea, but without that building's concessions to conventional proportion. In all this, we see the key ingredients of Hawksmoor's style emerging: the sense of dislocation between the adjacent wings; the robust, but at the same time delicate handling of architectural detailing; and the dramatic, almost violent changes of scale. It is an odd sensation taking in all this architectural drama as people quietly picnic in the summer on the lawn in front.

Walking around to the courtyard side, we find a facade that is arguably even more extreme. The central five-bay block appears to be based on a triumphal arch, but with the attic stage lopped off and a thin one-bay temple front perching on high rusticated pedestals inserted beneath the arch. It is a highly complex, almost unnerving arrangement that features no fewer than nine different window forms. Standing in the courtyard and trying to comprehend this facade is

West front of the King William Block, Greenwich.

near impossible, with one's eye unable to focus or settle on any element within it.

The courtyard range of the King William courtyard, Greenwich.

So perverse have these two facades appeared to many observers, their authorship has sometimes been questioned, both contemporaneously and by scholars today.[43] Could an architect so learned and well trained as Hawksmoor have really come up with designs that so wilfully, and apparently aimlessly, broke architectural convention? Given Wren's official control at Greenwich, we might imagine these facades as the target of the third Earl of Shaftesbury's damning critique of the 'devastation' apparently wrought by 'one single Court-Architect' – Wren.[44] But while Wren must have countenanced these two designs, perhaps even admiring their daring sense of invention, they could scarcely have come from his mind. If one compares them to Hawksmoor's almost contemporary design for the north front of Easton Neston in Northamptonshire, his hand – and the place of these designs within his broader career – are impossible to ignore.

Back to the country

Hawksmoor owed his involvement at Easton Neston entirely to Wren, who had been approached by his distant relative Sir William

Fermor, first Baron Leominster, for advice on the building of a new country seat. Heavily detained elsewhere, as ever, though also, it seems, little concerned with country house design, Wren passed the commission on to Hawksmoor. The design and construction of the house is relatively undocumented (it was probably begun in 1694 and roofed in 1702), but its attribution to Hawksmoor seems certain given how he described his relationship to it in a remark made some years later: 'One can hardly avoy'd loveing ones owne children.'[45]

Although the house was Hawksmoor's, the wings were not. They predate his involvement, and their attribution to Wren that is sometimes put forward can be discounted by Hawksmoor's description of them, in the same letter as the remark just quoted, as 'good for nothing'. It seems rather unlikely that the always respectful Hawksmoor would have referred to the work of his master, even after his death, in such a way. Whatever their origin, the wings had the effect of limiting the house to 125 ft wide. This comparatively small footprint resulted in a necessarily complex internal arrangement and it was perhaps for that reason a model was produced, which still survives, and was acquired by the RIBA in 2005. Though it is impossible to say for sure at which point the model came in the design process, its interior configuration is close to what was eventually built; its requirements shaped as much as anything by the need to house the Arundel marbles adequately, acquired by Fermor in 1691.[46]

The key difference between the model and the design as built is the presence of a giant order – a series of pilasters and applied columns that circumvent the building's cuboidal form, giving it a grandeur almost unprecedented in British country house architecture at that time. It is a building that bursts with energy, appearing to resist its compression into a comparatively small site. This effect becomes even more apparent when one considers the north front, which, like the King William court at Greenwich, contains a huge number of different window types: here, eight in total. At Easton Neston, this can be rationalized as a consequence of the presence of the grand staircase at the north end of the house.[47] Yet Hawksmoor could have quite easily maintained the external appearance of the two-storey arrangement of the other fronts with floors discreetly running across the tall windows, as Wren might have done and in fact did at Hampton

Court. The north front arrangement was clearly a conscious choice, a marked preference for effects of tension and ambiguity over and above classical order and harmony.

In the context of Hawksmoor's development, his work at Easton Neston ensured that he now had experience of the full repertoire of building types under his belt – ecclesiastical architecture at a range of scales; the collegiate type with the Writing School; palaces and grand public buildings; and now country houses. By the turn of the century he stood as arguably the best-trained architect Britain had ever seen. He had the skills of a project manager, quantity surveyor, draughtsman capable of producing everything from highly resolved presentation drawings to working drawings for craftsmen and, perhaps above all, the extraordinary ability to visualize on paper how a building might appear in reality. These skills and experience made Hawksmoor the ideal candidate to assist Sir John Vanbrugh, who had won the commission to build a grand Yorkshire house for the third Earl of Carlisle. As Castle Howard began to take shape, Hawksmoor quickly became indispensable.

Looking back over the course of Hawksmoor's early career, we see his relationship to Wren as largely that of the teacher and the pupil. The teacher trained his pupil up, offered him opportunities as his experience grew and in later years saw him develop his own creative path. This is, of course, rather simplifying things, overlooking in some ways how the working environments Wren created helped fuel Hawksmoor's fire. Nevertheless, the relationship between Wren and Hawksmoor is much easier to pin down than that between Vanbrugh and Hawksmoor. It seems clear that Hawksmoor was initially brought in by Vanbrugh to look after all the practicalities and details that were required to realize as monumental a building as Castle Howard. But the two soon forged a creative partnership that belied their different backgrounds, social standings and personalities and which was to prove a vital catalyst for Hawksmoor's independent career.

From what we can glean of Hawksmoor's character from his letters, we imagine a hard-working, diffident yet quietly determined man, a retiring figure who was far happier to let his buildings do the talking. Vanbrugh, it is fair to say, was the opposite. He was just

The complex north front of Easton Neston in Northamptonshire.

a couple of years younger than Hawksmoor, but by the time they met, almost certainly in 1699, he had already lived several lives. An early career as a merchant culminated in five years with the East India Company, with a year spent in Surat.[48] Returning to London in 1685, he entered the military. In 1688 he was arrested in France on a charge of spying and imprisoned, spending time incarcerated in Calais, Vincennes and the Bastille, before being released in 1692. Back in London, Vanbrugh then found success as a playwright, notably with *The Relapse* (1696) and *The Provok'd Wife* (1697); these plays demonstrated his quick wit and wry observations of social convention and behaviour.

During this time Vanbrugh, ever the socialite, renewed his acquaintances with fellow members of the Kit-Cat Club, the group of politicians and literary figures who had come together to promote Whig causes, notably the assertion of parliament's primacy and the securing of the Protestant succession. Among their members were several future patrons of Vanbrugh the architect, including the Earl of Carlisle, Viscount Cobham, the Duke of Newcastle and the Duke of Marlborough. It was perhaps at one such club meeting that Vanbrugh heard of Carlisle's intention of building himself a new country pile, and how he was having problems with William Talman, his initial choice of architect. Upon immediately offering his own services instead, Vanbrugh must have had some idea of what he hoped to create, but untrained and with no architectural experience he was far from equipped to take on a project of this magnitude. Hawksmoor was, therefore, the natural choice for Vanbrugh to help him realize his loose vision.

Hawksmoor's role at Castle Howard began and in part remained as what we would see today as 'executive architect'. Vanbrugh conceived the overall composition and his name remained attached to the scheme. Hawksmoor did all the behind-the-scenes work, such as negotiating with workmen, overseeing the quality of the work, sorting out the practicalities and taking on the innumerable small design decisions that arise during any building project.[49] Hawksmoor was no mere assistant, though, and the house at Castle Howard is in many ways a true collaboration, as different from Vanbrugh's later houses completed without Hawksmoor's help as it is from Hawksmoor's own works. The working relationship between the two architects was close. Hawksmoor's letters to Carlisle reveal his involvement in almost every sort of decision and also a clear understanding of what Vanbrugh himself wanted or what view he was likely to take. Like all the best partnerships, it was more than the sum of its parts, the fitting testament being how, even today, that great pile on a Yorkshire hill still takes one's breath away as its oversized cupola and sweeping courtyards swing into view on the approach down its long, undulating drive.[50]

Vanbrugh's transformation from soldier to playwright to architect did not happen unobserved. In 1706 the poet Jonathan Swift described in his satirical poem 'The History of Vanbrug's House' how 'Van's Genius, without Thought or Lecture/ Is hugely turnd to Architecture.'[51] One of the targets of Swift's satire was the admittedly rather odd house Vanbrugh built for himself on ground cleared by the destruction of Whitehall Palace. In another version of the poem Swift described the house as 'A Thing resembling a Goose Py' – and the name has stuck.[52] Swift's satire emerged both from his political opposition to Vanbrugh and the Kit-Cat Club, and from the not unreasonable insinuation that Vanbrugh had won the commission for Castle Howard as a consequence of his social connections and not his talent as an architect. So, when Vanbrugh went on to land the even more prestigious commission for Blenheim Palace, it is no surprise to see Swift observe, dripping with irony: 'And now the Duke has wisely ta'ne him / To be his Architect at Blenheim.'[53]

The Duke of Marlborough had originally intended to build a house from his own means, and seeing the success of Castle Howard, engaged Vanbrugh to do so. But the grant of the Royal Manor at Woodstock by Queen Anne and an agreement to pay for the works ensured that Blenheim soon turned into an odd hybrid – part private house and part monument to Marlborough's national victories during the War of Spanish Succession.[54]

Unlike at Castle Howard, arrangements were formalized, with Vanbrugh appointed as surveyor and Hawksmoor his deputy. Working arrangements between the two, however, continued in much the same way.[55] Hawksmoor remained engaged at Blenheim into the 1720s and even following Vanbrugh's resignation in 1716, after he

previous: Castle Howard's garden front.

The garden front at Blenheim photographed by Edwin Smith in 1956.

fell out with the Duchess of Marlborough for the final time. The nature of Hawksmoor's involvement at Blenheim is best summed up in his own words: while he regarded Easton Neston as one of his 'owne children', Blenheim was 'like the loving nurse, that almost thinks the Child her own'.[56]

Ornament and association

Given the collaborative nature of their relationship, it is difficult to talk of the influence Vanbrugh might have had on Hawksmoor. There is always the danger of going too far and risking a return to the view widespread in the early twentieth century that Vanbrugh was responsible for all of Hawksmoor's best ideas – or, conversely, of seeing Hawksmoor as Vanbrugh's guiding hand. In reality, they were opposite and complementary characters. But they also shared many similar concerns, notably a deep interest in the nature and role of architectural ornament and the capacity of buildings to evoke associations of time and place. These ideas figured in both Hawksmoor and Vanbrugh's architecture, though often in quite different ways. Hawksmoor, however, never articulated his ideas as eloquently or as evocatively as Vanbrugh did. So, here, we focus on two of Vanbrugh's most revealing statements for the light they shed, indirectly, on Hawksmoor's own thinking, especially as it diverged from Wren's.

The first is a now famous remark Vanbrugh made in a letter to Lord Manchester concerning additions to Kimbolton Castle, his Tudor manor house in Huntingdonshire. 'As to the Outside,' wrote Vanbrugh, 'I thought 'twas absolutely best, to give it Something of the Castle Air, tho' at the Same time to make it regular.'[57] Vanbrugh's use of 'Air' as opposed to style was quite deliberate. 'Air' was about the allusions a building might have, rather than how it conformed to the specifics of one particular style. Vanbrugh's additions of thick plain castellations were, therefore, deliberately in keeping with the 'air' of the rest of the castle, while at the same time helping to make it symmetrical, or 'regular', as Vanbrugh put it, thus remaining in keeping with the chief tenet of classical architecture. For Vanbrugh, the overall impression of a building was of far greater importance than style or ornament, as he made clear in a remark in a subsequent letter: ''tis certainly the Figure and Proportions that make the most pleasing Fabrick, And not the delicacy of the Ornaments'.[58] In this Hawksmoor was in firm agreement with his colleague. Throughout his work, but perhaps especially in the three churches he built in East London, Hawksmoor repeatedly preferred the effects of bold forms and massing over a reliance on ornament and decoration.

The second statement of Vanbrugh's that helps illuminate Hawksmoor's thinking focuses on association. This is the notion that our experience of a building might bring to one's mind whole hosts of associated ideas, images and memories. The possibilities of association came to the fore in an argument Vanbrugh made in a letter to the Duchess of Marlborough 'for preserving the Small Remains of ancient Woodstock Manour' – the ruins of a former royal palace in the grounds of Blenheim which had been the site of several notable events, including the romantic trysts of Henry II and his mistress, Rosamund Clifford. Vanbrugh reminded the Duchess how Woodstock Manor

> was rais'd by One the Bravest and most Warlike of the English Kings; And tho' it has not been Fam'd, as a Monument of his arms; it has been tenderly regarded as the Scene of his Affections. Nor amongst the Multitude of People who come daily to View what is raising to the Memory of the Great Battle of Blenheim; Are there any that do not run eagerly to See, what Ancient Remains are to be found, of Rosamonds Bower. It may perhaps be worth some Little Reflection Upon what may be said, if the Very footsteps of it Are no more to be found.[59]

It is a fascinating remark, particularly for the way Vanbrugh's argument for the preservation of Woodstock Manor rested on its historical associations, rather than on the quality of the building itself. Moreover, by extending his argument to Blenheim, noting how it would itself stand as a monument to Marlborough's victories, Vanbrugh was clear that associations were not necessarily confined to old buildings, but could be imparted by new ones too, a view firmly shared by Hawksmoor and, once again, attested particularly through his London churches.

Association was certainly a concept that Wren was aware of. He equated it with what he called 'customary' beauty, which he saw as 'begotten by the Use of our Senses to those Objects which are usually pleasing to us for other Causes'. In contrast to 'natural' beauty, which for Wren constituted proportion and geometry, and ultimately derived from nature, 'customary' beauty was contingent, informed by prior experience. Wren cautioned, though, that this 'familiarity breeds a Love to Things not in themselves lovely. Here lies the great Occasion of Errors [and] is tried the Architect's Judgment'.[60] Though Wren was clearly wary of its implications, for Vanbrugh and for Hawksmoor, too, association was fundamental to both how they designed and how they built. To their minds buildings could hold a power over the imagination that far exceeded the materiality of their stone.[61]

Fundamentals

Vanbrugh clearly revelled in the associative capacities of historic architecture, and was similarly fascinated by the possibilities of creating associations in new buildings by taking ideas and elements from many sources and deploying them in ways to maximize their effect.[62] To what extent these interests, which differed considerably to those of Wren, actually *influenced* Hawksmoor is difficult to ascertain. Hawksmoor would not have become the architect he did without the patronage and education provided by Wren. But how do we class Vanbrugh's quite different role in Hawksmoor's development as an architect? Would he have charted the course he subsequently did without encountering Vanbrugh? Hawksmoor's evocative wash drawings from the mid-1690s suggest that he was already thinking, albeit in different and rather more abstract ways, about what Vanbrugh articulated as 'air' and association. If Vanbrugh did not alter the course on which Hawksmoor was already set, he did, however, accelerate the development of his thinking and the boldness of his style. Perhaps the best way of describing Vanbrugh's creative influence over Hawksmoor is as a kind of catalyst for his architectural imagination, helping at this pivotal stage in his development towards a clearer sense of his own ideas.

Hawksmoor and Vanbrugh were far from exploring ideas of 'air', association and effect in a vacuum. A contemporary philosophical backdrop can be seen in the work of Thomas Hobbes, and in particular the elemental psychology explored in the first part of *Leviathan* (1651).[63] Hobbes's architectural analogies are, though, most apparent in a passage from another work, *Answer to Davenant* (1650): 'Time and Education begets experience; Experience begets memory; Memory begets Judgement and Fancy: Judgment begets the strength and structure, and Fancy begets the Ornaments of a Poem'.[64] In place of 'poem' we might substitute 'architecture' and be left with a near-perfect description of Hawksmoor's design process and its development over his career. This is not to say that Hawksmoor, Vanbrugh – or Wren, for that matter – were 'Hobbesian' architects; rather, both Hobbes and the architects shared an interest that followed the zeitgeist of their era: the rethinking of fundamentals – of philosophy, politics, science and, of course, architecture.[65]

If there was any place where the zeitgeist was crystallized, it was Wren's office during the 1690s – a place where architecture's political and structural possibilities were being rethought from the ground up. But, whereas Wren's architectural ideas ultimately emerged as a logical response to a particular problem, Hawksmoor's were powerfully shaped by his visual imagination, to encompass the fundamental experience of light and shade on form and mass and the allusions and associations they might evoke. Hawksmoor's very existence as an architect owed everything to Wren, yet it was undoubtedly a second piece of good fortune in his career that he came to work with a figure like Vanbrugh, whose energy and exuberance helped open up the possibilities of what this architect of lowly origins and upbringing might achieve. His experiences with both mentors proved vital for Hawksmoor when he gained a set of commissions that he himself must have sensed would be his most important: his great London churches.

TWO

ACHIEVEMENT

IN 1711 AT THE AGE OF FORTY-NINE, and at the peak of his powers, Hawksmoor became involved with an endeavour that would play a large part in defining him as an architect. On 10 October Hawksmoor was appointed, along with William Dickinson, as surveyor to the Commission to Build Fifty New Churches. Dickinson was soon supplanted by James Gibbs, who in turn was replaced by John James, but Hawksmoor remained in his post until the '1711 Commission' was more or less wound up in 1733. In that time Hawksmoor designed and oversaw the building of six of the twelve churches that were completed and had a hand in two others, which he co-designed with John James. Together, these churches were undoubtedly Hawksmoor's most important commission, one of a quite different order to his work in Wren's office, or in partnership with Vanbrugh. It was an opportunity that allowed Hawksmoor to design with the autonomy that his powerful architectural imagination warranted and deserved.

Being confronted by one of Hawksmoor's churches today, it is still hard not to be bowled over by their colossal, almost overblown scale and the sheer intensity of their layered, abstract masonry. Thinking particularly of his three East London churches, approaching them from the side we see vast expanses of smooth white Portland stone, punctuated by windows and doors that are seemingly punched through the masonry. Exaggerated keystones weigh heavy, almost teetering above them. The towers and spires, too, resist the force of gravity with an almost tangible energy as they push upwards from the main body of each of the churches. Rarely do we see conventional ornamentation, with Hawksmoor instead relying on the purity of his formal geometry and its vivid effects on light and shadow. In form and silhouette we detect allusions to the native Gothic past, but further back and further afield too, to the very origins of Christianity in the near East. If a Wren church is ultimately an intellectual solution, a Hawksmoor church is perhaps above all an emotional one. It is architecture that wears its heart on its sleeve; it has a vigour and richness with few peers in London or beyond.

Despite the almost otherworldly effect of his churches, it is important to remember that Hawksmoor was working to a brief – one informed by the needs and particularities of the urban environment in which his churches were to stand and the immediate political context. While the latter provided the impetus to the founding of the Commission to Build Fifty New Churches in 1711, the Commission's subsequent direction reflected longstanding and deeply rooted social and moral anxieties about London's expansion.[1] This was a period when politics and religion, morality and commerce, were all entwined. To explain Hawksmoor's churches – their design and how they came about – requires seeing them as urban and social interventions as much as religious or moral ones.

Whereas Wren's churches were almost all located in the City of London, replacing those destroyed in the Great Fire, the Commission's churches were to be located in the new suburbs outside the City's medieval walls. The number of churches initially aspired to – the nice round number of fifty – was clearly chosen to emulate Wren's achievements a generation before. It was no coincidence that the Commission was established just as St Paul's Cathedral was coming to completion. Its decades-long construction had been paid for by a tax on the coal that was brought into the city, and these proceeds could now be channelled to another round of church building. This had the interesting and important effect of directly linking London's architectural magnificence to its economic success. As trade flourished, so the demand for coal increased; more money was thereby levied from the tax and became available for the successive building campaigns.

Indicative of its increasing importance as a commercial centre, London's population grew tremendously over the seventeenth century, reaching a crescendo in its final decades. A city of 200,000 in 1600, by 1700 London was home to nearly 500,000 people, with some estimates even putting the number as high as 641,000.[2] In 1600 Londoners made up 5 per cent of the nation's population, but by 1700 that proportion had doubled to 10 per cent.[3] So great was the city's prominence that Edward Hatton in his *A New View of London* of 1708 remarked that

> London is generally believed, not only to be one of the most Ancient, but the most Spacious, Populous, Rich, Beautiful, Renowned and Noble Citys that we know of at this day in the World: 'Tis the seat of the *British* Empire, the Exchange of *Great Britain* and *Ireland*; the Compendium of the Kingdom, the Vitals of the Commonwealth, and the Principal Town of Traffic ... and was of so great Esteem in the time of the *Roman* conquest, as to be honoured by them with the Title of *Augusta*.[4]

London was beginning to rival ancient Rome in size, if not, despite Hatton's grandiloquence, in beauty. Hawksmoor himself lamented that if Wren's post-Great Fire plan for rebuilding the city had been followed with 'the Police Architectonical [the Office of Works] ... supported ... and the Legislature been pleased to restrain the exorbitant Growth of the Out-Parts and Suburbs, or reduced them to the regularity of the New City ... [then] As London excels in Extent, Commerce, ... so it would have excell'd in Beauty, and Accommodation', becoming 'foremost at this Day amongst the Wonders of the World'.[5]

As Hawksmoor observed, most of London's population growth over the seventeenth century had been in newly developed suburbs, outside the confines of its medieval walls. Indeed, the population of the City, as opposed to the rest of London, had actually remained fairly constant over the seventeenth century.[6] When he wrote these words Hawksmoor probably did not have in mind the ordered, affluent districts to the west, like Covent Garden, St James's, Piccadilly and Mayfair. Instead he was most likely referring to the unplanned suburbs to the east of the City: Clerkenwell, Spitalfields, Stepney and as far as Limehouse to the east, and to a lesser extent Bermondsey and Southwark to the south of the river. Even today, though long since enveloped as the city has grown, these places retain a distinctive character and history, one that strongly sets them apart in terms of social – and architectural – variety from their west-end counterparts.

By the early 1700s it was becoming increasingly apparent that the existing churches in London's then suburbs were insufficient to cater for the influx of people into their parishes. The growth of dissenting religious groups in the areas that lacked adequate church accommodation was a keenly felt concern for the Anglican authorities. This situation provided the immediate and practical justification for commissioning new churches. Yet like all architectural commissions, straightforward practical need is never the whole story, and, indeed, in this instance it offers little indication of what form the churches might take, other than their needing to accommodate a lot of people.

Despite their number and variety, Wren's City churches did not provide much of a model to follow. Unlike the new churches the Commission planned to build, Wren's were almost always built on enclosed sites and often on the foundations of the churches they replaced. Wren and also Vanbrugh did, however, put forward recommendations to the Commission regarding how the churches might be built. These were then assimilated into what was for all intents and purposes a well-defined brief from which the architects should work – a relatively unusual situation at the time. The brief was mainly concerned with planning and the general suggestion that the churches should stand out from the surrounding cityscape and be visible from afar.

But the vital question remained of how this was to be achieved. Hawksmoor's answer was to create a series of striking designs that drew from a wide range of sources: early Christian architecture, the Gothic and even elements from ancient Egypt. Despite never leaving his native shores, Hawksmoor was fascinated by and well versed in the origins of Christian architecture, which he worked into a historical narrative that connected it to medieval Gothic architecture. While the latter was shunned by many contemporaries, Hawksmoor recognized the Gothic's inherent worth and its associational qualities, which played an important role when he used that style in his work at Westminster Abbey and All Souls College, Oxford.

Hawksmoor's genius was to bring these various references and allusions together to create an architecture that was rich, resonant and eclectic, and imbued with the authority of the past. In the case of his churches this played the vital role of distinguishing them from the other forms of classical architecture then in currency in London, especially those being employed by those lower down the social ranks. For the people who lived in the streets surrounding the churches and who worshipped in their vast interiors, there was to be no mistaking where power and authority lay.

It was fitting that Hawksmoor worked from a brief that was influenced by both Wren and Vanbrugh, given the key roles played by both architects in shaping how he thought about and practised architecture. But despite Hawksmoor's debt to Wren and Vanbrugh on both creative and professional levels, neither architect would have been able to deliver quite what Hawksmoor managed to achieve with his London churches.

Impetus

During the night of 28 November 1710, a great storm ripped through London. Perhaps already weakened by the 'Great Infamous Wind' that had plagued Britain the previous month or maybe by excavations in the churchyard, the roof of the medieval church of St Alfege in Greenwich collapsed.[7]

The church was in fact the second on the site marking the martyrdom of Alfege, archbishop of Canterbury, who was killed by Viking raiders in 1012. Henry VIII was baptized in the church in 1491, which lay in close proximity to the then thriving Tudor palace. By 1710 Greenwich was dominated by the Royal Naval Hospital and the medieval church of St Alfege must have seemed rather quaint in comparison to the grand, classical complex nearby.

Perhaps with an eye on the coal tax now available after St Paul's completion, St Alfege's parishioners petitioned parliament for funds to rebuild. This was an opportune moment for such a plea. The election earlier that year had seen the Tories returned to power for the first time since 1688.[8] As far as one can project a cogent set of views on the many factions grouped under the descriptive banner of 'Tory', the Tories were the party of traditional landed interests and strong supporters of the established Church. They therefore stood firmly against the proliferation of dissenting religious groups and, during this time, clearly sensed the opportunity of a church building campaign in London's suburbs. Not only would the new churches help prevent local populations from falling into the arms of dissenters, they would also provide a powerful symbolic marker of the Tories' political victory and ideals.

The next year an Act of Parliament was passed that assigned the coal tax money towards 'building fifty new churches in the cities of London and Westminster and the suburbs thereof'.[9] The Act allocated funds towards acquiring sites for churches, their churchyards and adjoining rectories. Existing chapels could also be assigned funds for conversion into parish churches. A further Act of Parliament in 1712 provided for the rebuilding of St Mary Woolnoth in the City of London, which had been patched up following the Great Fire but was now in a precarious state, and money was also put towards the completion of Greenwich Hospital and work at Westminster Abbey.[10]

A commission was formed to put the Act into practice.[11] Of the 52 original commissioners, politicians, perhaps unsurprisingly, formed the largest contingent, but it also contained a number of clergymen and other prominent citizens, including architects. His son Christopher, Sir John Vanbrugh and Thomas Archer were all appointed, with Hawksmoor and William Dickinson installed as surveyors.[12] The surveyors were charged with all aspects of the church building process. Possible sites were identified, contracts negotiated, suppliers brought in and labourers employed. Although the precise locations of the churches still needed to the identified, the general need for churches in London's suburbs was immediate and apparent.

Writing in 1725, Daniel Defoe estimated that 350 acres of fields around Spitalfields were populated with buildings, 'which are all now close built, and well inhabited with an Infinite Number of people, I say, all these have been built new from the Ground, since the Year 1666'.[13] It was increasingly obvious that the existing churches were insufficient to cater for this influx of people into their parishes. In 1711 the Revd George Stanhope, vicar of the Parish of Deptford, appealed to parliament on behalf of the

12,000 souls who cannot possibly be accommodated in the said church . . . for want of which . . . many have wholly neglected their duty on the sabbath day . . . and many others go to meeting houses . . . of Quakers . . . Presbyterians, and . . . Anabaptists.[14]

In the same year Jonathan Swift claimed that in the city as a whole over 300,000 people were left unaccommodated by the existing stock of churches.[15]

While the practical need for churches to cater for these congregations was clear, the impulse to build was bound up with complex and deep-seated anxieties about the city's expansion and, in particular, the role of commerce in driving it. Although perhaps most keenly felt by those of a Tory persuasion, such anxieties ran far deeper than party politics. Looking back from our twenty-first-century vantage point, in which a majority of the world's population now lives in cities, it is often hard to see the growth of cites as anything other than inevitable. Yet for many during the seventeenth and into the eighteenth centuries, this was far from the case. From the mid-sixteenth century, new building in London was tightly regulated and at times entirely prohibited, with restrictions only slightly eased after the Restoration.[16] As Elizabeth McKellar suggests in a compelling account of London's development during the period, 'the desire to regulate and control building can be seen as part of a much more widespread anxiety about the growth of the city'.[17] The anxieties were partly environmental, but derived also from long-standing moral concerns.[18]

The environmental anxieties are perhaps easier to immediately understand. London in the seventeenth and early eighteenth centuries was a dangerous place – and not just from the risk of crime. In many areas the water supply was irregular and a comprehensive sewerage system was still nearly 200 years away. Disease was rife, especially in the overcrowded slums occupied by the significant majority of the city's inhabitants. Many, including Wren, viewed the Great Fire, which had followed the Great Plague, as an opportunity to rebuild the city afresh and in such a way that would alleviate many of these environmental problems. But as Hawksmoor himself remarked several decades later:

When London was Burnt in 1666, out of that fatall acci-
dentall mischief one might have expected some good when
ye Phoenix was to rise again, vitz a convenient regular
well built Citty, excellent, skillful, honest Artificers made
by ye greatness & Quality of ye worke in rebuilding such a
Capital. but instead of these, we have noe city, nor Streets,
nor Houses, but a Chaos of Dirty Rotten Sheds, allways
Tumbling or takeing fire, with winding Crooked passages
(Scarse practicable) Lakes of Mud and Rills of Stinking
Mire Running through them.[19]

This was no doubt something of a caricature; not all of London was
like this. Yet many of the areas along the river east of the City –
where Hawksmoor would build three mighty churches – would
have certainly been recognizable in his description. And even today,
when East London has undergone waves of regeneration and invest-
ment, there still remain many pockets of dereliction and decay.

Moral anxieties around London's expansion stemmed in several
ways from the social consequences of the growth of trade and commerce. As new wealth poured into London and consumption increased,
the existing social and economic hierarchies began to destabilize.
Traditional signifiers of social status – such as clothing and fashion,
cultural and artistic products – were increasingly appropriated by
those lower down the social ladder with newfound financial means.
This forced the re-evaluation of how authority itself was represented,
with new fashions, strategies and behaviours emerging in a variety
of spheres, including the very public art of architecture.[20]

'Scoundrell Streets'

The most visible and controversial manifestation of this phenomenon
was personified by the notorious figure of Nicholas Barbon. Barbon
was born around 1640, the son of Praise-God Barbon, 'known to
his contemporaries', John Summerson noted, 'as leatherseller, paedo-
baptist, Member of Parliament, fanatical anti-monarchist, mob-raiser
and general nuisance'.[21] Given the hostility to figures like his father
in the immediate aftermath of the Restoration, Nicholas wisely

departed for the Netherlands to take a medical degree, returning to London in the slightly less fevered climate of the late 1660s. Like his father, the younger Barbon was a conspicuous character all his life and, like his father, skilled in raising a mob to his advantage.

We know a relatively great deal about Barbon thanks to the autobiography of a sometime friend, the lawyer Roger North. According to North, Barbon was

> the inventor of this new method of building by casting of ground into streets and small houses, and to augment their number with as little front as possible, and selling the ground to workmen by so much per foot front, and what he could not sell build himself. This has made ground rents high for the sake of mortgaging, and others following his steps have refined and improved upon it, and made a super-foetation of houses in London.[22]

As Summerson observed, Barbon was hardly the 'inventor' of what we would now describe as speculative property development, but he was its most visible and advanced exponent; almost proudly unscrupulous in his business affairs, he was unapologetic in his conduct, brazen in his (usually successful) attempts to take whatever financial or legal advantage he could find, and would happily resort to intimidation tactics.[23] Contrary to established opinion, Barbon argued that London's expansion would in fact have numerous positive effects, not just for the city itself but for the country as a whole. New development would improve the city's environmental conditions, increase land values, enlarge existing markets and also create new ones.

Barbon was, therefore, quite prepared to redevelop sites well inside London's existing expanse when he could see the potential for profit. One such example was Essex Street, on the strip of land running south from the Strand to the Thames, which had formerly been the site of Essex House and its elaborate garden parterres. Here, on the quiet backstreet that originally ran down to the river just beside the Temple, remain some of the few surviving (though altered) examples of the sorts of heavily standardized houses Barbon built. Externally they are relatively plain: simple red brick frontages

Barbon's still surviving 49 Great Ormond Street. Barbon Close is named after him.

enlivened by white horizontal bands between the floors, casement windows topped by small ornamental keystones, and a thick cornice below a pitched roof. Most architectural attention was reserved for the door cases, which were loosely classical, perhaps copied from a pattern book, but often crude in interpretation. Inside, layouts were economical. Rooms were generally panelled, with tight dimensions, and the staircase balusters were carved in exactly the same way in almost every example. Though it is hard to believe now with so few of them surviving, Barbon's houses were the products of a well-oiled development machine that made frequent and early use of standardization in order to reduce costs and maximize profit.[24]

Barbon's developments, while often formulaic, hardly constituted the 'Chaos of Dirty Rotten Sheds' in Hawksmoor's description of London's new suburbs. However, in the same passage Hawksmoor also took aim at the 'workmen' who were enabling the city's expansion. Although he did not reveal the individual targets of his attack, by referring to the mechanics of development Hawksmoor clearly had figures like Barbon – perhaps even the man himself – in his sights:

> The Workmen soe far from skill or honesty that ye Generall part of 'em are more brutall & Stupid then [sic], in the remotest part of Britain and the longer they worke the worse they grow, as you may see in all ye Additional Scoundrell Streets they are Continuously Cobling up. to Sell by whole-sale and this is not all in London, for this sort of Vermin has run, & spread all over ye Country, and as they have Ruind ye Capitall Soe have they all ye Other Citys & Townes in Engld.[25]

The description of developers' pursuit of profit consequently 'ruining' the places where they built is of course a familiar one over history. The vehemence of Hawksmoor's phrasing – the 'Scoundrell Streets' created by 'Vermin' – indicates that it was not just the built consequences of developers' activities that raised alarm and anxiety, but their very behaviour. Hawksmoor alluded to the way the city's expansion was creating a circle of immoral and unscrupulous conduct. Thus the patently unvirtuous behaviour of the likes of Barbon was both a consequence and cause of London's expansion.

The most striking example of this conflation of moral conduct and urban growth appears in one particularly infamous episode concerning Barbon's development at Red Lion Fields in 1684. The Society of Gray's Inn, whose houses backed onto the fields, had protested that the loss of the fields to Barbon's development would be considerably detrimental to their nearby buildings and to the area as a whole. Matters came to a head when Barbon's workmen began to dig trenches in the field before any resolution had been found. Although the lawyers were surely all too aware that building had begun, Barbon could not resist rubbing their noses in it, as a representation to the Privy Council explains:

> The said Barbon did of late and particularly upon the 11th day of June last march about the fields in the head of two hundred men, shouting and hallowing within the hearing

of Grays Inn, and waving their hats as by way of challenge
to the gentlemen of the Society to come out and encounter
them, the said Barbon himself exhorting them that they
should not be discouraged for he would back them with a
thousand the next morning.[26]

Barbon's provocation proved intolerable for the lawyers, who swarmed
into the Fields and physically assaulted several of his workmen, ultimately driving them from the site. Barbon was to have the last laugh,
however, as despite the Society's protestations, Red Lion Square
soon emerged on the site of the Red Lion Fields.

Taming the city

Barbon's victory at Red Lion Fields was symptomatic of the tide of
development that, by the 1710s, must have appeared near impossible to resist. The nascent forces of capitalism had already firmly
established London as the world's first modern city. Growth in
trade and commerce had overturned long-standing moral certainties
and social hierarchies, which in many ways takes us to the core of
the broader circumstances that led to the establishment of the
Commission to Build Fifty New Churches. Indeed, the very act of
establishing the Commission can be read as an attempt at assuaging
anxieties about the city's expansion: these grand and imposing new
churches could be a way of re-imposing social and spiritual order – and
salvation – on London's suburbs. Perhaps inevitably this endeavour
lost some of its early impetus when the Tories fell from power in
1714 and the Commission itself was reconfigured. However, the
huge amounts of money that continued to be spent illustrate just
how deeply felt was the belief that architecture, in the form of these
new churches, had the power to tame the city's vices.

   While Wren's City churches were not a particularly useful model
for churches that would be built on open sites, they did at least set
the precedent of classical-style Anglican churches. This was the
underlying assumption that united both Wren and Vanbrugh's recommendations, despite their unsurprising differences in both tone
and detail.[27]

Informed by his long experience, Wren's suggestions were characteristically practical, including stipulations regarding materials, fire protection, sites and capacity. He also argued strongly that graves be kept well away from the churches, and, ideally, in 'cemeteries seated in the outskirts of the town'. If allowed in the church itself (as was common in medieval churches) 'the pavements can never be kept even, nor pews upright'. Burying in a nearby churchyard was 'also inconvenient, because the ground being continually raised by graves, occasions, in time, a descent by steps into the church, which renders it damp, and the walls green, as appears evidently in old churches'.[28] Wren specified the appropriate model to be his elegant if rather plain church of St James, Piccadilly, which 'may be found beautiful and convenient, and as such the cheapest of any form I could invent'.[29]

In stark contrast to Wren, Vanbrugh, ever the dramatist, couched his advice in terms of 'magnificence', 'dignity' and 'strength', arguing that the churches 'shou'd ever have the most Solemn & Awfull Appearance both without and within'.[30] He agreed with Wren that burials should be confined to cemeteries on the outskirts of the town, which he envisaged as necropolises filled with grand mausolea. Vanbrugh developed Wren's suggestion that the churches 'be brought as forward as possible into the larger and more open streets', demanding that the churches be 'so plac'd, to be fairly View'd at such proper distance, as is necessary to shew their Exterior Form, to the best Advantage'. Moreover, each should be adorned with a 'High and Bold' tower and grand porticoes so that the churches would become 'Ornaments to the Towne, and a Credit to the Nation'.[31]

A number of 'observations' on Vanbrugh's recommendations were made by the Anglican scholar George Hickes.[32] Reflecting an important and influential strand in contemporary ecclesiology, Hickes argued that 'the plans of the most primitive structure of churches ... [are] capable of most if not all the state, and graces of architecture, and as that way of building was the most ancient: so it is most fit to be imitated.'[33] The churches of the so-called Primitive Christians would have an important role to play in Hawksmoor's church designs, but it is also interesting to note that Hickes's other recommendations were very much rooted in the realities of his present moment. 'Square

pewes wherein in [sic] men, and women sit together, contrary to ancient order and decency, looking upon one another is not only a great but a scandalous hindrance to devotion', while 'high pewes are most indecent, and the occasion of much deplorable irreverence in churches'.[34]

For Hickes, the interior function of the churches was seemingly more important than the symbolic role they might hold in the city-scape; he actually began his observations by stating that 'devotions will depend upon the fabric of seats, or pewes more than that of

Wren's plain but elegant church of St James, Piccadilly.

churches'.[35] The Commission, in contrast, was very much concerned with the churches' urban role, indicated by their broad acceptance of Vanbrugh's recommendations, which were incorporated into a number of official 'rules' to be followed.[36] As well as specifying that each church should, as Vanbrugh recommended, be 'insular', that is free-standing on an open site, and adorned with 'handsome Porticoes' and steeples, the 'rules' stipulated that 'the Churches be all built with Stone on the Outside'. The Commission was fully aware that monumental scale and expensive materials (stone as opposed to standard brick) were clear ways of differentiating the churches from their urban contexts – a strategy that Hawksmoor developed in their design. However, within this brief, there existed a discernible tension between the churches' function as liturgical spaces and their role on an urban scale. This conflict was borne out, especially, in the arrangement of their interiors.

Difficulties in brief

One of the chief tenets of the Anglican liturgy was the importance of the full and active participation of the congregation in all aspects of the services. Clear and ordered planning, an open space that could carry the lone voice of the clergyman conducting the service and ample light were all vital requirements. The Commission's 'rules' stipulated that all the churches must be orientated east–west and there should be at the 'East end of Each Church two Roomes. One for the Vestments, another for the Vessels & other Consecrated things' and that 'the Chancels [at the east end] be raised up three Steps above the Nave or Body of the Churches'.[37] It went without saying that the altar would be placed in the east end. But various elements of services were also conducted at the reading desk, which was positioned in the main body of the church, while the pulpit, for preaching purposes, was also important. A further consideration was fonts, which were to 'be so large as to be capable to have Baptism administered in them by dipping, when desir'd'.[38] The brief, therefore, was for a church interior with many centres of focus.

Hawksmoor's natural inclination was almost certainly towards centralized or centrally-planned church designs. In contrast to the essentially Gothic longitudinal plan, with long nave, transept arms and choir, centralized designs are symmetrical along two (or more) axes. Wren's centralized designs – and here we might think of St Mary Abchurch, St Mary-at-Hill and early designs for St Paul's – were typically rational solutions to the peculiarities of the sites he had to contend with and the general problem of how to span and draw together large interior spaces. For Wren, as it no doubt was for Hawksmoor, longitudinal spaces, even those as elegant as St James, Piccadilly, were always and inevitably compromises that allowed part of the church to be brought into use before the completion of the whole, but without the overall integrity of centralized spaces.

However, the Commission's straightforward stipulation that 'no scite ought to be pitched upon for Erecting a New Church, where the same will not admit that the Church be placed East and West' put centralized plans essentially out of the question.[39] Moreover, the many centres of focus required in the churches, combined with galleries, which irrevocably imposed asymmetry on the interior space, further ensured that the interior spatial unity that centralized plans offered and that appealed to both Hawksmoor and Wren would be nigh on impossible to achieve. One solution was a plan defined by a cross-axis, which Wren had actually explored to a degree in his own churches from the 1670s. Hawksmoor's six churches can be seen as a series of interpretations of this idea, increasing in sophistication as he gained more and more confidence in his handling of church planning.

At St Alfege, Greenwich, the interior, including the galleries and pulpit, is much as it would have been in Hawksmoor's time, having been carefully restored after the Blitz by Sir Albert Richardson. The low pews are an important exception. Their original layout included not only the existing central aisle, which one walks down into the centre of the church, but another running perpendicular to it, between the subsidiary entrances on the church's north and south sides. These two intersecting aisles created a cross-axis that partially mitigated the otherwise insistent focus towards the east end.

St Alfege is in many ways the least sophisticated interior of any of Hawksmoor's churches: aside from the apse at the east end with its elegant *trompe-l'œil* coffering, it is quite clearly a rectangular box in which the altar, pulpit, reading desk and galleries coexist. However,

imagining for a moment the ambiguity created by the cross-axis of the original pew layout, we can see a conscious decision on Hawksmoor's part to evoke the sensation of a centralized plan in an essentially longitudinal space. Progressing in succession through the Stepney churches of St Anne, Limehouse, St George-in-the-East and Christ Church, Spitalfields, to St Mary Woolnoth in the City and then St George's, Bloomsbury, the last of Hawksmoor's churches to be begun, this effect only gets more sophisticated and intense.

At St Anne, Limehouse and St George-in-the-East Hawksmoor defined an inner cuboidal space with four columns set into the corners that rise up through the galleries. At St Anne's, despite the peeling Victorian paint scheme, monumental compound piers quite clearly serve to define an outer volume and screen the chancel at the east end and a narthex-like space at the west. At St George, where we have to rely on photographs to get a sense of its original interior, this outer volume is instead defined by four wide barrel vaults that we might read as vestigial transept arms. While the ceiling at St Anne's comprises an oval panel, as at St Alfege, the main ceiling at

The interior of St Alfege, Greenwich, restored after Blitz damage by Sir Albert Richardson.

St George takes the form of a massive groin vault, creating tension between the competing axes.

All of Hawksmoor's churches had multiple entrances to cater for the huge numbers of people attending services. In addition to the main west end entrance, at St Anne's entrances are set in each of the church's four corners, while at St George the entrances are far more integrated into the body of the church. Before the destruction of the church's interior, the colossal side doors led directly into the body of the church while also providing access to the galleries through spiral stairs in each of the 'pepper-pot' towers. Just entering the church would have been an extraordinary experience for those who lived in the timber shacks that made up most of the buildings around it.

When both St Anne's and St George are looked at from the side, their west towers still appear distinct from the main body of the church. At Christ Church, Spitalfields, in contrast, the tower is almost totally integrated, so that inside the church the effect is to compress the east–west space and enhance the prominence of the north–south cross axis. Grand colonnades run longitudinally from

The still rather dilapidated interior of St Anne, Limehouse.

east to west, with an inner volume marked in each corner by thicker compound piers that punctuate, rather than completely disrupt, the sense of rhythm. As in the other churches, this centralizing effect would have been heightened by the original pew layout but, here, also by the presence of two entrances, running across the central east–west axis. Meanwhile, at the east and west ends, the cornice lines are extended across the church to create what are, in effect, two screens that help define the interior volume of the church, with the space beyond appearing as quite separate.

The interior of St George-in-the-East photographed by the National Monuments Record just before it was bombed in 1941.

The cleverness of these various techniques becomes apparent when standing on the church floor: one actually reads the space almost as a cube, which is exaggerated by the taller central ceiling that is pierced by clerestory windows. When one ventures up to the newly reinstated galleries, one is suddenly able to comprehend the full body of the church, seeing beyond the colonnades to take in a space that feels far wider and far larger than it does from the church floor; it is a startling experience.

St Mary Woolnoth was begun in 1716, two years after the three Stepney churches, and is the only one of Hawksmoor's churches to be situated in the City of London. In plan and interior configuration it, therefore, diverges from Hawksmoor's other churches, being the most overtly centralized, though still shaped by the tension between cross-axes. Even in its current, quite considerably altered state, St Mary Woolnoth vividly illustrates how adept Hawksmoor had become by this point in his handling of space and light for dramatic effect.

At St George's, Bloomsbury – Hawksmoor's final and westernmost church – the interior is closer now to Hawksmoor's original layout than it has been since only a few decades after the church's completion – thanks to the recent restoration led by the World Monuments Fund. Here, a restricted site meant that Hawksmoor had to arrange the church in such a way that the main entrance was to the south but the altar remained in the east. Thus, one enters the church under the south galleries and emerges into a central cube space, lit by clerestory windows from above, with the altar appearing in a recessed apse on the right and further galleries in front to the north. The dark wood of the galleries acts as a kind of buffer to the eye, dissuading it from trying to comprehend the space beyond. It is something of a surprise, therefore, when one becomes aware from the plan that the space beyond the north galleries extends almost as far as the portico does south. All around the architecture is working in concert to stretch the space along the east-west and squash it along the north and south.[40] It is an interior of stunning drama and rich spatial tension, which could only have been conceived and executed by an architect with the experience of designing five earlier churches already under his belt.[41]

overleaf: St Mary Woolnoth's lunette clerestory windows, invisible from the outside.

'The Basilica after the Primitive Christians'

If the planning of Hawksmoor's churches was shaped to a large degree by the requirements of the brief, the look of their exteriors was left relatively open. Beyond the stipulations of the scale, use of stone and the presence of spires and porticos, Hawksmoor was given relatively free rein. One possible direction was that suggested by the Reverend George Hickes, who had argued that the churches should imitate those of the Primitive Christians of the Middle East. Hickes was far from the only one of the 'divines' to be fascinated with the origins and history of the Primitive Church.[42] As the architectural historian Pierre du Prey has exhaustively outlined, many theologians around this time sought to establish links between the practices of the Primitive Church and contemporary Anglicanism, and so construct a parallel history of Christianity that was, vitally, untainted by Rome and popery.

This line of thinking had important architectural implications. In *An Account of the Churches, or Places of Assembly of the Primitive Christians* (1689), Sir George Wheler proposed several models for

The reinstated north galleries at St George, Bloomsbury.

Byzantine-esque 'primitive churches'.[43] Hawksmoor perhaps had these or other speculative models in mind when, likely in the latter half of 1711, he drew up a plan for a church to be situated at the top of Brick Lane, titling it 'The Basilica after the Primitive Christians'.[44] The church depicted is probably closest to St George-in-the-East in plan, but arguably the most interesting features of the drawing are the marginalia under the title 'Manner of Building the Church – as it was in ye fourth century in ye purest times of Christianity'. Hawksmoor's notes largely followed the specifications outlined by Hickes in his 'observations' and it seems certain that Hawksmoor and Hickes must here have been in close consultation.

One interesting departure is the proximity of the 'Coemetery', as Hawksmoor labelled it, which lies just to the east of the church, rather than being some distance away as Wren, Vanbrugh and Hickes had all recommended.[45] Given that cemeteries were not mentioned at all in the Commission's 'rules', it seems that Hawksmoor was reflecting the fact that this particular recommendation had not been taken up. In the end, the three 'Stepney churches' were built with large adjoining churchyards that allowed them to be 'insular', as had been suggested, though their eventual use for burials contravened Wren's recommendations.

It is, though, more in the external appearance of Hawksmoor's churches, rather than their plans or situations, that an interest in the architecture of the Primitive Christians can really be detected. In this, as du Prey has suggested, the work of Reverend Joseph Bingham, cited by Hickes in his 'observations', was arguably the most influential. Bingham's masterwork was his *Origines Ecclesiasticae*, an epic summation of early texts and contemporary theological debate about the Primitive Church, which began to be published in 1708.[46] Bingham explained how the Primitive Christians had converted pagan temples for the purpose of Christian worship, observing,

> If they were well built they should not be destroyed, but only be converted from the worship of devils to the service of the true God . . . Sometimes the temples were pulled down, and the materials given to the church, out of which new edifices were erected.[47]

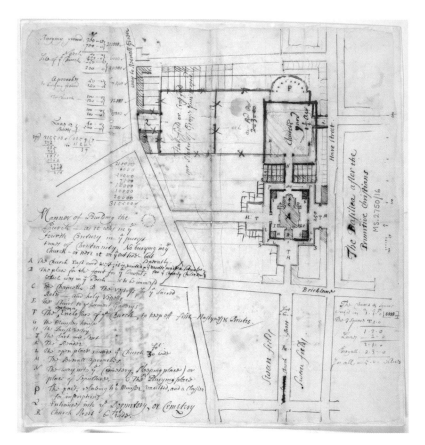

The Basilica after the Primitive Christians', likely drawn by Hawksmoor in the latter half of 1711.

Importantly, Bingham identified the way that the churches of the Primitive Christians made frequent use of spolia – reusing the materials, elements and adornments, like columns, bits of entablature and sculpture, appropriated from existing buildings or structures. Whether Hawksmoor read Bingham's works cover to cover or not, he would certainly have been familiar with many of their insights, including the use of spolia by the Primitive Christians – and it is to this interest that many historians have sought to attribute some of the more unusual elements of Hawksmoor's churches.

Looking at Hawksmoor's churches through this 'Primitivist' lens, therefore, we can begin to construct interpretations of many otherwise hard to comprehend aspects of the churches' designs. For example, the funereal altars that we see acting as oversized bollards outside the east end of St Alfege might be understood as evoking –

or even recreating – how the Primitive Christians incorporated such elements into their own churches. In fact, we see the same altar form deployed in the finials atop the octagonal coronet at St George-in-the-East – an even more overt example of this kind of architectural quotation.

Several other examples can be found in the churches' skylines. At St Anne's, a rather remarkable drawing reveals that Hawksmoor toyed with the idea of placing a pair of pyramids atop the church's east end. A lone pyramid standing in the churchyard is often said to have been one of those originally intended for this purpose. Continuing this theme, the famous stepped pyramidal spire at St George's, Blooms-bury, which is topped by a statue of George I, is clearly a quotation of the Mausoleum at Halicarnassus, the great monument of antiquity

The east front of St Alfege, Greenwich, with Roman funereal altars.

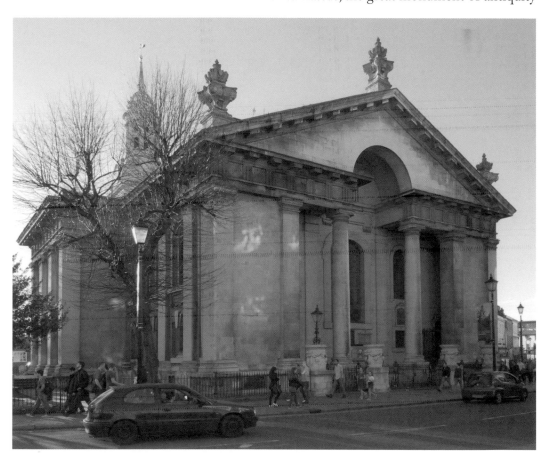

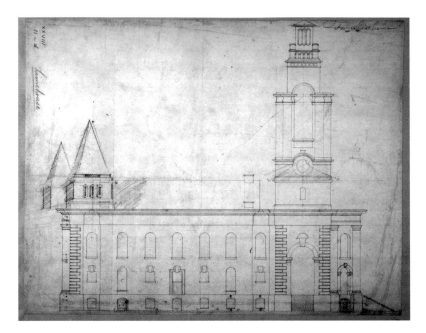

North elevation of St
Anne, Limehouse, with
pyramids, drawn in pen
and brown ink and
pencil *c.* 1712–19.

that Hawksmoor knew from written accounts. More generally,
the elemental starkness we see in the side elevations of St Anne's
and especially at Christ Church, Spitalfields, can be read as inspired
by a similar rawness in Primitive church architecture. The argument
went that Primitive Christians drew much of their strength from
the simplicity and purity of their faith, which was figured in and, in
turn, shaped by their churches.

The idea that Hawksmoor was somehow trying to re-create
or evoke the spirit of the architecture of the Primitive Christians is
a beguiling hypothesis, especially as it actually offers two interpretations. The first sees Hawksmoor literally trying to re-create the
churches of the Primitive Christians; while the second holds that he
sought to evoke their spirit in a way that provided a context for his
own eclectic quotations and references – a kind of 'synthetic spoli-
ation'. We can easily discount the first argument, given the multitude
of other pressures and influences on the brief. The second, while
clearly seductive in its theoretical elegance, is, I would argue, too
much of a conceptual leap to be the sole explanation. As with most
of Hawksmoor's architecture, so singular an interpretation is rarely
adequate. Indeed, neither Primitivist argument accounts for the way

The west tower of St
George-in-the-East,
seen from the west.

84

The west front and
spire of St George,
Bloomsbury.

Hawksmoor combined overt architectural quotations, with other
references that were subtly assimilated into his compositions of form
and mass to create more allusive effects. The latter was the case, in
particular, with Hawksmoor's recurring references to the Gothic.

Gothic

It was not just for theological reasons that Hawksmoor was interested
in the churches of the Primitive Christians, but architectural ones as

well. Like Wren, Hawksmoor was fascinated by architecture distant in time and place, as well also by that closer to home, notably the native Gothic tradition. He designed in the Gothic at both All Souls College and Westminster Abbey, but creating wholly new buildings in the style at a time when classical architecture otherwise reigned supreme was out of the question. Despite the absence of any characteristically Gothic elements, when we look upon Hawksmoor's churches we can detect a variety of references and allusions to medieval architecture weaved into their forms and massing. To see why this might be the case, we need to look more closely at Hawksmoor's understanding of the Gothic and its history, and also the instances where he explicitly designed in the style.

Hawksmoor's interest in Gothic architecture was relatively unusual. Most views of the Gothic were still clouded by the writings of the Renaissance painter and art historian Giorgio Vasari, who linked medieval architecture to the 'Goths' and 'Visigoths', the great destroyers of ancient Roman civilization. In Randle Cotgrave's *Dictionarie* of 1611, 'Gothic' was defined as 'rude, cruell, barbarous'.[48] By the late seventeenth century, Roger North was able to observe that 'The distinction now of building in the world, is reducible to Gothick and Regular ... [with the former term] apply'd to all that is not Regular'.[49] For North, as it was for many others, the Gothic was everything classical architecture was not: ungainly, barbarous and synonymous, even, with the destruction of civilization itself. This view was most vehemently summed up by Wren's friend John Evelyn:

> It is the Ancient *Greek* and *Roman Architecture* only, which is ... most entirely answering all those Perfections requir'd in a Faultless and Accomplish'd Building ... of the Civiliz'd World, and would doubtless have still subsisted ... had not the *Goths, Vandals* and other Barbarous Nations, Subverted and Demolish'd them, together with that Glorious *Empire* ... Introducing in their stead, a certain Fanatical and Licencious manner of Building, which we have since call'd *Modern* (or *Gothic* rather) [which consisted, he suggested, of] Congestions of Heavy, Dark, Melancholy and *Monkish Piles,* without any just Proportion, Use or Beauty.[50]

In contrast to Evelyn, Wren was far more open to the Gothic.[51] Inspecting Salisbury Cathedral in 1668 for its bishop and former Oxford colleague Dr Seth Ward, Wren observed that 'The whole Pile is large & magnificent, and may be justly accounted one of the best patterns of Architecture in that age wherein it was built'.[52] He did, though, qualify this enthusiasm on account of the structural faults he found in the building, adding, 'Notwithstanding this commendation of our Architect there are some original errours [sic] which I must lay to his charge, the discovery of which will give us light to the cause of the present decay'.[53]

In the various repairs and proposals he made for Westminster Abbey as Surveyor, Wren proposed adhering to the Gothic 'throughout the whole intention: to deviate from the old form, would be to run into a disagreeable Mixture [of styles], which no person of good Taste could relish'.[54] But Wren had little concern for archaeological accuracy in the way a nineteenth-century revivalist would have had, and was far more restrained in his use of ornament than any medieval variant of the Gothic.[55] In the words of the architectural critic Ian Nairn, 'Wren treated the Gothic like a cantankerous old aunt: with affectionate disrespect.'[56]

While Wren understood the Gothic, and sought to improve it in purely classical terms, Hawksmoor was far more attuned to the resonances it held and in the creative possibilities it presented. This came to the fore on the occasions when he designed in the style, with the Gothic shaping both the nature of his designs and the way they related to their surroundings. This was especially the case in his designs for All Souls College, Oxford.

Hawksmoor produced a variety of schemes for All Souls from around 1708 to 1716, yielding his most significant contribution to Oxford's many centuries of architecture. Hawksmoor owed his introduction in Oxford to Dr George Clarke, a fellow of the college and a Tory politician, who was also involved with the Navy, eventually rising to Joint Secretary of the Admiralty.[57] The first proposals for All Souls followed a plan devised by Clarke to create a new quadrangle to the north of the existing one. The existing chapel would be matched by a new hall to the east. A colonnade with a library on top would run across the enlarged south quadrangle, thus providing an axial link to the new north quadrangle and the fellows' building on its north side.[58] Designs for the buildings were solicited from several architects, including Hawksmoor.[59]

Hawksmoor produced several grandly classical elevations for the fellows building to the north, but like his similarly epic proposals for nearby Queen's College, also created around this time, they went unbuilt.[60] In any case, the plans changed when, in 1710, Christopher Codrington bequeathed £10,000 to All Souls, of which £6,000 was granted to build a new library and the remainder intended to furnish it with books.[61] Given the size of the bequest, the idea to position the library rather unsatisfactorily above the colonnade across the old quadrangle was dropped, and instead it was decided to place it on the north side of the new quadrangle. This necessitated the quadrangle's reorientation, so that it would now be aligned along an east-west axis, looking west over Radcliffe Square.[62]

On 19 February 1715 the College resolved that the 'Library ... [be] built as the College Chappell was, according to the model [design] that was then shown to the Society'.[63] As the resolution indicates, Hawksmoor's idea was for the design of the library to match that of the chapel, while the fellows' building, shifted to the east side, would incorporate two huge Gothic towers. The foundation stone was laid on 21 June and, although Hawksmoor was to make several changes to the designs as built, the north quadrangle was completed more or less according to this scheme.

If the library was to match the chapel, then Hawksmoor's hand in terms of the choice of style was essentially forced; Gothic was the only way to go. But, as ever with Hawksmoor, it was rarely that simple, as revealed by careful inspection of the library window. The tracery is designed in such a way that it might be read as Gothic from the outside but is in fact a tripartite Venetian window on the inside. A rather beautiful drawing illustrates the stylistic gymnastics to which Hawksmoor had to resort in order to make this stylistic collision work.

This interaction between the Gothic and the classical is even more clearly observable in the west range, which lies between the north quadrangle and Radcliffe Square. In a letter to Dr Clarke, Hawksmoor reported that 'I have designed a Portico and Gate (next the Great Piazza) after the Roman Order, to shew that we are not quite out of charity with that manner of building'.[64] Although this particular design is lost, another similarly classical design, described by Hawksmoor as 'after the Greek', does survive, showing the central gateway with a high buttressed dome flanked on either side by screens of Corinthian columns.[65]

As built, the gateway is topped by an ogee dome and Gothic pinnacles, but the difference in stylistic effect when viewed from either side is quite surprising. Looking east towards the quadrangle, the ogee dome and pinnacles neatly correlate with the Gothic towers beyond. However, looking west from within the quadrangle, the effect is quite different. Beyond we see the Radcliffe Camera, the circular library built by James Gibbs, though very much inspired by earlier designs by Hawksmoor. Nearby, Hawksmoor had just realized the Clarendon Building, a classical temple-like building, intended to be a purpose-built home for the university press.[66] From the beginning, it seems Hawksmoor had imagined Radcliffe Square and its surrounding area as a kind of 'classical precinct' and this shaped his thinking for the inside of the gateway range.[67]

On its Radcliffe Square side the gateway is flanked by a tall medieval-like crenellated wall, while the inside is a Romanesque-style, round-arched cloister, with the crenellations on the other side obscured. This has the effect of presenting the ogee dome in a different light, alluding to a latent classicism that is brought to the fore by the more flamboyantly classical Radcliffe Camera beyond. Drawing from and marshalling a variety of references and allusions

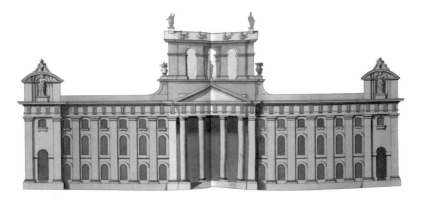

One of several elevations for the fellows' building in the north quadrangle at All Soul's, drawn by Hawksmoor in brown ink and grey wash, c. 1708–9.

Elevation and plan for
the Gothic–classical
west window of the
Codrington Library,
c. 1717–18.

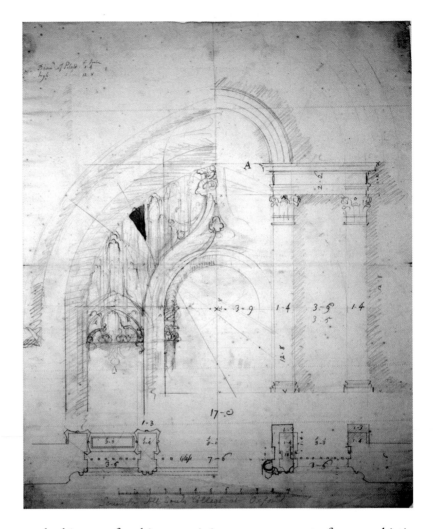

to the history of architecture, it is an arrangement of rare sophistication and the product of a mind able to see beyond stylistic labels
and categorizations.

Lines of descent

It was not until two decades later that Hawksmoor, in a letter to Joseph
Wilcocks, Dean of Westminster Abbey, actually articulated his particular version of the history of architecture that had so informed
the thinking behind his designs for All Souls.

Hawksmoor was appointed Surveyor of the Fabric at Westminster on Wren's death in 1723, but it was not until the arrival of Joseph Wilcocks as Dean in June 1731 that thoughts once again turned seriously towards building work.[68] As well as continuing the series of repairs that Wren had begun, Hawksmoor produced several designs for the completion of the Abbey, whose crossing had been left without a spire while its west-end towers were, Wren observed, 'left imperfect . . . one much higher than the other'.[69] It was in defence – and justification – of these designs that Hawksmoor was moved to write at length about the history and origins of Gothic architecture.

Intriguingly, Hawksmoor saw Gothic architecture as actually deriving from 'the Primitive Christians [who] wanted Churches [but] wou'd not, or cou'd not make use of the Temples of the Gentiles'.[70] While the Primitive Christians did 'make use of some of the Basilica's for Churches . . . they cou'd not, or wou'd not, go to the expence at

View from the north quadrangle of All Souls College looking towards Radcliffe Square.

that time, To build in the Antient Way'. Instead, they used 'stones of less dimensions . . . and sometimes patch'd up aukward Buildings, out of the Ruins of Old Magnificent Structures'.[71] This bears striking similarity to Bingham's account of the spoliated architecture of the Primitive Christians.

Hawksmoor did not, however, leave this history there. The ways the Primitive Christians built evolved, as Hawksmoor continued: 'if you observe the different periods of time, you'll find the Workmen, took the liberty to change the style & manner, of this new invention, on sundry occasions, and sometimes built as the materials could be had, to suit their purposes'.[72] Over time appeared 'a manner of Building . . . with sharp pointed Arches, and the Pillars dress'd with small Torus's', which, Hawksmoor noted, 'Mr Evelyn, Sir Chrisr: Wren . . . beleiv'd [sic] was brought from ye Saracens (in the holy war).'[73] Using Westminster Abbey as his example, Hawksmoor then traced further distinct phases in the so-called Saracen style: the 'Tracery' style (Decorated), 'Filigrane' (roughly correlating with our Perpendicular) and 'Ditterlyn' (equating to late Gothic or Tudor).[74]

In this way, Hawksmoor charted a line of descent through the native Gothic tradition all the way back to the architecture of the Primitive Christians. This architectural lineage correlated almost exactly with those being forged by contemporary divines seeking to link the Anglican Church with the early apostolic Church of the Primitive Christians. The implications of this, as far as our understanding of Hawksmoor's churches is concerned, is that we should not view the references Hawksmoor made to the architecture of the Primitive Christians in isolation, but as part of his interest in a broader continuum of the history of architecture. Indeed, they should be seen as equivalent and in the same light as the important allusions Hawksmoor made also to medieval Gothic architecture.

Given how often their Gothic qualities are remarked upon today, it is surprising that Hawksmoor's churches contain not a single pointed arch, flying buttress or pinnacle between them. Rather than relying on such 'signifiers' of Gothic architecture, Hawksmoor's churches evoke the Gothic through feeling, mood, and light and shade, an effect most apparent in the three churches he built in the old parish of Stepney.

Setting aside its Roman funereal altar finials, the octagonal coronet of the spire at St George-in-the-East that first appeared in his designs for St Alfege, has often been viewed as one of Hawksmoor's more direct borrowings from Gothic architecture. Similar forms are found in the medieval Boston 'Stump' in Lincolnshire and perhaps more significantly in the crossing at Ely Cathedral.[75] In his design for St George, Hawksmoor combined this feature with four other subsidiary 'pepper-pot' towers which stand above the spiral staircases on the north and south facades. For the source of this unusual configuration we might very well look at Ely too, and in particular its west end. As at St George, Ely's west-end tower is almost square in plan. To the south protrudes a transept arm topped by two smaller, octagonal towers which are almost exactly equivalent to Hawksmoor's 'pepper-pots', and sit in a similar relationship with the tower. Originally, Ely's southwest transept would have been matched by an identical one to the north, whose presence is still visible through the noticeable 'scar' left on that side of the building following its collapse in the Middle Ages, all but confirming it as a likely source.[76]

The link to the Gothic at St George is all about the use of configuration and handling of mass and volume; it is suggestive and allusive, rather than direct or explicit. The spires of St Anne, Limehouse, and Christ Church, Spitalfields are, in contrast, rather clearer in their more obvious Gothic silhouettes. The spire at St Anne's bears quite close resemblance to the pair Hawksmoor built at All Souls College, Oxford. The motif of repeating patterns of lozenge shapes and small circles which appears embossed on St Anne's two east end turrets (the ones Hawksmoor toyed with the idea of topping with pyramids) appears throughout his Gothic work – especially in his designs for Westminster Abbey and, again, at All Souls. Though it eschews this motif, the spire at Christ Church remains perhaps the most conventionally Gothic of any of Hawksmoor's churches, roughly equivalent to an elongated medieval broach spire. Its original form of three stages of dormer windows with ornate hood moulds is remarkably similar to one of Hawksmoor's near contemporary spire designs for Westminster Abbey.[77]

The more one looks at these buildings the more striking their allusions to the Gothic become: in the arrangement of their forms

The early Gothic west
end of Ely Cathedral.

overleaf:
Hawksmoor's twin
Gothic towers at
Westminster Abbey,
completed after his
death.

Looking up from the
base of the tower of
St Anne, Limehouse.

and massing; their silhouettes; and perhaps above all how they
seem to almost actively interact with light and shade, coming alive
in different guises as the sun rises and falls. That Hawksmoor was
fascinated by such effects is confirmed not only by his buildings, but
by his drawings too. An interest in light and shade and how they
determine the appearance of a building's form recurs throughout
his drawings. In one in particular, part of a small group of drawings
that Hawksmoor produced in 1697 for the rebuilding of St Mary
at Warwick, we see the design distilled into little more than pure

Outline elevation from 1714–20 of the west front and tower of Christ Church, Spitalfields, showing the spire as built.

Design for a west end spire at Westminster Abbey, drawn by Hawksmoor in pen and brown and yellow ink and brown wash, *c.* 1731.

architectural essence.[78] The church is shown in a dramatic perspective view rendered in the evocative pencil and grey wash technique that Hawksmoor was developing in his drawing for St Paul's. All architectural detail appears subservient to Hawksmoor's study of the building's form and massing and different layers of shade. It is a visualization of architecture as light and shadow, plane and recession, allusion rather than ornament, which has much in common with what he was actually able to translate into stone with his London churches.

Architecture and authority

By abstracting the forms and massing of Gothic architecture and wrapping them into his church designs, Hawksmoor was able to evoke the spirit of the Gothic – the Gothic 'air', as Vanbrugh might have called it – without having to resort to explicit 'signifiers' of the style. But why, we might reasonably ask, would Hawksmoor allude to the Gothic at all, if the style was so thoroughly discredited? And why, moreover, did he go to such considerable trouble and expense to make references to early Christian architecture other than to satisfy the interests of a group of ecclesiologists involved in the '1711 Commission'? What, if anything, did these references and allusions

Hawksmoor's evocative perspective view looking northeast of St Mary, Warwick, drawn in pencil and grey wash, *c.* 1695–7.

mean to those for whom these churches were part of their day-to-day experience of London – for those who worshipped in their cavernous interiors and lived and worked around their hulking white masses? The answers, I would argue, can be found through analysing the architectural and urban contexts of the areas the churches were designed, above all, to dominate.

By the early eighteenth century, the classical style was universally observed as indicating the elevated status of a building and its owners.[79] But the way the classical language was employed was by no means consistent or understood as such. Pattern books and the enterprising skills of common craftsman saw classical elements – pedimented door-cases, applied pilasters, keystones – appearing in the most ordinary of private dwellings. Such types of discrete, self-contained elements, which could easily be applied to otherwise plain facades and frontages, were used frequently in the standardized houses produced by developers like Nicholas Barbon. Classical elements in these sorts of dwellings, which were generally built by or for the aspiring middle or merchant classes, were not deployed as part of a coherent architectural system. Rather, they were used as symbols intended to confer status by giving the surface appearance of conformance to the elevated classical style.

Thus, following the arguments of the historian Peter Borsay, as classical architecture filtered down the social ranks its position as a signifier of elite status was increasingly eroded.[80] By the turn of the century even the houses of immigrant Huguenot cloth weavers in Spitalfields were beginning to spring up adorned with all manner of classical detailing. It was this architectural and urban context that Hawksmoor found himself having to deal with. A conventional classical church design, such as Wren's St James, Piccadilly, which Hawksmoor's former master had in fact put forward as a model to be followed for the churches of 1711, would have been too close to its neighbours in scale, materials and design. While striking in the 1680s, by the 1710s its red brick facades, simple cornice, white Portland stone window dressings, quoining and horizontal bands between floors had been emulated all over London, and become a key part of the architectural vocabulary of the types of houses built by the likes of Barbon.

How, then, might buildings that were intended to stand as embodiments of power and authority be distinguished in terms of their design from those further down the social ladder? Rather than relying on the conventions of classical architecture, Hawksmoor's response was to create a kind of 'hybrid architecture' – a visually complex and monumental form of classical architecture enriched by references from styles outside the classical canon and imbued with the authority of the past. It is therefore in this light that we should understand Hawksmoor's allusions and references to the Gothic and to early Christian architecture. Coupled with their towering scale and construction in brilliant white stone as opposed to the red brick of what lay around them, this was architecture that simply could not be emulated.

Several theories have been put forward to explain why Hawksmoor resorted to architectural past in quite the way he did. One of the most seductive is that suggested by Vaughan Hart, who sees the churches' towers and rooftops as monumental 'gardens of remembrance', interpreting their urns, altars, obelisks and statues as an iconography of memorialization, deriving from the general interest in death arising during the period.[81] 'Hawksmoor,' Hart suggests, 'would have been well aware of the memorial origin and meaning of the forms he used on his churches.'[82] Certainly an architect as learned and thoughtful as Hawksmoor would have understood the associations of the elements he was using, even if we have no confirmation that Hart's interpretations reflect Hawksmoor's intentions. But it seems highly unlikely that the churches' users would have comprehended the obscure and rarefied meanings that Hart argues Hawksmoor was trying to impart.[83]

While Hart's interpretation has some credence, it is, I would argue, only by understanding Hawksmoor churches more generally as aspiring towards an architecture of authority that we might draw together the desires of the Commission, the interests and outlook of the architect and, pivotally, the roles the churches were designed to play on an urban scale for their local population. Moreover, it is the only explanation that offers a convincing case for why Hawksmoor might have recourse to Gothic architecture at a time when many questioned its status as architecture at all.

Despite the widespread aspersions on the Gothic, Hawksmoor recognized how medieval buildings continued to have important civic and symbolic functions.[84] He concluded his letter to Dean Wilcocks of 1734–5, in which he outlined his account of the history of the Gothic, by stating

> These are the different modes of this modern way (if I may
> call it so) that we have us'd in England which is in most of
> our Great Churches and Publick Buildings, and what the
> people call in general (and without distinction) Gothick.[85]

Medieval churches remained the focus of village life. Learning was still very much associated with medieval establishments, where classical architecture was only just beginning to penetrate. A building as venerable and historically significant as Westminster Abbey, for example, would still have held real power, with which its Gothic-ness, as symbolic of its ancestry, was intertwined. This is confirmed by the nature of Hawksmoor's 'Gothic vocabulary' and one particularly favoured element.

The best known of Hawksmoor's drawings for the completion of Westminster Abbey is a perspective view from the north. The drawing literally builds upon Wenceslaus Hollar's view of 1654 that depicted the abbey in its unfinished state. Little visible had changed in the intervening 80 years and Hollar's view was copied and enlarged, likely by one of Hawksmoor's assistants. To this, as a note makes clear, Hawksmoor added 'the West Towers and the middle Lantern as intended'.[86] The west towers appear relatively close to their completed form. In contrast, three different designs for the lantern, which all went unbuilt, were included on fold-out flaps. The outermost version shows a highly ornate octagonal lantern supported by buttresses and pinnacles, with small ogee domes set into the four corner recesses. Underneath and lesser known are two variants of an ogee dome: one tall and elongated, the other squat; and both supported on a low tower by battlements and pinnacles.[87]

Together with pinnacles projecting above the roof line, panels with thick reveals and heavy cornicing, the ogee dome was a mainstay in Hawksmoor's Gothic works, appearing in designs for All Souls

Perspective view of
Westminster Abbey
from the north with one
version of Hawksmoor's
proposals for completing
the crossing and west
end. Drawn in pen and
brown and grey ink and
brown wash, *c.* 1731.

College, Oxford, and for St Mary, Warwick. Though to our eyes the
ogee dome has connotations of Middle Eastern architecture, it had
a long history in British architecture (with two even visible in Hollar's
engraving of the abbey). It is a common feature of Elizabethan architecture, notably at Burghley Hall in Lincolnshire, where multiple
ogee domes animate the roofline, along with a pyramid that tops a
courtyard gateway. It even appears in coded form in Wren's architecture: in Tom Tower at Christ Church College, Oxford, and also at St
Mary le Bow. But in the context of London there were perhaps few
more clear landmarks than the ogee domes that topped the corners
of the White Tower at the Tower of London, renewed in the 1530s.[88]
It is hard to imagine that Hawksmoor did not have this major land-
mark in mind when he proposed using the ogee dome for the crossing
at Westminster Abbey.

    Hawksmoor, it would seem, saw little difference between his
work at Westminster Abbey and on his London churches – and, for
us, it makes sense to see them in the same light. Despite the quite radically different contexts of the royal seat of Westminster and London's
emerging suburbs, Hawksmoor's overriding concern remained in

creating an architecture of authority. Working within the existing Gothic context at Westminster Abbey, Hawksmoor was relatively direct in his references to and interpretation of medieval architecture. But when it came to his churches – new buildings that had to remain within the conventional decorum of classical architecture – Hawksmoor was necessarily much more allusive, giving them a Gothic 'air'. Because it lacked the Gothic's taint, Hawksmoor could be rather more explicit in quotations from early Christian architecture, and thus more overtly eclectic. But to Hawksmoor's mind these references and allusions all derived from this broader continuum of Gothic history that paralleled the alternative lineage constructed by the likes of Hickes and Bingham from the contemporary Anglican Church back to the origins of Christianity.

Whether we look at Hawksmoor's churches, his work at Westminster Abbey or, indeed, at All Souls College, Oxford, it is clear that these buildings and interventions were not constructed for the here and now, though they were, of course, shaped by that context. This was architecture that was designed from the very beginning to stand the test of time and aspire to 'eternity' as Wren would have seen it. Standing in new and emerging parts of London where no architectural monuments yet existed, Hawksmoor's churches were designed to take on the role played by buildings such as Westminster Abbey in the older parts of the city. Looming as vital symbols of public good, Hawksmoor's churches were to provide a powerful counterpoint to the social and moral uncertainties sparked by the private priorities of trade and commerce.

For their builders, the '1711 churches' were always intended to be colossal structures, set on open sites, visible from miles around – physically dominating the city and standing as social and moral beacons for its populace.[89] Yet their striking design has seen Hawksmoor's churches have a profounder and more enduring effect on Londoners then and over history than the Commission could have imagined.

For anyone getting off the bus amid the hustle and bustle of Commercial Road, the short walk south down Cannon Street Road towards Hawksmoor's St George-in-the-East is a comparatively calm one. There still remain a few late Georgian houses either side, though their peeling stuccoed fronts now house computer repair shops and the like. As one approaches the rail bridge, the curious octagonal coronet of St George's west tower appears in glimpses, its funereal altars glistening in the sunlight. After one has crossed Cable Street, the three towers and multitudinous lower-rise blocks of the St George's Estate dominate the view to the right, while to the east a certain regularity now appears in the modest Georgian-style terrace. Built in the late 1960s, St George's Estate incorporated Wellclose Square, which had been built up in the 1680s by Barbon and others. Little if anything from that time survives, but the estate's layout still revolves around the vestigial square.

St George-in-the-East's looming presence is now hard to ignore, but it is always revelatory when one turns the corner to be confronted by its towering layered west face, which unnervingly appears to rest on four comparatively undersized Ionic pilasters. Only towards the Highway does the church finally have the wide open site that Hawksmoor always wanted for it, after the small run of terraced houses along its south side was destroyed in the Blitz.

On the opposing corner of Cannon Street Road and the Highway, a new housing development is just nearing completion. Seeking to

The view looking down Fournier Street towards Christ Church, Spitalfields, in 1909.

overleaf: St George-in-the-East viewed from the south.

cash-in on the proximity of Hawksmoor's architectural marvel, the developer has enterprisingly named the complex of flats 'The Hawksmoors'. It is boxy, brick and metal panel clad and a deeply lacklustre affair that is a limp affront to St George-in-the-East across the road.

This is a church that seems to repel whatever one throws at it, like paint dripping off a shiny surface. In keeping with all Hawksmoor's churches, this is architecture conceived in the grandest terms – both in its visual appearance and its perceived power to shape and mould ideas and behaviour on an individual and social level. Having seen off the likes of Barbon long ago, not even the 1960s housing estate or its adjacent bastard child (not to mention the Luftwaffe) have been able to overcome it. For the motorists speeding their way in and out of the City along the Highway, the way Hawksmoor's church suddenly rears up and then disappears from view is a familiar sight, but one whose power does not easily diminish.

THREE
FALLING INTO SHADOW

ONE OF THE BEST WAYS to get a sense of the full sweep of Hawksmoor's London churches is actually by train on the approach into London Bridge Station from the southeast. It is a stretch of track familiar to millions of commuters as trains from Kent and Sussex, not to mention the outer parts of London, converge around New Cross before they head northwest into London Bridge, towered over today by the Shard.

Passing Deptford and then Southwark parks, St Anne, Limehouse, suddenly emerges out of the window to the right, peering between the trees from the other side of the Thames. Even from this distance, its white stone seems far more resilient than the oversized mass of glass towers of Canary Wharf, which try, but can never quite manage, to overcome it. As the train progresses now through Bermondsey, St George-in-the-East looms up from across the river, catching the light whatever the weather. Christ Church remains hidden, but, having already been assailed by its two sister churches, one can almost feel its presence.

As the train gently slows down just before pulling into London Bridge, it passes the surreal sight of a modern building of brown brick and glass set upon a shining plinth of Portland stone. This is the headquarters of the London City Mission and it stands upon the base of Hawksmoor and John James' St John, Horsleydown, a church famous before its demolition for its spire, which took the form of a tapering Ionic column. For architect and current Surveyor of the Fabric at Westminster Abbey, Ptolemy Dean, who makes the

St John, Horsleydown,
which stood just off
Tower Bridge Road
until its demolition. The
London City Mission
offices now on the site
were built 1972–6.

journey into London Bridge regularly, the presence of this withered brown building makes it appear 'as if nothing will grow on that stone plinth, it has an indestructible power'.[1] The church's former presence has seemingly salted the earth below it, denying life to anything that might take its place in the cityscape.

Still standing tall as the cityscape has changed irrevocably around them, Hawksmoor's churches have today achieved the eternity that

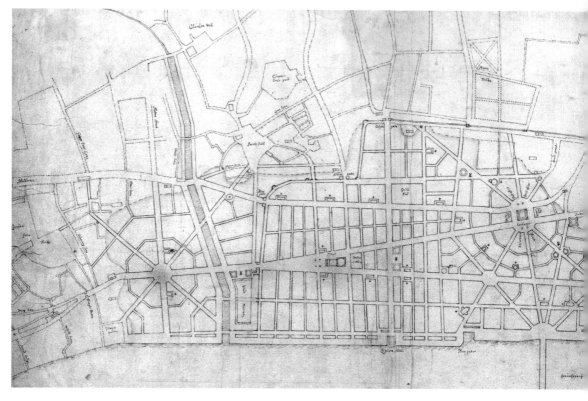

Wren argued architecture should aim at. Hawksmoor's ideas about cities, however, ran far deeper than simply building churches. Like his master, he was fascinated by the possibilities of city planning, and produced city plans for Oxford, Cambridge and parts of London – the focus of the first part of this chapter. However, when we compare Hawksmoor's city plans with Wren's familiar post-Great Fire plan for London, key differences between them quickly become apparent. Wren's principal concern was to impose spatial order through the plan itself. The buildings that sat between the great radiating boulevards with which he proposed to replace London's mix-mash of medieval streets were really of secondary importance. Hawksmoor's approach was essentially the reverse. For him the architectural monument was everything. Rather than using the plan to determine where buildings would be sited, Hawksmoor began with the buildings first, with whatever new interventions he proposed devised in order to accentuate the spatial relationships between the most important buildings

Wren's design for replacing the City of London after the Great Fire, 1666.

in the cityscape. He was far less concerned with what lay between these grand architectural monuments – both in terms of the street plan and particular buildings. In this, therefore, Hawksmoor's approach to town planning was in many ways the natural progression of ideas that informed his churches.

Despite their grandiosity – though we could also say because of it – Hawksmoor's city plans were never realized. Time and again, Hawksmoor's ideas exceeded what was practically feasible, as well as politically or economically possible. In a letter to the third Earl of Carlisle just two years before his death, Hawksmoor despaired that Greenwich Hospital had, in his view, been left unfinished: 'I once thought it wou'd have been a publick Building, but it will sink into a deformed Barrac'.[2] It is not a description that many familiar with Greenwich would recognize, yet it illustrates rather clearly the extent to which Hawksmoor's insatiable imagination frequently ran much further than most would deem realistic.

However, it was not just their impracticality that left some of Hawksmoor's grander ideas unrealized. In his later years he found himself increasingly having to contend with an architectural climate that he saw as frequently conspiring against him. With Vanbrugh's death in 1726 and Wren's, at 91 years old, three years before, Hawksmoor ploughed an increasingly lonely furrow for the last decade of his life. Professionally, he was frequently under attack from a range of ambitious, yet often patently unqualified men, who wanted his official positions. The hold that Wren and his followers had had over the Office of Works and, indeed, the nascent profession of architecture itself, had passed. This situation was, though, not solely to do with politics and personality. Taste itself was changing in a way that was to have important repercussions for the remainder of Hawksmoor's career and subsequent reputation.

As Hawksmoor's churches rose across London, his grand, eclectic form of classical architecture was increasingly under attack from proponents of a calm, ordered and restrained architecture that took inspiration from the work of the sixteenth-century Italian architect Andrea Palladio and his British interpreter, Inigo Jones. Led by Lord Burlington, the Palladians aimed at redefining British architectural taste and succeeded by holding almost complete sway from the mid-1720s. Far from being revered, the architecture of Wren, Vanbrugh and Hawksmoor became the style against which the Palladians defined their own architectural ideas. Hawksmoor became yesterday's man with his architecture increasingly considered irrational, idiosyncratic and, by some, frankly bizarre, ensuring that even before his death Hawksmoor's reputation began to fall into shadow.

Despite this, however, the Earl of Carlisle remained faithful to Hawksmoor, who had been involved at Castle Howard since before the first stone was laid. With the bulk of the house complete, attention turned towards the garden where Hawksmoor realized several buildings and structures, notably the great Mausoleum. Completed after Hawksmoor's death, and though subject to interference from Lord Burlington himself, the Mausoleum crystallized, perhaps above all else, Hawksmoor's innate feeling for architecture of form, mass and effect that haunts and enraptures in equal measure. It was testament to Hawksmoor's steely determination that, despite declining health and ever more frequent attacks upon his work, he was still able to realize a building of such enduring power, one that is in many ways his masterpiece.

London plans

Hawksmoor was never in the position to create an overall plan for London in the way Wren had done the generation before, nor would it, in any case, have seemed appropriate. The uneasy political position of the restored monarch and priorities of private property put paid to Wren's plan. By the early eighteenth century private commercial interests were so well entrenched that any kind of overall plan for London would have been seen as – and probably would have been – counterproductive to the city's economic fortunes.[3] However, plans on a more local scale were possible, even if those that Hawksmoor proposed went unrealized. The ones of most interest were for the areas around St Paul's Cathedral, Westminster and Greenwich. From these episodes, taken from different moments of his career, it is possible to deduce the broader, overriding principles that shaped Hawksmoor's approach to city planning.

In 1728 Hawksmoor published *Remarks on the Founding and Carrying on the Buildings of the Royal Hospital at Greenwich*, a report he had presented to the Admiralty the previous year in which he pleaded for the completion of the Hospital on the scale originally intended. 'We may instance *Rome*,' Hawksmoor stated,

for tho' there are many Devices to draw in Foreigners, yet their admirable and stupendous Buildings have no small

Hawksmoor's plan for completing Greenwich Hospital, which accompanied his *Remarks on the Founding and Carrying on the Buildings of the Royal Hospital at Greenwich* (1728).

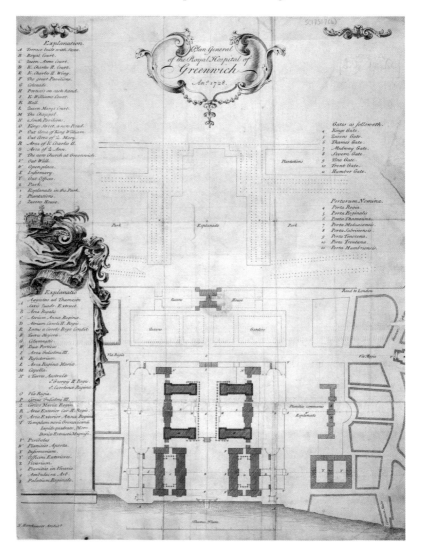

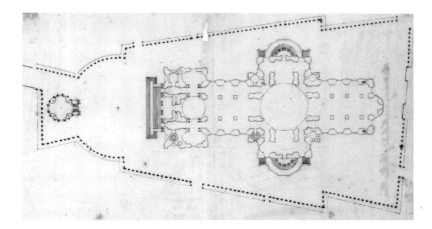

Plan for a colonnaded precinct around St Paul's, drawn by Hawksmoor. *c.* 1696–7.

Share in captivating the Attention of Strangers, to the great Advantage of the Inhabitants, and greatly owing to the Encouragement of Arts and Architecture . . .[4]

Included with Hawksmoor's text was a plan showing how he proposed to replace the Romney Road, which originally, and rather oddly, ran underneath the Queen's House, with a new *Via Regia* that would pass adjacent to the Hospital. Not only would this improve the situation of the Queen's House, to which we can see he planned to add radiating wings, but it would extend an axial line to the east front of his church of St Alfege. Although more modest than his earlier designs for creating a huge domed church or colossal tower, Hawksmoor's *Via Regia* proposal succinctly illustrates the extent to which he thought about the relationship between buildings. Here, it was on a relatively local level, but the principal remained the same even when extended to the city scale, as revealed in his proposals for the area around St Paul's.

We know from his post-Fire plan that Wren had intended the rebuilt St Paul's Cathedral to sit at the intersection of two great boulevards. As constructed, however, it was enclosed by buildings, largely rebuilt on the same plots as the ones which had burned. The effect of this remains to this day. The approach to St Paul's up Ludgate Hill is one of revelation as the cathedral suddenly appears in sight as the road snakes around; it is an experience quite unlike approaching a grand public building in a European capital.

As early as 1696–7, as Gordon Higgott has recently identified, Hawksmoor produced a design for a colonnaded precinct around the cathedral.[5] Like his later designs for a domed chapel at Greenwich, its angles and curves recall Bernini's Piazza San Pietro; it is hard to believe Hawksmoor did not have that example in his mind when he designed it. At the west end of the precinct sits a circular colonnaded structure, which was intended as a baptistry or possibly a royal mausoleum. Its design, known also from an elevation, is close to Wren's design in the 1670s for a mausoleum for Charles I, while also anticipating the mausoleum Hawksmoor designed at Castle Howard.[6]

Heading from St Paul's down Ludgate Hill to the west, up Fleet Street and onto the Strand we come to James Gibbs's St Mary le Strand, one of the four 1711 churches Hawksmoor was not involved in designing. Here, Hawksmoor proposed to the erect a column in the Roman manner in honour of Queen Anne, following a stipulation by the Commission.[7] Although conceived at different times, it seems likely that Hawksmoor was thinking of his design for the St Paul's precinct and baptistry/mausoleum when proposing this new monumental column. Indeed, by considering them in relation to each other, we see the same principle of creating axial linkages as at Greenwich, but here extending across the city.

If both had been built, the St Paul's precinct coupled with the Strand column would have constituted a powerful urban intervention. But it was arguably at Westminster that we find what would have been Hawksmoor's most significant work in urban rather than purely architectural terms. Engaged at Westminster Abbey from Wren's death in 1723, and though there was much work to be done on the Abbey itself, not to mention his obligations elsewhere, Hawksmoor's thoughts soon turned to rethinking the surrounding urban site and, more specifically, the idea of building a new bridge.

The possibility of a new bridge at Westminster was a popular discussion during the 1730s. Daniel Defoe had talked of the need for a bridge in his *A Tour thro' the Whole Island of Great Britain* while Alexander Pope hinted at the idea in his famous *Epistle to Burlington* (1731).[8] Amid a crescendo of debate during 1736, concerned principally with whether the bridge should be of wood or stone, Hawksmoor published a pamphlet entitled *A Short Historical Account of London-Bridge with A Proposition for a New Stone-Bridge at Westminster.* The account included a description of both the history and structure of London Bridge, and a detailed proposal for a new bridge at Westminster, which Hawksmoor supported with designs and a description by Charles Labelye, to whose designs the bridge was eventually begun in 1739, on the predicted 'Fall of the Water . . . and some Conjectures of the Effects it will probably have on Navigation of the River'.[9]

There was, Hawksmoor wrote, 'nothing conducing more to facilitate and promote the Trade and Prosperity of Towns or Cities than such commodious Edifices for an easy and publick Access' than 'Bridges of Stone'.[10] To his mind, the bridge represented an opportunity of squaring the circle of London's expansion. The new bridge would aid businesses and individuals alike by alleviating the 'Badness and Inconveniency of *Lambeth-Ferry*, since there is scarce any one ignorant of it, and some have found it to their Cost'.[11] As well as being a functional structure, the bridge could also stand as a powerful public symbol, of one nation united under George II, reconciling the destabilizing forces of trade and commerce with civic virtue and public good. As Hawksmoor continued,

> The several publick Buildings advanced by him, testify the great Pleasure he has in magnificent and useful Works; and

Hawksmoor's proposed design for the central archway of a new bridge at Westminster, *c.* 1736.

An outline plan of
Westminster showing
various sites for a
bridge, included in
Hawksmoor's *A Short
Historical Account of
London-Bridge* (1736).

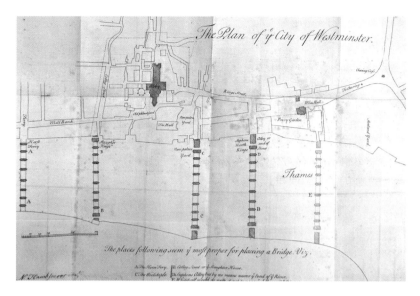

a Bridge of Stone built over the *Thames* in his Reign, for the
Good of his People, will be . . . an everlasting Trophy to his
Honour and Memory in times to come.[12]

Alongside designs for the bridge itself, Hawksmoor also published a plan of Westminster that indicated several locations where
the bridge could feasibly be sited. The site marked C – 'New Palace
Yard' – was clearly his favoured location, prominently positioned
near Westminster Hall.[13] A dotted line marks the outer limits of
what Hawksmoor no doubt imagined as a new forum akin to the
Roman model. The areas around the Abbey would be cleared of the
various buildings that had grown up over the centuries, thereby
allowing it be viewed in the round, just as he hoped his Stepney
churches would be. Westminster, however, was a site of national
importance, and here Hawksmoor's proposals took on a further level
of grandeur. Had it been built, Hawksmoor's bridge at Westminster
would have surely constituted the grand culmination of his ideas
on how buildings contribute to the cityscape: a structure facilitat-
ing private enterprise while at the same time standing as a powerful
symbol of the public good.

Reactions

Despite his many disappointments at Westminster and elsewhere, it was obvious from what Hawksmoor actually did get built in London – principally his churches – were architectural statements of the grandest kind. They were, after all, conceived from the very beginning to stand out in the cityscape – and did so. It therefore came as no surprise that such grand and, in some ways, ostentatious buildings would attract criticism, especially as architectural taste began to change.

A watershed moment was the publication in 1715 of *Vitruvius Britannicus* by the Scottish architect Colen Campbell. Best described as an architectural manifesto, this documented the current state of British architecture and offered a new exemplar for it to follow:

> above all, the great *Palladio*, who has exceeded all that were gone before him, and surpass'd his Contemporaries, whose ingenious Labours will eclipse many, and rival most of the Ancients. And indeed, this excellent *Architect* seems to have arrived to a *Ne plus ultra* of his Art.[14]

Why did Campbell ascribe such importance for contemporary British architecture to the work of an Italian architect who had been dead for over 130 years? On the surface it seems a rather strange position, but there were several reasons for it. Firstly, Palladio's architecture, notably his famous villas around Vicenza, had proved especially formative for Inigo Jones, the early seventeenth-century architect who was credited as the first to introduce an Italianate form of classical architecture into Britain and is usually assumed to be the 'Vitruvius Britannicus' of the book's title, the great architect of Augustan Rome reborn. Jones had brought back many of Palladio's drawings from his travels, and the Italian's work was well known in Britain and elsewhere through his hugely influential treatise *I quattro libri dell'architettura*, published in 1570. Furthermore, the political and geographical separation of Palladio's work in and around Vicenza and Venice from Papal Rome, and the fact that he was most famous for his villas, rather than ecclesiastical architecture, made his work a little more palatable for a nation still riven by a distrust of Catholics.

Despite his promotion of Palladio and Jones in the first volume of *Vitruvius Britannicus*, Campbell also reflected on what he described as the 'Happiness of the *British Nation*, that at present abounds so many learned and ingenious Gentlemen', mentioning Wren, Vanbrugh and Hawksmoor, among others of that generation. Campbell could scarcely have criticized them. As a survey of both British architecture as it was then, as well as a manifesto of where it should head, *Vitruvius Britannicus* included many examples of their work, but in the succeeding volumes that appeared in 1717 and 1725 Campbell increasingly focused on and advocated the building of designs inspired by Palladio. These included several by his sometime patron, Lord Burlington, in whose buildings we find perhaps the clearest expression of the Palladian taste that was conceived from the outset in direct opposition to the architecture of Hawksmoor and his colleagues.

Famously described by Horace Walpole as the 'Apollo of the Arts', Richard Boyle, the third Earl of Burlington, was an important patron of art and music; indeed, the composer Handel actually lived for a time at Burlington's town residence on Piccadilly. It was, however, in architecture that Burlington had his great impact and influence.

Elevation of Burlington House by Colen Campbell from volume III (1725) of his *Vitruvius Britannicus*.

As a young man Burlington visited Italy three times, immersing himself in Palladio's architecture. Upon his return from one of these Italian trips, Burlington commissioned Campbell to reface the 1660s Burlington House on Piccadilly in the new Palladian style. While

following Palladio, Campbell's design also drew from works by Jones, notably the Banqueting House at Whitehall. The resulting facade still survives, despite the addition of a further storey in the 1860s by the Royal Academy of Arts (RA), the building's present occupiers. We see all the facade's constituent elements acting in concert to create a coherent, overriding sense of rhythm and order, quite unlike Hawksmoor's intuitive handling of mass.

From its outset at Burlington House, Palladian architecture was conceived as a distinctly aristocratic style, with Burlington himself, by the early 1720s, the chief arbiter of Palladian taste. The most convincing way to read Palladian architecture is as an attempt to wrest the classical language away from the market and out of the hands of commercial builders like Barbon and his successors. In this aim it was equivalent to Hawksmoor's own architectural strategies. However, while Hawksmoor sought to differentiate his architecture through bold sculptural effects and wide-ranging references, Palladian architecture was marked by its uniformity. Adhering to Palladian strictures was a way of marking out one's place in, and conformance to, the decorum of an elite social group. While Palladio and Jones stood as the main exemplars, in the words of Robert Morris, its foremost theorist, Palladian taste was guided above all else by 'symmetry', 'concordance' and 'reason' to create architecture that was 'beautiful', 'harmonious' and 'agreeable'.[15] Such abstract concepts were intended to be comprehensible only to those of noble sensibility and learning.[16]

Although true Palladian taste could not be reduced to a series of forms or motifs to be copied from a pattern book, in time it was emulated and ultimately commodified. This did not, however, happen in the usual way and was actually begun by a hack journalist with no architectural training, James Ralph. Given the way Palladian taste was conceived through particular terms or concepts, such as those coined by Morris, it is unsurprising that Ralph sought to appropriate not the aesthetics of Palladian architecture, but the very language in which it was understood. Central to this was Ralph's *Critical Review*, sometimes overlooked by architectural historians, but which is vital to understanding the architectural climate of the time. Strewn across its pages were several vitriolic attacks on Hawksmoor's churches, which did much to set the tone in how those buildings and their architect were viewed over subsequent decades.

Critics

Born from a number of articles published over the previous year, Ralph's *A Critical Review of the Publick Buildings, Statues and Ornaments in, and about London and Westminster*, to give it its full title, was published as a single volume in 1734.[17] Ralph stated in the dedication that 'beauty is first founded in simplicity, and harmony; and [is] magnificent in propriety of ornament, and nobleness of imagination'.[18] These series of terms recur throughout the *Review*, employed as authoritative yardsticks of taste according to which Ralph constructed his critiques. In a similar way to being dressed in the latest fashionable attire or possessing a popular print, these terms would – their users hoped – express the appearance of cultural education and social status. This was particularly important given that the *Review* was, after all, aimed at a broad journal readership, few of whom had the means actually to build their own Palladian mansion.

Ralph launched numerous attacks against a variety of targets, but quite possibly reserved his harshest words for Hawksmoor's architecture, in particular

> the four following churches which have been built at *Limehouse*, *Ratcliff*, *Horsley-down*, and *Spittle-fields*, tho' they have all the advantage of ground which can be desired, are not to be looked at without displeasure. They are mere Gothique heaps of stone, without form or order; and meet with contempt from the best and worst tastes alike. The last, especially, deserves the severest condemnation, in that 'tis built at a monstrous expence, and yet is, beyond question, one of the most absurd piles in *Europe*.[19]

The churches to which Ralph referred were, of course, St Anne, Limehouse, St George-in-the-East, St John, Horsleydown, which Hawksmoor designed with John James, and Christ Church, Spitalfields, for which 'Gothique' is used quite simply here as a term of abuse, in the way that can be traced back to Vasari. To his assessment of Hawksmoor's churches, we might contrast Ralph's comments on the epitome of 'good taste' – Campbell's facade at Burlington House – which he described as 'simple and magnificent . . . august and beautiful'.

Ralph's criticisms of Hawksmoor's churches did not go un-answered. A concerted rebuttal appeared in the *Grub Street Journal* from July 1734 to March 1735 by the wonderfully named commentator Batty Langley. Writing under the masonic pseudonym 'Mr Hiram', Langley stood up for Hawksmoor's work as part of a general defence of native British architecture, including the Gothic, against what he saw as the imported Palladian style. His views on Hawksmoor's 'Stepney churches' are particularly fascinating for just how close his description came to Hawksmoor's intentions:

> That stile or mode, after which the churches at *Limehouse* and *Ratcliff* are built, is a mean between the Greek and Gothique architecture; and was first invented and practiced by NATHANIEL HAWKSMOOR, Esq; under whose direction those structures were erected; and to whom this kingdom is greatly obliged for many other strong and magnificent piles . . . every judge of architecture, who has viewed and examined those buildings, at a proper distance, where their parts may be distinctly seen, has always agreed, that their stiles or modes were truly strong and magnificent, and at the same time light and genteel.[20]

We can attribute the mistake in Hawksmoor's first name to a moment-ary lapse; Hawksmoor's son-in-law, Nathaniel Blackerby, treasurer to the Fifty New Churches Commission, was a patron of Langley's. It was in any case corrected in the next issue.[21] Despite this mistake, the perceptiveness of Langley's remarks – notably their appreci-ation of Hawksmoor's use of both classical and Gothic forms, and the way his churches were in many ways intended to be viewed from afar – illustrate that he clearly understood what Hawksmoor was trying to achieve with these buildings. In fact he almost certainly knew Hawksmoor personally and judging from some of his later comments on the 'Stepney churches' very likely discussed these buildings with him, so accurate are his descriptions. At St George-in-the-East, Langley described how the

> tower is of a more solum aspect than that of *Lime-house,* being crown'd with a group of square columns affix'd to a Cylinder, each supporting an ornament in manner of an altar, on which the ancients made their offerings.

While a little further down the river at St Anne, Limehouse,

> The tower is a most magnificent pile, exhibiting the most solemn reverend aspect when viewed in front; and when at an angle ... the most gay and airy. This different appearance upon changing the point of view, is surprisingly delight-ful. To this I could add much more in praise of this building: but as this is sufficient to prove our pretended Critic an *ignoramus* ...[22]

Surprisingly, despite the personal nature of his attacks, not all of Ralph's remarks concerning Hawksmoor's churches were con-demnatory. The not remotely Palladian tower of St Vedast, Foster Lane, though described by the Earl of Shaftesbury as of the 'Gothick kind', received quite a positive appraisal from Ralph:[23]

> the beautiful pyramid it forms, and the just and well-proportion'd simplicity of all its parts, satisfy the mind so effectually, that nothing seems to be wanting, and nothing can be spare.[24]

Langley made sure to pick Ralph up on his inconsistency, especially when it crossed into his own personal and professional interests in the Gothic:

> 'Tis very surprising, that this gentleman should think *the tower of St Michael's Cornhill a magnificent pile,* since 'tis in the Gothic stile, which he so much condemns. To this may

be added, that beautiful Gothic tower of St Mary Aldermary in St Thomas Apostles; which his lofty eyes over-looked, and which I think was built by the immortal Sir CHRISTOPHER WREN.[25]

Langley was perhaps motivated in these rebuttals by his personal connection to Hawksmoor, but he was also concerned with his own career as an architectural writer, no doubt anxious to ensure that no single voice could hold a monopoly on architectural taste in the public sphere, especially when that taste so contrasted with his own ideas.[26]

'Mistook whim for genius'

When he came to St George's, Bloomsbury, Ralph was simply at a loss to explain its design:

Twill be impossible to pass by the new church of *St George, Bloomsbury*, without giving it a very particular survey; 'tis built all of stone, is adorn'd with a pompous portico, can boast many other decorations, has been stinted in no expence; and yet, upon the whole, is ridiculous and absurd even to a proverb. The reason is this, the builder mistook whim for genius, and ornament for taste: he has even err'd so much, that the very portico does not seem to be in the middle of the church, and as to the steeple, it is stuck on like a wen to the rest of the building; then the execrable conceit of setting up the King on the top of it, excites nothing but laughter in the ignorant, and contempt in the judge. In short, 'tis a lasting reflection on the fame of the architect, and the understanding of those who employed him.[27]

To be fair to Ralph, the spire is certainly Hawksmoor's strangest. Its stepped pyramidal form derives from the Mausoleum at Halicarnassus, a tomb built in the mid-fourth century BC in what is now Turkey by Mausolus, a provincial governor in the Persian empire. The descriptions of it by Vitruvius and Pliny were well known to Wren and Hawksmoor. Wren described the Mausoleum in his fourth *Tract* and Hawksmoor in fact produced a drawing to illustrate that description.[28] As for the sculpture, the spire featured the lion and the unicorn of the royal coat of arms engaged in playful combat, with the pyramid topped, as Ralph observed, by a statue of George 1 himself. It seems Hawksmoor had actually proceeded with the sculpture without the permission of the Commission, which admonished him for it, though it did concede that 'Some Sort of Decorations were necessary in these Places'.[29]

Ralph was not the only observer to note the idiosyncrasy of St George's, Bloomsbury. While his disparaging critique of Hawksmoor's church was framed in purely visual terms, criticism, or rather satire, of its moral imperatives came from none other than William Hogarth.

As Hawksmoor's churches were coming to completion in the early 1730s and their architect, by now in his late sixties, was increasingly infirm and afflicted with gout, Hogarth was achieving his greatest period of success. *A Harlot's Progress* appeared in 1731, followed by *A Rake's Progress* in 1735 and *Marriage à-la-mode* in 1743. These cycles of paintings were engraved, taking their images and stories far and wide. In 1751 Hogarth published a pair of engravings – *Beer Street* and *Gin Lane* – in support of the soon to be passed Gin Act that aimed to curb excessive gin consumption among London's poor.

Gin Lane was a fictional street yet one quite clearly situated among the infamous rookeries of the parish of St Giles around Seven Dials, north of Covent Garden. Amid the various incidents unfolding in the foreground, the city is depicted crumbling and filthy, a literal heap of dilapidated ruins. To the right a collapsed wall reveals a man hanging from a rafter, while further along a house is shown in the very process of collapsing. Gripe's pawnbrokers is ironically the only building in good repair and adorned with comparatively luxurious classical adornments. In the background, rising high over the mass of collapsed buildings, we see the stepped pyramidal spire of St George's, viewed by Hogarth as an ironic symbol of the impotence of the monarch and the state to cure the maladies afflicting the city and its people.

Hogarth's architectural analogy becomes even clearer when *Beer Street* and *Gin Lane* are compared. In the latter, the city is in a

William Hogarth's *Gin Lane*, published in 1751.

well-tended state, only the pawnbroker is in disrepair. The distiller and undertaker are replaced by the blacksmith, pavior (paver) and butcher, while those drinking the wholesome native beer are doing so after a long day's productive work.

There were clearly some similarities in the ways Hogarth and Hawksmoor equated the physical state of the city and the moral standing of its inhabitants. But they differed fundamentally on the point of whether architectural interventions had the ability to engender moral or social reform. Hogarth certainly understood what Hawksmoor and the Commission were trying to achieve, but vehemently disagreed that such grand and highly symbolic architectural statements as Hawksmoor's churches had any real impact, other than standing, in his view, as vainglorious monuments while London rotted both physically and morally around them.[30]

Gin Lane was published after Hawksmoor's death, so the effects of its satire on the spire of St George's, Bloomsbury were felt only on his posthumous reputation. Hogarth had similarly few sympathies with the Palladians and directed his satire at Burlington's rule of taste in an early print, *Masquerades and Operas*, published in 1724. Nevertheless during the 1720s, under Lord Burlington's influence, Palladian architects gained increasing prominence and patronage, and on several occasions shut Hawksmoor out of positions that he felt were rightfully his.

Matters had already come to a head in 1718, when Wren was deposed as Surveyor to the Office of Works and Hawksmoor, too, was relieved of his role as Secretary. Wren's replacement was the amateur William Benson, who, Hawksmoor wrote, 'in extreme Need of an employment . . . disguising himself under the pretence of an Architect, got himself made Surveyor Generall'.[31] Hawksmoor's position was taken by Benson's brother. Their reign over the Office was, however, rather short, lasting just one notorious year, and finally ending with a scandal over repairs to the House of Lords, in which, somewhat ironically, Colen Campbell was also implicated.

Campbell did not give up though, and upon Vanbrugh's death in 1726, engineered to replace him as Surveyor at Greenwich. This clearly irked Hawksmoor. He felt the position should have been his own, relaying in a letter to Carlisle how Campbell, 'smelling this out, in spite of all ye Lords of ye Admiralty could doe, got ye place Sr John, had made at Greenwich'.[32]

Despite being passed over repeatedly as others far less qualified jostled for positions, Hawksmoor was able to regain his position as Secretary to the Office of Works in 1726 thanks to the 'kinde assistance' of the Earl of Carlisle. By then, with his friend and ally Vanbrugh dead, Hawksmoor was heavily outnumbered by the sinecurists and Palladians, and it was with mocking irony that he reported to Carlisle how he had 'ye honor to be the Secretary to his honble Board'.[33]

Return to Castle Howard

Throughout the 1720s and until Hawksmoor's death in 1736, Carlisle remained loyal to the architect who had worked at Castle Howard from the beginning. From the tranche of letters that survives, it seems the two developed a close personal affinity, even friendship, despite the huge difference in their social standings. After Vanbrugh's death in 1726 Hawksmoor was Carlisle's only architect, and, with the house largely complete, their attention turned towards the garden.

The first designs of significance are those for the belvedere, which became the Temple of the Four Winds on the edge of Wray Wood. It was ultimately realized to Vanbrugh's design, with the building work supervised by Hawksmoor after his friend's death. Vanbrugh envisaged a 'Temple of smooth freestone with a portico each way, and Dom'd over ye center' – a loose interpretation of Palladio's Villa Rotunda.[34] Hawksmoor produced designs for Carlisle's 'amusement', no doubt conscious that his patron was already happy with what Vanbrugh had produced. Hawksmoor's first design was 'in a Square forme built with rough stone, except ye apertures, which are ornaments after ye Greek manner'. In its title Hawksmoor cited

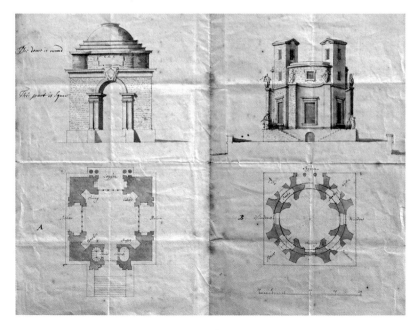

Hawksmoor's unbuilt design for a 'belvedere' at Castle Howard, 1724.

Hawksmoor's pyramid
at Castle Howard.

Herodotus, Pliny and Varo as sources, but its design is in fact most
obviously after the church of S. Andrea in Via Flaminia by Vignola.[35]
Hawksmoor described his other design as sitting on a base 'after
ye Manner Antique', though in a swipe at his doctrinaire Palladian
opponents, who were gaining more and more influence, added that
'he wou'd not mention Authors and Antiquity, but that we have so
many conceited Gentlemen full of this science, ready to knock you
down, unless you have some old father to stand by you'.[36]

Despite his designs for the belvedere going unbuilt, Hawksmoor
did realize several other garden structures before and after Vanbrugh's
death. These included pedestals for statuary, obelisks, the rusticated
pyramid and Four Faces in Pretty Wood, and the quasi-medieval
Carrmire Gate, which stands on the approach road to the south
before one reaches Vanbrugh's earlier Pyramid Gate. On the stretch
of road between the two gates one can just glimpse through the gaps
in the trees a further pyramid, its silhouette clearly visible. This one,
which stands alone, was built as a monument to the earl's grand-
father Lord William Howard, and in many ways acts as a prelude for
the largest and most important building of the whole garden: the
Mausoleum.

With both architect and patron increasingly afflicted by gout, meetings between them were infrequent, leaving the story of the Mausoleum to unfold in wonderful detail in Hawksmoor's letters to Carlisle.[37] We read in them the criticisms with which Hawksmoor had to contend, emanating from the Palladian coterie around Lord Burlington at Chiswick. Carlisle's son-in-law, Sir Thomas Robinson, an amateur architect of some pretension, showed Hawksmoor's designs to Burlington on several occasions, clearly worried that the earl and his architect were straying too far from the true Palladian path. It is a fascinating and quite unusual instance of two competing visions of architecture being brought into direct contact. Despite his declining health and death before the Mausoleum's completion, this was a fight that Hawksmoor would ultimately win.

We first hear of the Mausoleum being mooted in a letter of 3 September 1726. Carlisle's preference at this stage was for a 'Greek Temple', though Hawksmoor noted that the Greeks 'never buryed near their temples, or built their tombs in the form of any temple dedicated to divine honours'. He cited, instead, the Mausoleum at Halicarnassus and the tomb of Porsenna as important precedents from antiquity.[38] Already the intention was to place the Mausoleum 'upon the hill in Yeomans Close, not farr from the Lake'.[39] Drawings were referred to in a letter of November 1727, which were, Hawksmoor noted, 'Authentic and what is According to the practice of ye antients', but none of these survive.[40]

Over the following months, during which time Carlisle and his son Henry, Viscount Morpeth, visited Hawksmoor in London, the design evolved rapidly, with patron and architect settling on a square basement that would support a round, domed structure above, based 'upon the Designe of . . . ye Tomb of Metella, a Noble person of Rome'.[41] Vaughan Hart has suggested that Hawksmoor knew of this building, also called the Capo di Bove, which stood on the Appian Way, from illustrations in Pietro Santi Bartoli's *Gli antichi sepolcri, overo Mausolei Romani et Etruschi* (1697). While this may well have been the source for the Mausoleum's overall form, its relative simplicity – a square base supporting a cylindrical superstructure – suggests that Hawksmoor looked to other models too.[42] There were, in any case, several more modern precedents for a circular design: Wren's mausoleum for Charles I; Hawksmoor's baptistry for St Paul's Cathedral; and the Radcliffe Library in Oxford, the circular design of which we might attribute to being part library and part monument to its benefactor.[43]

Several of the early drawings show that Hawksmoor's first inclination was for an arcade enclosing an inner drum. Responding in March 1729 to Carlisle's suggestion 'to make a collonade around the Temple or Mausoleum', Hawksmoor was 'entirely for a Colonade', provided that stones of sufficient size could be found to construct the architrave.[44] A two-fold elevation shows these two variations side by side, the columns and thick Doric entablature carrying the colonnaded version much higher. The choice of Doric, we discover in a letter of 6 May 1729, was justified on account of the 'difficulty of the Entablement'. The other option considered was the Ionic, but its intercolum-

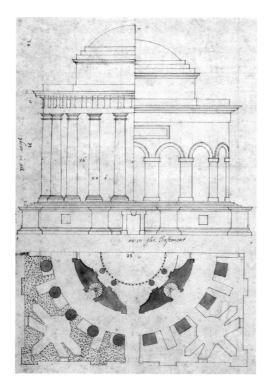

Two-fold elevation for the Mausoleum at Castle Howard, showing both arcade and colonnaded versions, relating to a letter of 1729.

niation – the distance between adjacent columns – is far wider and Hawksmoor still had reservations about securing stones large enough to make the spans. This letter seems to correspond with several of the surviving drawings and marks the point when the main aspects of the design were resolved and foundations then laid. The work was overseen by William Etty, Clerk of the Works at Castle Howard, who was a near ever-present figure in Hawksmoor's correspondence with Carlisle.

Building work continued while the finer points of the design were resolved. Hawksmoor visited Castle Howard with his son-in-law, Nathaniel Blackerby, in July 1731, when further design changes were almost certainly made. This was, in fact, to be Hawksmoor's last visit to Castle Howard. Correspondence continued regularly between patron and architect, though building work all but ceased during the winter months. Word was spreading and the Mausoleum was clearly gathering some interest, with Hawksmoor noting in a letter of 4 January 1732, with inadvertent prescience, that he hoped 'the poet Mr Pope will not set his satire upon us for it'.[45]

Interference and setbacks

By the autumn of 1732 things began to take a turn for the worse. Writing to Carlisle on 3 October, Hawksmoor reported 'At my Comeing to Towne, I found your Lordships Letter giving me an account of Ld. B.–s Observations on our Performances'.[46] These observations were likely made on a visit by Lord Burlington to Castle Howard a few days before, no doubt in the company of Robinson.[47] Burlington's objections centred on the width of the intercolumniation. There was apparently no ancient precedent for a circular colonnade with the comparatively small intercolumniation that Hawksmoor had designed. Moreover, as Robinson later relayed to Carlisle,

> the reason Ld B. gave why a Diameter and a half for the Dorick Order, was not proper in a round building, because from the nature of a Circular Colonade the Columns must appear to stand closer, let the Spectator examine it from what point of view he will, than they would do in a Square building . . .[48]

In many ways this is a rather strange inversion of positions: on the one hand, we have Burlington, for whom antique precedent was the defining criterion in architecture, arguing in terms of a building's effect; and Hawksmoor, on the other, moved to produce several pages of justifications for his design (despite stating that he would 'be as short as possible'), citing authors ancient and modern: Vitruvius, Pliny, Fréart de Chambray (via Evelyn's translation), Perrault and Wren.

Vaughan Hart has argued that Hawksmoor's clinging to the Doric order in face of this opposition, when a change to the Corinthian or Composite would sate his detractors, is evidence of the symbolic importance it held for Hawksmoor and Carlisle. According to Hart, the Doric's significance in this context lay in its ancestry in the architecture and democratic ideals of ancient Greece, which made it particularly appropriate for a building that was intended, so his argument proceeds, to commemorate Carlisle's Whig non-conformism.[49] However, no mention of this idea appears in Hawksmoor's 'account' on Burlington's 'observations', where if this really was the overriding concern of both architect and patron, we would expect to see at least a mention. In fact, little of Hawksmoor's letter was relevant to the matter at hand. Like the letter to Dean Wilcocks concerning his work at Westminster, its purpose was mainly to reassert his own qualifications amid mounting criticism.

The most important remark actually comes towards the end of Hawksmoor's letter, offering a clear statement as to how his approach to architecture differed to that of Burlington and the Palladians:

> Men have generally different ways of thinking and the Opinion of the Professours of Arts are exceeding various, so that if you will not agree to this Maxim, that all Rules should proceed, from Reason Experience and necessity, (as well as Laws) then we must Submit to the many Caprices of the World.[50]

For Hawksmoor, there were no absolutes, no antique source nor any author from which one might derive fixed guidelines for the 'correct' appearance of a building. It was 'reason' above all that determined Hawksmoor's choice of the Doric order, informed by his long personal 'experience' in building and construction. Antiquity was both a source of knowledge and ideas for Hawksmoor but, unlike the Palladians, it was really just the starting point for an architecture shaped by the 'Reason Experience and necessity' of the present age. In this it seems that Carlisle concurred, endorsing the letter: 'Mr Hawksmoor's judicious remarks in answer to ye objection made by Ld Burlington for . . . ye disposition of ye columns being contrary to ye rules as my Ld asserts . . . has shewn great reading and knowledge.'[51]

Though Burlington had been held at bay for the moment, further bad news followed. The inner walls of the basement settled, with the rubble core causing the masonry to bulge out. This was tantamount to disaster as the inner walls were required to support the drum and dome above. A flurry of letters in the last months of 1732 saw Hawksmoor relaying anxious instructions for the urgent repair and strengthening of the masonry. News of the problems inevitably reached Burlington. Robinson reported to Carlisle that he had discussed the matter over dinner with Burlington, who had enquired with equal degrees of mischief and condescension as to what deficiencies in the design had caused the structural problems.[52] Burlington's questions were, however, largely irrelevant to the problems, the fault of which was very likely due to poor workmanship and materials.

Despite these difficulties, work continued steadily, if rather slowly. Hawksmoor's letters were increasingly punctuated by descriptions of the bouts of gout with which he was often afflicted, and also enquiries after the health of his correspondent, Carlisle. Reading the letters it is hard not to be struck by the poignancy of the correspondence between two men of longstanding friendship both reaching the end of their lives. There is an almost tangible frustration in Hawksmoor's words at not being able to visit the site and oversee the work himself.

The death of William Etty in summer 1734, therefore, hit Hawksmoor hard. They had known each other and worked together at Castle Howard for many years. Etty was Hawksmoor's man on-site and a close friend.[53] In his subsequent letters, he hardly ever referred to Etty's replacement – Mr Doe – instead preferring Mr Hodgeson, who had been mason since 1731.[54] With Hawksmoor unable to travel to Yorkshire, he and Hodgeson met in London in August 1734, and reported to Carlisle that 'Your Mason I think is a promising Workman, and I fancy I shall make him a Master'.[55]

Although Hawksmoor had won the battle over the intercolumniation, Robinson's interfering continued, going so far as to produce his own designs. In a letter of 20 July 1734, Robinson relayed to his father-in-law that

> I have spent this whole morn with Mr Hawksmoor and have shewn him my design for the Basement of the Mausoleum, he flatters me with his approbation of it, I am sorry I can't return him the complyment by approving the scheme he shewed me for finishing the entablature of the Colonade ...[56]

Robinson reported that he would show both designs to Lord Burlington and 'let yr Ldshp know what he says of it'. For an architect as proud, accomplished and knowledgeable as he such interferences would have been near intolerable. Yet Hawksmoor remained stoic, even while his designs were under assault, and ultimately acquiesced to his fate:

> Sr Thomas Robinson has half a score of papers for your Lordship which I hope he has shewn My Lord Burlington. they concern the Mosoleum. I would rather have all ye World see the designe before the thing is done, and finde all the faults they can (possibly) rather than condemn when 'tis too late.[57]

Hawksmoor's letters over the next year record the building's progress as discussions turned towards the cornice modillions, stone for the vaulting, the guttering and the roof lead with the occasional barb against his enemies and their obsessions with 'Palladio's humble Villas'.[58] Hampered by various rivals and his declining health, time was increasingly against Hawksmoor.

On 17 February 1736 Hawksmoor wrote to Carlisle:

> I am Much concernd that your Lordship is any way indisposed with that great enemy the Gout, I hope the summer season will set you a better way; I have had a sad Winter, and the more so because the Worthy Squire Rip-y has had power from his great Friends to Destroy me at Greenwch: Hospitall. and the H. of Commons. have suspended our fund for Repairing the Abby, so that adding the Loss of my Limbs to my Misfortunes I am in a fine situation. And the World is determined to starve me. for my good services.[59]

In a further letter sent less than two weeks later, Hawksmoor reported that his work in preparing drawings for the work at Castle Howard had 'bin so hinder'd by propls conceding our intended bridge at Westminster: that I can hardly have any Respit'. A bill was before Parliament for a bridge, which, as mentioned earlier, Hawksmoor hoped might be made of stone, unless it was opposed by some 'wooden-headed carpenter'.[60] Hawksmoor closed the letter with a few words in his own favour:

I must entreat your Lordship recommendations to your friends, that I may be employd in Some Shape or other if I shall be alive in Building the Bridge I have taken as much pains for.[61]

Yet, this was not to be. Less than two weeks later, on Thursday 25 March, Hawksmoor died from 'gout in his stomach' at his home on Millbank.[62] The affliction, which 'for many years he laboured under', finally overcame this most determined and indefatigable of men.[63] He was survived by his wife, Hester, and his daughter, Elizabeth.

Realization

When Hawksmoor died in London work at the Mausoleum would have been beginning afresh for the new season. By this time it was more or less complete up to the cornice level of the colonnade. Over the next few years, the attic and dome were added according to Hawksmoor's designs, as well as the coffered ceiling of the interior.[64] The steps and outer court were, however, the work of Daniel Garrett, a sometime clerk and draughtsman to Lord Burlington, who had been installed by Robinson after Hawksmoor's death. The Mausoleum was finally under complete Palladian control and the steps down to the court closely resemble those at Burlington's Chiswick Villa.[65] They jar somewhat with the Mausoleum above, and we might imagine that Hawksmoor had in mind something along the lines of the original concealed steps at St George-in-the-East.[66] Yet when viewed from afar with the dome rising above the trees, the Mausoleum's silhouette against the sky, the effect of isolation that was so central to Hawksmoor's vision remains undiminished.

How his buildings would appear in the landscape or cityscape consumed Hawksmoor perhaps above all else over his career: from his early topographical sketchbook to his plans for London. The contrast between the disappointment of these grand visions going unrealized and his ultimate success at Castle Howard was one that Hawksmoor himself clearly recognized, as he noted in a letter to Carlisle, 'I hope your Lordship got safe downe and that ye Beautys of castle Howard will make amends, for ye Deformitys of ye most ill contrived Towne in the World'.[67] Despite – or perhaps because of – the meddlesome interference of Robinson and Burlington, the Mausoleum is arguably Hawksmoor's greatest achievement, dominating the landscape physically and, we might add, psychologically. The Mausoleum's power is no less keenly felt even today, as I discovered the first time I visited it.

From the steps of Vanbrugh's Temple of Four Winds, we see the Mausoleum across the valley standing tall on its lonely hilltop. We jump the fence and make our way hurriedly down the valley, conscious that other visitors, whom we have now left behind, will be watching our progress towards Hawksmoor's great masterpiece. At the bottom of the valley, there is a fence and open gate and a sign: 'Bull in field'. Fortunately, there is no indication of one nearby and we proceed, now uphill, towards the Mausoleum itself.

As we climb, our hearts steadily beating, I cannot but help think of how this was a journey Hawksmoor never made himself, dying several years before the Mausoleum was completed. It is, though, one he must have made countless times in his mind, his vivid imagination conjuring into near reality the sight that we see unfolding before us today. I think also of the frustrations that Hawksmoor felt in his later years, as the Palladian coterie closed around him, aiming to smother his intuitive feel for how blocks of stone could be moulded into some of the most powerful buildings Britain has ever seen. Although the Palladian rule of taste in the years following Hawksmoor's death ensured that as an architect he was soon forgotten, it could not erase his buildings.

By now, we are a stone's throw from the Mausoleum itself and we can hear the wind rushing through its colonnade. We dare not go any nearer. As the sunlight flickers between the adjacent columns, just looking at this rugged yet perfectly composed mass of stone, one is overcome by a sensation not unlike standing on the edge of a precipice. The Mausoleum is perhaps the clearest built manifestation of Hawksmoor's architectural philosophy and we see in it many of the ideas and formal devices he used over his career. While Hawksmoor took inspiration from ancient precedent – a key and recurring interest of his work – he did not try to recreate his sources but to assimilate them into a broader composition. Indeed, the building's overall form

overleaf: The Mausoleum at Castle Howard peering over the rambling Yorkshire landscape.

and effect is far more important than its ornament. Yet the ornament which is present, principally that relating to the Doric order, is carefully chosen and precisely carved. The detailing amplifies the changes in scale we experience on approaching the Mausoleum: when we get up close, the entablature appears to grow in weight, teetering above the Doric columns that seem increasingly slender, with the domed cap, in contrast, becoming less and less prominent.

As we circle the Mausoleum, it becomes abundantly clear why Hawksmoor insisted on the Doric order. Corinthian would have been too ornate and the columns too slender, while the triglyphs running around the entablature lend the building a sense of rhythm, energy and dynamism that would have been absent with the plainer Tuscan order. The way Hawksmoor used the Doric places the building on the very cusp of abstraction; it is quite obviously a classical building, born from that tradition, yet it also evades stylistic categorization altogether, becoming almost pure architectural form.

Beginning our descent away from the Mausoleum we cannot help but feel quietly observed. The building's presence remains far more keenly felt than its size might suggest as we look back from the bridge that crosses the river in the valley. The Mausoleum's assault is not just on our senses, but on our minds and our imaginations, on our very psyches. It has the unsettling presence of revealing something to us about our inner selves. Although built as a monument to Carlisle and the Howard family, the Mausoleum stands rather like St Paul's does for Wren, as a monument to its architect, yet one forever bathed in shadow.

FOUR

NEGLECT AND REHABILITATION

HAWKSMOOR WAS THE LAST of a generation that redefined British architecture. The finest achievements of the epoch – St Paul's Cathedral, the City churches, Greenwich Hospital, Castle Howard, Blenheim and, of course, Hawksmoor's churches – put Britain on the map as an architectural force for the first time since arguably the great cathedrals of the Middle Ages. This did not, however, prevent the architecture of Wren, Vanbrugh and Hawksmoor from being assailed by the change in architectural taste, even as its greatest monuments were still rising. Nor did it save several still-born building projects that, if realized, might very well have been regarded among the most important achievements of the age. These included several by Hawksmoor, some of which we can piece together through drawings and others whose existence is known only through the most tantalizing of references.

Among the 2,000 of Hawksmoor's drawings sold at auction after his death, 43 were catalogued as depicting the 'Parliament House by Mr Hawksmoor'. Little else is known about them apart from a note in the *Grub Street Journal* of March 1732, reporting, rather unfortunately for Hawksmoor, that 'The plan for building the new parliament house is the design of Nicholas Hawksmoor Esq., one of the surveyors of his Majesty's Works, which is said to be very grand and beautiful, and is now under the inspection of the right hon. the Earl of Burlington, for his approbation'.[1] With or without Burlington's interference, this project was, of course, never to be and we can only wonder now as to what might have been.

Given the originality and sheer scale of his architectural ambition, in retrospect it is perhaps unsurprising that at the end of his life Hawksmoor was disappointed that this ambition was left unfulfilled. So powerful was Hawksmoor's imagination, there was simply no way – practically, financially or politically – that some of his more outlandish ideas (as well as some of his lesser ones) could be translated into stone. The multitude of opportunities that had come Wren's way was exceptional: partly a quirk of history, and partly a consequence of his undoubted genius and the practicality of his designs. Wren also had the advantage of being a gentleman, and, like Vanbrugh, of being extremely well connected. Hawksmoor's own genius was, unfortunately, not enough to secure him the necessary professional posts and positions of influence. It is perhaps indicative of his career that he is most closely associated with a Commission whose towering ambition aimed at building 50 new churches, but which, in the end, realized only twelve.

Despite suffering frequent professional setbacks, during the 1720s and 1730s especially, Hawksmoor rarely ever complained. His comments to the Duchess of Marlborough, in a letter of 1722, were an exception: 'I have been also very ill Treated by Some persons that I have raised in ye World [likely colleagues in the Office of Works], in return for the great Favours I bestowed upon them I did think them poorest, but I have found them very ungratefull knaves.'[2] The Duchess had in fact summed up Hawksmoor's situation well in a letter of 1715, in which she noted how 'everybody that knows him will allow him to bee one one of the most able in his profession'.[3] Those who knew Hawksmoor personally were in no doubt as to his ability. But Hawksmoor's natural modesty and reticence prevented him from promoting himself in the ways his rivals were quite prepared to do.

This almost self-deprecating aspect of Hawksmoor's character was captured clearly in a letter of July 1734 from Thomas Robinson to his father-in-law, Carlisle, concerning the Mausoleum at Castle Howard. Although Robinson outlined the deficiencies of Hawksmoor's designs in a rather self-regarding and patronizing manner, he added in a postscript: 'I must say one thing in fav'r of Mr Hawksmoor I never talk'd with a more reasonable man, nor with one so little prejudiced in favour of his own performances'.[4] Others recognized this too. In

1709 Arthur Maynwaring, a close associate of the Duchess, wrote to remind her that 'I have often heard you wish for some opportunity to do him good; which he is the more worthy of, because he does not seem to be very solicitous to do if for himself; but has two qualities that are not often joined, modesty and merit.'[5]

In many ways Hawksmoor was the sort of architect and character who would have truly prospered under the consistent patronage of the absolutist regimes of the continent. Vanbrugh had made this very point. 'Poor Hawksmoor', he wrote, 'What a Barbarous Age have his fine, ingenious Parts fallen into. What would Monsr: Colbert in France have given for Such a Man? I don't Speak as to his Architecture alone, but the Aids he cou'd have given him, in almost all his brave Designs for the Police'.[6] Colbert was Jean-Baptiste Colbert, Louis XIV's powerful minister, under whose patronage many of the great building projects of the Sun King's reign were completed. Colbert recognized the unique potential of state-sponsored buildings – what Vanbrugh meant by 'police' – to express the king's dominion over France and, especially, its capital city. In this there was some overlap with Hawksmoor's own ideas, particularly those expressed in his *Remarks* on Greenwich in 1728. But it seems rather doubtful that the ever cost-conscious Colbert would have looked on Hawksmoor's ambitious designs in a particularly favourable light.

In the same summer that Vanbrugh lamented Hawksmoor's lack of a Colbert-type patron, his friend was mounting a campaign to save the ruinous St Alban's Abbey and 'Support this venerable pile from being Martyr'd by ye Neglect of a Slouthfull generation'.[7] In an odd way, the fate of St Alban's Abbey stands as something of a metaphor for the way Hawksmoor's achievements were to suffer similar neglect and be largely forgotten soon after his death. Hawksmoor was certainly a victim, even in his own life, of historical circumstance and changing architectural taste. Yet he also did little to promote his ideas in print, unlike his contemporary Gibbs, whose *Book of Architecture* (1728) carried his influence across Britain and the American colonies. Moreover, whether wilfully or naively, Hawksmoor avoided the politicking that would have helped further his career, instead preferring to spend his time advancing more esoteric interests and causes, as with St Alban's Abbey.

This chapter charts how Hawksmoor stayed in the shadows, largely forgotten for much of the remainder of the eighteenth century and, indeed, almost all of the nineteenth. Occasionally, a light was shone towards him, but almost always far too fleetingly to make much, if any, difference to the broader awareness and appreciation of his work. Three important members of the Royal Academy of Arts – Sir John Soane, J.M.W. Turner and C. R. Cockerell – were aware at least of some aspects of Hawksmoor's work, even if, in Soane's case, he never mentioned him by name, despite discussing his work in his RA lectures. But even for these rarefied and enlightened cultural circles, Hawksmoor's architecture just did not fit in with the concerns or interests of the time. Even with the revival of interest in Wren's architecture towards the end of the century, Hawksmoor remained largely overlooked.

It was not until the 1920s that Hawksmoor began to step out of the shadows. This was heralded by the threat of demolition to his church of St Mary Woolnoth in the City of London – in many ways his most conspicuous building – and the enthusiasm for his work propagated by the maverick architect H. S. Goodhart-Rendel. This combination played a vital role in helping begin Hawksmoor's steady ascent that would see him re-emerge in the decades after the Second World War as a major figure in the history of British architecture.

Walpole's *Anecdotes*

Blackerby's obituary of Hawksmoor that appeared in *Read's Weekly Journal* did not go unnoticed. It was copied down, albeit with some inaccuracies, by the engraver and antiquarian George Vertue.[8] After his death, Vertue's notebooks were acquired by Horace Walpole, the famous antiquarian, politician and dilettante. Son of Sir Robert Walpole, Britain's first Prime Minister, Walpole was an avid collector and conversationalist, famous both for his Gothic fantasy house, Strawberry Hill in Twickenham, and his witty and voluminous correspondence. Of his published works, *The Castle of Otranto* (1764), usually considered the first Gothic novel, is the most significant, but Walpole also wrote extensively on the arts.

Between 1762 and 1771, Walpole published his *Anecdotes of Painting in England*, a collection of entries and observances, heavily based on Vertue's notes. Walpole was thus able to include a sizeable entry on Hawksmoor, giving a broad, if occasionally erroneous, account of his career and works. Walpole listed Hawksmoor's churches without comment until he reached St George's, Blooms-bury, 'the steeple of which is a master-stroke of absurdity, consisting of an obelisk, crowned with the statue of King George the First, and hugged by the royal supporters. A lion, a unicorn, and a king on such an eminence are very surprising.' So surprising, in fact, that Walpole was moved to write the couplet, 'The things, we know, are neither rich nor rare, / But wonder how the devil they got there.'[9]

He described the Mausoleum at Castle Howard as 'magnificent', and went into more detail about the house and garden in a letter of 1772:

> Nobody had informed me that I should at one view see
> a palace, a town, a fortified city, temples on high places,
> woods worthy of being each a metropolis of the Druids,
> vales connected to hills by other woods, the noblest lawn
> in the world fenced by half the horizon, and a mausoleum
> that would tempt one to be buried alive; in short I have
> seen gigantic places before, but never a sublime one.[10]

In summing up the *Anecdotes* entry, Walpole concluded that Hawksmoor's 'knowledge in every science connected with his art is much commended, and his character remains unblemished'.[11] He did, however, qualify his comment, adding, 'Hawksmoor deviated a little from the lessons and practice of his master, and certainly did not improve on them'.[12]

More generally, Walpole was careful to emphasize that the *Anecdotes* were only 'intended as an impartial register of, not as a panegyric on, our artists. When I have erred on either side, in commending or blaming, I offer but my own judgment, which is authority to nobody else, and ought to be canvassed or set right by abler decisions'.[13] The latter, however, rarely happened. Walpole's *Anecdotes* were frequently copied, plagiarized and republished over subsequent decades with barely any comment, qualification or correction.

Hawksmoor's twin Gothic towers at All Souls College, Oxford.

London Transport poster featuring St George, Bloomsbury, by
Richard Beer, 1976.

Drawing by John Harvey from 1958 illustrating Arthur Bailey's
design for building a smaller modern church within the shell of
Hawksmoor's St George-in-the-East.

Photograph of Brushfield Street in 1990 by David Secombe.

Lithograph of Christ Church, Spitalfields, by John Piper from his
A Retrospect of Churches (1964).

The restored interior of Christ Church, Spitalfields.

Opposite: The openwork spire of St Anne, Limehouse, from the west.

Christ Church, Spitalfields, from the southwest.

The west front and spire of St George, Bloomsbury.

St George-in-the-East, from St George's Gardens to the east.

An edition of Walpole's *Anecdotes* that did contain 'considerable editions', as the title page put it, was the one published by James Dallaway, a Sussex vicar and antiquary. Though Dallaway added an extensive commentary to Walpole's original text, he was not averse to reciting earlier opinions or even outright plagiarism.[14] In another work, for instance, Dallaway lifted directly from James Ralph of all people, whose criticisms of St George's, Bloomsbury, he reproduced almost word for word.[15] Dallaway did manage to attribute All Souls correctly to Hawksmoor, which was quite unusual, but in his assessment described it as an 'imperfect idea of the true gothic style'.[16]

Changing contexts

Dallaway's remarks concerning All Souls prefigured much of how eighteenth-century Gothic architecture was viewed during the nineteenth century. To Victorian eyes 'Gothick', as it became known, echoing Langley and then Walpole's nomenclature, was a fanciful bastardization of the true forms and spirit of medieval architecture.

This climate naturally clouded views of Hawksmoor's 'Gothick' work. In *A History of the Gothic Revival* (1871), Charles Locke Eastlake, architect, designer and Keeper of the National Gallery (1878–98), lambasted the west towers at Westminster Abbey as 'hideous', 'clumsy' and 'bungling'.[17] To complete the humiliation for Hawksmoor, he mistook their architect as Wren, stating 'we can but lament that a man whose fame has been transmitted to posterity as the greatest architect whom England has produced should have been thus associated with the degradation of one of her fairest monuments'.[18]

Such assessments were, however, rarely consistent. At almost the same time, the Scottish architectural historian James Fergusson got himself into a terrible muddle of attribution:

> From what we know of the pupil's own works, we may certainly assert that the double spires of All Souls' College at Oxford were designed by the master. They display the same intimate appreciation of the essential qualities of Gothic art, combined with the same disregard of its details, which characterise the western towers of Westminster Abbey or the

towers at Warwick or in Cornhill and Wren's Gothic work generally.[19]

Preconceived positions rather than careful study determined Fergusson's responses; all the examples he cites are, of course, by Hawksmoor, except St Mary, Warwick, which was ultimately realized by William Wilson. The overriding point, though, was that for many Victorian revivalists archaeological accuracy in Gothic architecture was not just a question of aesthetics. It was a moral one, in which 'Gothick' was an abomination. As Eastlake concluded:

> Gothic architecture had its vicissitudes in this country . . . But in the days of its lowest degradation, it may be questioned whether it would not have been better that the cause should have remained unespoused than have been sustained by such a champion as Batty Langley.[20]

Even though Hawksmoor was largely forgotten, his churches could not fail to be noticed by the stream of topographical writers who documented London's cityscape as it quickly evolved. For nineteenth-century observers accustomed to the academic certainties of the Gothic or Greek revivals, Hawksmoor's churches appeared perhaps more bewildering than they had even to their eighteenth-century forbears. However, they were on occasion greeted with enthusiasm.

Joseph Gwilt, writing in John Britton and Augustus Pugin's *Illustrations of the Public Buildings of London*, first published in 1825, claimed St Mary Woolnoth as an 'exquisite example' of what he called the 'Christian style', while its 'interior, in some respects, is unrivalled by most of those by Sir Christopher Wren'.[21] He concluded in effusive terms, noting how the church 'has such exquisite beauties that it is irksome to dwell on its few and trifling faults'.[22]

Other observers were much less positive. Another commentator in the same volume, writing under the initials H. A. about St George-in-the-East, was quick to point out that the church was 'selected not so much as a specimen of its fine design, as an example of the peculiar style of its architect, and characteristic of the taste of the age in which it was erected'.[23]

This edifice is a specimen of that ponderous and singular architecture which marked the public buildings of Vanbrugh, and which Hawksmoor imitated in its worst features. It has fortunately never acquired much favour with the public, nor is there reason to apprehend it will ever regain even the short-lived estimation in which it was held when the present edifice was erected. Massiveness in quantity of materials, and grotesque features, are its characteristics; and though these may seem to assimilate with the prisons and work-houses, they have few pretensions to be approved in designs for churches or private mansions.[24]

H. A.'s association of 'massiveness in quantity of materials, and grotesque features' with 'prisons and work-houses' was revealing of the period in which he was writing. Looking back, we now see the imagery of prisons and work-houses – physical and psychological repositories for the dangerous and socially and economically useless – was inseparable from the emerging Victorian psyche. Intriguingly, H. A. was not the only writer to make this link to Hawksmoor's by now soot-blackened churches.

James Peller Malcolm, the American-English antiquary and topographical draughtsman, had also seen numerous prison-like qualities in Hawksmoor's work in his *Londinium Redivivum* (1802–7).[25] Again at St George-in-the-East, he noted how the windows 'are those of a prison', while the church itself 'appears enormous when compared to the neighbouring diminutive houses', which he described as 'mere hovels', occupied by the 'dregs of the community':[26]

the labouring part of Wapping society, and seamen who lodge on shore. Those, and their inmates, being of the roughest and most unpolished manners, rendered offensive by numbers of infamous women interspersed throughout most of the streets, are below description.[27]

Malcolm saw the church's prison-like features seeping into and poisoning its surroundings, rendering the local inhabitants as 'inmates', seemingly trapped by its magnetic pull. The 'strange ponderous walls of the church and steeple . . . [which] cannot be described for want of terms' were for Malcolm the fitting emblem for such a deprived and depraved area.

Different perspectives

While several of his buildings were noticed and recorded by topographical writers, in architectural and artistic circles Hawksmoor remained largely unknown. Vanbrugh, in contrast, was still receiving some attention, in particular from Robert Adam, the Scottish architect renowned for the wonderfully ornate and colourful neoclassical interiors that became the trademark of his office from the 1760s. Adam's architectural imagination had space for multiplicity and diversity and he was intrigued by Vanbrugh's work, though with certain caveats, as he wrote in the preface of the first volume of *Works in Architecture* (1778), co-written with his brother James:

> Sir John Vanbrugh's genius was of the first class; and, in point of movement, novelty and ingenuity, his works have not been exceeded by anything in modern times. We should certainly quote Blenheim and Castle Howard as great examples of these perfections in preference to any work of our own, or of any other modern architect; but unluckily for the reputation of this excellent artist, his taste kept no pace with his genius, and his works are so crowded with barbarisms and absurdities, and so borne down by their own preposterous weight, that none but the discerning can separate their merits from their defects. In the hands of the ingenious artist, who knows how to polish and refine and bring them into use, we have always regarded his productions as rough jewels of inestimable value.[28]

Hawksmoor, however, went unmentioned.

Around this time, Vanbrugh also received praise from the painter Sir Joshua Reynolds, in his famous *Discourses*, which he delivered to the Royal Academy of Arts in his capacity as its first President. In his thirteenth discourse (1786), Reynolds stated how 'in the buildings of Vanbrugh, who was a Poet as well as an Architect, there is a greater display of imagination, than we shall find perhaps in any other'.[29] The poetic quality of Vanbrugh's architecture was also noticed by the architect Sir John Soane, for whom Vanbrugh was no less than 'the Shakespeare of architects'.[30]

Soane's remark came in one of his own addresses to the RA in his capacity as Professor of Architecture. In the same lecture in 1810, Soane did in fact make one reference to Hawksmoor, though referred to him only as Vanbrugh's 'pupil' and claimed the Mausoleum at Castle Howard as Vanbrugh's design.[31]

Soane's only other reference to a building by Hawksmoor came in a passage concerning the ornamentation of buildings with paintings and statues:

> The summit of the steeple of Bloomsbury church is crowned with a statue of King George the Second, which occasioned the following epigram.
>
> > When Harry the eighth, left the Pope in the lurch,
> > His Parliament made him the head of the Church,
> > But George's good subjects, the Bloomsbury people,
> > Instead of the Church, made him head of the Steeple.[32]

These lines are a strange interlude in Soane's lectures and it was surely no coincidence that their inspiration was the same highly idiosyncratic spire – that of St George's, Bloomsbury – that had moved Walpole to break into verse in his *Anecdotes* 50 years earlier.

At almost the exact time Soane was drawing attention to St George's, the painter J.M.W. Turner was creating views of the church for his own RA lectures, which he began delivering on 7 January 1811, in the capacity of Professor of Perspective.[33] That Soane and Turner were concerned with the church at the same time may have been a coincidence; simply because its spire was visible from all sides. But there is the possibility that Turner saw Soane's lecture and perhaps called on his friend's architectural knowledge in the preparation of his lectures, especially lectures three and four, which have a quite technical architectural focus.[34]

Whatever the case, Turner's sketchbooks of 1808–11 include several drawings of the spire in graphite or pen and ink that are roughly contemporary with a further sketch of the Mausoleum at Halicarnassus which he compared in a note to 'Bloomsbury Ch'.[35] These sketches were worked up into two watercolour 'Lecture Diagrams' for his first lecture. One shows the porch and spire from the north, which Turner noted reveals that the 'proportion is positively marked in the spire of Bloomsbury where the steps comprising it increase as they recede from the eye'.[36] The second is from the south and depicts the spire at an oblique angle from below. Both 'diagrams' were used to help describe to the RA students the adjustments needed to be made when viewing objects – here, sculpture – at different angles. The effect, especially of the second, is powerful. Turner's manipulation of perspective allowed him to create the effect of the height, almost of the vertigo that overcomes one when looking up at a soaring spire – an effect especially acute in Hawksmoor's churches.[37]

The 'Lecture Diagrams' were not Turner's only depictions of Hawksmoor buildings, though the others are rather more incidental. A graphite and watercolour sketch from around 1808–9, depicting the view from One Tree Hill in Greenwich Park, show the spires of St Alfege, Greenwich and St Anne, Limehouse and, just visible, the west towers of Westminster Abbey. The principal focus of the image was, however, the twin domes of Wren's Greenwich Hospital and their formal relationship to St Paul's beyond.

The west towers of Westminster Abbey in fact appeared much more prominently in two early watercolours prepared for *Copper-Plate Magazine*, a publication with which Turner was involved from 1794.[38] In one, the towers take centre stage, rising above the mass of the Abbey and Westminster Bridge in the foreground. The subject was likely chosen by the publication rather than Turner, and in any case, was due to its topographical prominence, rather than their architect's fame. However, it is intriguing how Turner's depiction of the towers in layered grey watercolour is evocatively reminiscent of Hawksmoor's own wash technique.

Perspective view of St George, Bloomsbury, produced by Soane's office in 1807 to illustrate his seventh Royal Academy lecture.

Turner's 'Lecture Diagram 7: St George's Church, Bloomsbury', created for his Royal Academy lectures in graphite and water-colour on paper, *c.* 1810.

Westminster Bridge, with the Abbey Seen across the River, by Turner depicted in graphite and watercolour *c.* 1796. The work is an unfinished study for the subject published in the *Copper-Plate Magazine* (1 August 1797).

Wren revived

Depictions of Hawksmoor's work remained nothing more than a mere footnote in Turner's larger and greater oeuvre. Similarly, there is no Soane building that could be said to follow Hawksmoor. It took another generation before an architect was to appreciate Hawksmoor's achievements properly and, indeed, take inspiration from aspects of his work.

That architect was Charles Robert Cockerell, today best known for designing Oxford's Ashmolean Museum and branches of the Bank of England in Liverpool and Manchester. Cockerell's work was polymorphous, separate from both the Greek and Gothic Revivals, though at times drawing from both. He was both an architect and archaeologist, an interest he developed through a long, seven-year Grand Tour during his twenties. Though fully cognizant of the Greek Revival, Cockerell resisted the binds of academic revivalism and had a far more eclectic appreciation and understanding of architecture than, arguably, any of his peers. These interests soon led him towards Wren, Vanbrugh and Hawksmoor.

In June 1821, two years after being appointed Surveyor of the Fabric at St Paul's Cathedral, Cockerell made a visit to St George-in-the-East and St Anne, Limehouse, recording the latter in detail.[39] Several drawings in the RIBA collection reveal the influence that St Anne's, and also St Mary Woolnoth, had on Cockerell's designs for the church of St Bartholomew, Moor Lane, which replaced Wren's St Bartholomew by the Exchange, following its demolition to widen the road. The influence also extended to Cockerell's now demolished Hanover Chapel on Regent Street (1823–5), his most significant early work. The chapel featured an innovative iron and glass dome, behind a loosely Grecian frontage. Its twin flanking towers, which created a glorious punctuation along John Nash's Regent Street, clearly echoed the two turrets sat atop the west tower of St Mary Woolnoth.[40]

Cockerell's Hawksmoor-inspired design for St Bartholomew, Moor Lane, drawn in the 1840s.

In 1829 Cockerell was elected to the RA, first as an associate and then, in 1836, as a full member. Soon after, work began on his University Library at Cambridge, and there we can detect an even more direct inspiration from Hawksmoor. Only the north wing of the library was completed, but its debt to Christ Church, Spitalfields is clear. The library's end elevations, in particular, strongly evoke the grand Venetian window motif of Christ Church's west front, complete with scooped-out niches.

Cockerell was appointed Professor of Architecture at the RA in 1839, the position coming to him after the death of William Wilkins, who had only recently succeeded Soane in the position after his death in 1837. Like Soane, Cockerell delivered lectures to the Academy's students and his fellow members. For the latter half of his stint Cockerell spoke in front of a large watercolour entitled *The Professor's Dream*. First shown in the Academy's annual exhibition in 1849, *The*

Perspective drawn by Cockerell in 1822 of the view looking down Regent Street and also inside his now-demolished Hanover Chapel.

Professor's Dream was a dramatic capriccio of the greatest monuments of architectural history: the pyramids, numerous Greek and Roman temples, Gothic cathedrals, great monuments of the Renaissance and some buildings of the present day. It followed an earlier work, *Tribute to the Memory of Sir Christopher Wren* (1838), which had similarly drawn together Wren's works, and also some by Hawksmoor, erroneously attributed to his master – notably the two Gothic towers of All Souls and Westminster Abbey.

Cockerell's almost hero-worship of Wren certainly overrode whatever interests he had in Hawksmoor. In part this was because, despite its own decline, Wren's posthumous reputation had never come close to reaching the nadir of Hawksmoor's. Even if one found the style of Wren's buildings to be distasteful (as many did during the nineteenth century), it was impossible to ignore the scale of his achievements.

As both the Greek and Gothic Revivals began to lose their hold over architectural taste during the end of the century, positive appraisals of Wren's work began appearing, especially of St Paul's and the City churches. One of the first, *Wren's City Churches*, was published in 1883 by the Arts and Crafts pioneer Arthur Heygate Mackmurdo. Today it is best remembered for its stunning and highly unusual cover that prefigured aspects of Art Nouveau, but its text offers several intriguing insights into Wren's revival and the place of Hawksmoor within it.

While to Mackmurdo's eyes Wren could do no wrong, he was careful to caution that 'The pupils of Wren saw only novelty in their master's work, as in our days the disciples of Norman Shaw see only picturesqueness in his architectural designs. Hence such monstrosities by the pupils of a Wren as St. John's, Horsely Down, and St.

Cockerell's Tribute to Sir Christoper Wren which was exhibited at the Royal Academy in 1838.

Luke's, Old Street Road.'[41] St Mary Woolnoth received an even harsher assessment:

> Here, one cannot refrain from referring to this mass of piled up plagiarism, put together by a pupil of Wren; whose training never was able to refine his native coarseness, that some, in their criticism of this composition, have glorified by the name of boldness: yet the gulf between this and Wren's work is too broad to need critical measurement. I mention it, only because it has been thought by some worthy of the praise it has received by archaeologists incapable of discriminating between what is fine and what is eccentric, – a praise likely to depreciate, while it lasts, all good work of this time.[42]

Mackmurdo's descriptions were clearly partisan; to his eyes the work of Wren's 'pupils' was automatically inferior to that of their master. This was even the case when he mistook the work of the pupil for that of the master. He was, for example, glowing in his estimations of St Michael, Cornhill ('There is no weak point') and was just as fulsome in his praise for St Vedast, Foster Lane ('one of the most beautiful specimens in the world').[43] Mackmurdo was also aware of the fluctuations in taste, noting how

> Wren's influence upon us to-day, upon you and me, as we walk day by day round and about his works . . . is not so great as we might at first suppose it to be, since there are many associations which prevent the influence of art working upon us freely.[44]

But the irony of how similar 'associations' were clouding his own views of Wren's pupils like Hawksmoor was clearly lost on him.

Even as appreciation of Wren's work was building, it did not automatically translate into a revival of interest in Hawksmoor's work. So, by the end of the nineteenth century, Hawksmoor's status was still essentially as described in an article in *The Builder* as far back as 1843: 'a name which, though not celebrated in the annals of British architecture, has indubitable claim to respectful mention'. He remained, at best, a second-rate talent: 'Hawksmoor's was one of those plodding minds content to labour diligently in its vocation, leaving few traces beyond those incidental to active, though subordinate, co-operation in great works'.[45]

Interest in Wren, in contrast, was steadily growing. Around the turn of the century many architects began to look to his work as a model for an architecture that would celebrate Britain's imperial power at the moment it was reaching its zenith. Borrowings from both St Paul's and Greenwich Hospital can be seen in a range of public buildings commissioned during the 1900s, such as Belfast City Hall (1906), the War Office in Whitehall (1906) and the Port of Liverpool Building (1907). As a rare instance of British cultural pre-eminence, the work of Wren and his school became the natural source for buildings that were intended to proclaim the might of the British Empire, with London at its centre.

In 1904 the artist Niels Møller Lund took this entwining of architecture and empire – what we call now the Edwardian Baroque – as the subject for his painting *The Heart of the Empire*, which depicts the view to the west of London, towered over by St Paul's Cathedral and City church spires, with Westminster and the Houses of Parliament visible in the distance. Intriguingly, in the immediate foreground, Lund has been careful to paint the vantage point from where he composed the image: one of the turrets of the tower of St Mary Woolnoth.

Numerous examples of the Edwardian Baroque revival can also be found in Britain's former colonies. One of the most striking is Sir Herbert Baker's Union Buildings in Pretoria (1910–13), whose twin domes and split-wing configuration obviously derive from Greenwich Hospital, though here they were imbued with significance symbolic to the new Union of South Africa. While work on the Union Buildings was coming to completion, another even grander example of architecture's 'political use', as Wren would have put it, was coming into view in the new Indian capital of New Delhi. Its architect was Edwin Lutyens.

Heart of Empire by Niels
Møller Lund, in oil on
canvas, 1904.

Lutyens

Lutyens is the central figure in the Edwardian Baroque and the
wider revival of Wren's work that is often described as the 'Wren-
aissance'. He was known initially for his country house designs, but
his practice soon branched out to encompass a range of building
types: from commercial buildings to the Cenotaph, the structure
built on Whitehall in London as a monument to the dead of the
First World War. To all his work Lutyens brought a sensitivity that
allowed him to adapt and reimagine traditional architectural styles
for his own age.

In January 1912 Lutyens became involved with the design of
New Dehli, which was to be the new capital of India following its
transfer from Calcutta. The plan for the city centre – all radiating lines
and grand boulevards – was reminiscent of Wren's plan for London.
Baker was drafted in to design the Secretariat buildings, while
Lutyens took responsibility for the centrepiece: the Viceroy's House
(now Rashtrapati Bhavan).[46]

The Viceroy's House powerfully fused classical, Mughal and
Hindu styles into an architectural language of monumental grandeur
not unlike Hawksmoor's proposals for completing Greenwich Hospital

Viceroy's House (now Rashtrapati Bhavan) in New Delhi by Sir Edwin Lutyens, 1912–29.

with a huge domed chapel. Although Lutyens was strongly influenced by Wren both here and elsewhere, he had a deeper, almost Hawksmoorian feeling for architecture's elemental power, expressed in the freedom with which he handled form and mass, texture and colour in the Viceroy's House.

Despite the fact that he was clearly aware of Hawksmoor's buildings, if not his authorship, there are no specific instances of Lutyens commenting on Hawksmoor. So it is interesting in light of their similarities to speculate whether Lutyens had in fact seen Hawksmoor's Greenwich drawings. Another specific example is the Orangery (1904–9) at Hestercombe, where Lutyens worked with his friend and collaborator Gertrude Jekyll, is obviously inspired by Hawksmoor's Orangery at Kensington Palace. However, this was probably an instance of Hawksmoor's work being mistaken for Wren's. More generally, the raw associative power that Lutyens created through his apparently rough yet deeply sophisticated handling of stone at Castle Drogo (1912–30) could be seen as equivalent to the similar qualities of Hawksmoor's faux-medieval garden walls at Castle Howard.[47] Though again, this is more indicative of a common approach, rather than causal link.

Midland Bank on
Poultry in the City of
London by Sir Edwin
Lutyens, 1924–39.

Probably the closest Lutyens came to emulating Hawksmoor
was in his Midland Bank on Poultry in the City of London (1924–39),
where he employed the symbolic, as opposed to systematic, use of
classical elements that Hawksmoor had explored 200 years before.
So close is Lutyens's use of banded rustication, elevated temple,
obelisks, round-arched windows and niches to Hawksmoor's nearby
St Mary Woolnoth, it is hard not to think that he had the work of
his architectural forebear in mind when he designed it.

The Lutyens-Baker collaboration at New Dehli was not always
a happy one. They fell out badly over the height of the Secretariat

buildings, which, from several viewpoints, ended up obscuring the Viceroy's House, much to Lutyens' consternation. The comparison to the seemingly easy and harmonious collaboration between Vanbrugh and Hawksmoor was an obvious one to make, as Laurence Whistler wrote in his book *The Imagination of Vanbrugh and his Fellow Artists*:

> The bitterness and, worse, the artistic harm that result when one architect calls in another, but is not given any least advantage over him, have been illustrated in our own entry at New Delhi, where Sir Edwin Lutyens called in Sir Herbert Baker . . .[48]

Whistler saw Hawksmoor as a 'submissive and melancholy' figure, but also 'a man of outstanding talent and far greater knowledge than his colleague'. By the 1950s, when Whistler's book appeared, Hawksmoor's star was indisputably on the rise. The Edwardian Baroque had at least given Hawksmoor some prominence, even if it was on the coat-tails of Wren. He would have remained largely in shadow without a champion to promote and enthuse about his architecture. He found that in the thoughtful and energetic architect Harry Stuart Goodhart-Rendel.

Goodhart-Rendel

Much of Goodhart-Rendel's early life was spent in France and this proved highly formative on his architectural ideas. He had an unconventional architectural education, beginning his studies at Cambridge in music before turning to architecture and training with Sir Charles Nicholson.[49] Since he was wealthy enough to never need to work, architecture was not so much a profession for Goodhart-Rendel as it was a vocation. He was deeply religious and built and repaired many churches over his career. This led him towards a pioneering reappraisal of the Victorian Gothic Revival at a moment when it was at its least fashionable. Although Goodhart-Rendel was an almost exact contemporary with the modernist generation born during the mid-1880s – which included Le Corbusier, Walter Gropius and Mies van der Rohe – he charted his own idiosyncratic course and the sophistication of his work often went unnoticed. As John Summerson remarked in his RIBA Gold Medal speech in 1976: 'Rendel was an architect whose buildings nobody understood and therefore nobody liked'.[50]

It is little surprise, in retrospect, that early in his career Goodhart-Rendel was drawn to an architect whose work was similarly misunderstood. In 1924, while President of the Architectural Association (AA), Goodhart-Rendel published a book simply titled *Nicholas Hawksmoor*.[51] The short text was copiously illustrated with photographs by the AA's Secretary, F. R. Yerbury. The book begins with Goodhart-Rendel lamenting the vagaries of fame and reputation:

> Fame deals partially with artists, robbing one to enrich another, bestowing and withholding favours according to her whim. Towards Nicholas Hawksmoor, architect, she has been especially unkind, ascribing much of his produce to other authorship and making little of the rest. Thus has she kept in the second rank a reputation which, had she chosen, might have equalled that of any of her favourites. If a building of Hawksmoor's please, Fame credits it to Wren: if it fail to please, then Hawksmoor can have it.[52]

Goodhart-Rendel's anthropomorphizing of fame belied the readily identifiable causes of how reputations rise and fall that we have begun to identify over this book. He did, however, cite the example of the historian James Fergusson, who had attributed Hawksmoor's Gothic work at All Souls solely to Wren: 'No doubt when Hawksmoor has come into his own many a Fergusson "from what he knows of the master's own works" will be able "almost certainly to assert that the dome of St Paul's Cathedral was designed by the pupil".'[53]

Goodhart-Rendel's stated intention was to get Hawksmoor 'recognized as one of the greatest masters of modern architecture'.[54] Quite what he meant by 'modern architecture' is not entirely clear, and certainly bears no relation to modernist architecture, but was rather to do with how buildings were perceived through both conscious and unconscious associations. Indeed, for Goodhart-Rendel Hawksmoor's buildings were 'aimed at the depths of the mind where response must be slow ... and prejudice must be gradually penetrated'.[55] Hawksmoor's was an architecture of raw form and even rawer emotion:

> Hawksmoor's great superiority over his contemporaries, then, lies in his greater consciousness than theirs of the emotional values of architectural forms. They were versifiers and he a poet, they were sophists and he a philosopher ... He was always inclined by his temperament toward that which is sombre and awe-inspring. Like Michael Angelo's, his architecture was great tragedy.[56]

Goodhart-Rendel's interest in Hawksmoor lasted his whole career and was one he was keen to impart in others. From 1933 to 1936 he served as Slade Professor of Fine Art at Oxford. The final year of his professorship coincided with the bicentenary of Hawksmoor's death and Goodhart-Rendel took the opportunity to deliver several lectures on 'The Works of Hawksmoor'. These were subsequently published over March and early April 1936 in the *Architect & Building News*, accompanied by copious illustrations, in the still likely instance of the reader being unfamiliar with the works being discussed.

While the earlier book had served as a brief and quite general introduction, Goodhart-Rendel went into much greater detail in his lectures, undertaking a relatively sophisticated formal analysis of Hawksmoor's buildings. He began by stating, 'Nicholas Hawksmoor ... very possibly may come to be regarded as the greatest British architect'. Though Hawksmoor's great abilities were being recognized, Goodhart-Rendel dangled a carrot before his aspiring students: 'For the student of architectural history here is a fascinating field of research, a field that although open, is almost unexplored'.[57] Most of Goodhart-Rendel's attention fell on the churches, though he afforded some space to Greenwich Hospital and Easton Neston. Of the latter, he noted, 'I think this design very far from being one of Hawksmoor's best, and I show it to you for its importance, for its general grandeur, and for its indefinable flavour of Hawksmoorism, a flavour', he told his students, 'you will come to recognise easily as we go on.'[58]

Despite his obvious enthusiasm, Goodhart-Rendel was not always glowing in his assessments of Hawksmoor's work. In his description of St Anne, Limehouse, he noted how 'The side portions of this facade are inharmonious with the rest, and as ill-designed as the rest is exquisite'. When introducing St George-in-the-East, he recalled a remark of twelve years before in which he described the church as 'one of the most profound and expressive designs in the whole range of modern architecture'. 'I still think this,' he continued, 'but I confess that a caprice in its design that worried me a little then now worries me a great deal more.' The pairs of pilasters framing the west door are 'uncomfortable to look at; the front of the magnificent tower seems to stand upon four inadequate legs. I am afraid that this cannot be defended.'[59]

These were probably minor quibbles on Goodhart-Rendel's part. Yet the abrupt dislocation in scale between the pilasters and tower above was a valid criticism of Hawksmoor's design for eyes used to more conventional systems of proportion, even if this unsettling effect was exactly what Hawksmoor was trying to achieve.

'I have left no time in this lecture', Goodhart-Rendel concluded, 'for any peroration, having said at the beginning of it what I believe about Hawksmoor's greatness and having, I hope, given you during its course some evidence in support of my claims for him.' As if to emphasize the point, with his final slide he left his audience a view of the 'heroic mausoleum at Castle Howard'.[60]

Reactions

Goodhart-Rendel's claims for Hawksmoor were far from universally accepted, especially by those who saw him as primarily Wren's subordinate and therefore of inferior talent. In their compendium of *English Homes*, H. Avray Tipping and Christopher Hussey asked 'is Mr. Goodhart Rendel justified in seeking to give Hawksmoor a place as "one of the greatest masters of modern architecture"? . . . Was he not an incomparable assistant rather than an originating genius?'[61] That the title of the section of the book was 'The Work of Sir John Vanbrugh and his School' is something of a giveaway as to where the authors' allegiances lay.[62]

Tipping took particular issue with Goodhart-Rendel's proposition that 'Hawksmoor could do without Vanbrugh a great deal more than Vanbrugh could do without Hawksmoor'. Although, as Tipping continued, Hawksmoor undoubtedly possessed

> a high degree of training and an abundance of information; it does not suggest creative qualities. He may have had a tendency to develop a more massive style than Wren, but would he ever have realised such a style had he remained with Wren and not come under the commanding personality of Vanbrugh? It was original to Vanbrugh to conceive and realise a remarkable combination of mass and movement as the preponderating and basic principle of an English phase of classic architecture . . . Hawksmoor fell completely under his influence.[63]

Tipping did, however, acknowledge the importance of the first volumes of the Wren Society, published in 1925 and 1926, in revealing Hawksmoor's hand in the drawings for St Paul's Cathedral, on which the first volumes focused.

> There can be little doubt that many of those that deal with the later portions of the Cathedral will be by him. One that is very interesting shows part of the West front, drawn by a careful draughtsman, and at the top of it, roughly put it in Indian ink wash, is a suggestion for one of the West towers. It is a fair surmise that the lower half was done by Hawksmoor, and that Wren set his suggestion for the tower on to it. But, as at Greenwich, Mr. Bolton sees here not Wren, but the bold and suggestive brush of Vanbrugh.[64]

This drawing was, of course, the one discussed in chapter Two, the top half of which, we now know, can only be Hawksmoor's. Yet the conception of Hawksmoor as the plodding assistant, creator of the elevation, and Vanbrugh the flamboyant artist, responsible for the watercolour, was still deeply ingrained at this time.

Although we now know that many of the drawings were in fact by Hawksmoor, the Wren Society editors, Arthur T. Bolton, curator of Sir John Soane's Museum, and H. Duncan Hendry, barely gave Hawksmoor a look in. It was not until volume IV, published in 1929, that Hawksmoor got a proper mention, when he was described, along with John James, as one of Vanbrugh's 'assistants'. Even though the volume reprinted Hawksmoor's *Remarks* on Greenwich from 1728, he was discussed in unfavourable terms, as the following makes clear:

> It seems pretty clear that Hawksmoor was a difficult person. He seems to have owed his appointment in the first place to Wren, against the probably greater merits of James, who appears to have been a very competent architect, with a better sense of detail and proportion than Hawksmoor ever acquired.[65]

Again, this was an assessment based on personal prejudice and conventional ways of understanding 'detail and proportion' rather than scholarship. Throughout the Society's volumes numerous Hawksmoor buildings, as well as a great many drawings, were unquestioningly attributed to Wren or Vanbrugh. In the introduction to volume VII (1930), it was noted how 'It has also been found possible to throw some fresh light on the design and building of *Kensington Palace;* and of the famous Orangery, the latter being the joint work of Sir Chr. Wren and Sir John Vanbrugh'.[66] Eight years earlier, in volume IX the editors included a reproduction of Cockerell's *Tribute to Wren*. All Cockerell's attributions to Wren, including the west towers at Westminster Abbey, remained intact, apart from All Souls, which was described 'as doubtful to-day' with Hawksmoor's name attached.[67] Even in 1940, in volume XVII, Hawksmoor was omitted from a list of 'Wren's contemporaries' that included Vanbrugh, Gibbs, Archer, Talman and even Dickinson.[68]

The Wren Society's editors' attempts at playing down Hawksmoor's talents and important role in Wren's office were in some ways understandable. The Society had been founded to celebrate and further the understanding of the architecture of Wren. To accept that there was another genius working in his office might, to them, have been to diminish Wren's achievements. Nevertheless, the light they shone on Wren's office and Hawksmoor's vital role within it, especially at St Paul's and Greenwich, was always going to reflect upon Hawksmoor too.[69]

At this stage, it was really the position that Hawksmoor was coming to occupy in architectural history, rather than his actual works, that was of most significance for his rehabilitation. He was an architect who quite obviously charted his own course, engaging directly with architecture's associative and emotional qualities – a figure whom someone like Goodhart-Rendel saw quite obvious affinities with for his own position.

Though he was becoming known as an architect, the influence of Hawksmoor's buildings on any practising architects remained slight. This was the case even for as great an enthusiast as Goodhart-Rendel, an architect who, in John Betjeman's words 'was not concerned with theories of architecture but with visual impressions made first by various shapes and materials and then by the work of individual architects and periods of architecture'.[70]

Perhaps the closest Goodhart-Rendel came was Holy Trinity, Dockhead (1951–60), the Catholic church situated on a junction of Jamaica Road just behind St Saviour's Dock in London's Bermondsey. For Goodhart-Rendel, style was really a question of context; one style might work well for one building but be an abomination for another. This gave him the flexibility to build in a French Romanesque style with a High Victorian polychromy at Holy Trinity, but in a modern style just down the road at St Olaf House (1928–32) on Tooley Street.[71] Perhaps in Goodhart-Rendel's equation there was simply no appropriate modern context for a style as singular as Hawksmoor's.

However, if we move beyond questions of style to talk in terms of form we might, in fact, see some affinities between Holy Trinity and Hawksmoor's St Mary Woolnoth. Both share the same wide, twin-turreted formation, a central, portal-like arch and the striking horizontal banding, rustication in Hawksmoor's case, polychromatic brick in Goodhart-Rendel's. This may, of course, simply be a case of common sources, but it is hard not to think that Goodhart-Rendel had Hawksmoor's church – 'the noblest street corner in London' –

The Most Holy Trinity Church on Dockhead, behind St Saviour's Dock, by H. S. Goodhart-Rendel, 1957–9.

in the back of his mind when he came to design Holy Trinity, itself situated prominently on a junction.[72]

St Mary Woolnoth

In his lectures Goodhart-Rendel had noted how St Mary's reputation had fared rather better than Hawksmoor's other churches: it had 'always been celebrated for its beauty, even during the years of Hawksmoor's eclipse'.[73] To say it was 'celebrated' was, perhaps, going a little too far, but it was certainly the case that St Mary Woolnoth had always been Hawksmoor's most conspicuous building.

Sited on the prominent crossroads adjacent to Mansion House, the Bank of England and the Royal Exchange, St Mary's is Hawksmoor's only church within the City of London, built to replace

a medieval church that had been unsatisfactorily patched up following the Great Fire. It was there, in the eighteenth century, that John
Newton, the former sailor turned evangelical preacher, spoke out
against the slave trade with which he had been involved during his
life on the sea. Among the congregation was a young Member of
Parliament, William Wilberforce, who would soon become a leading
figure in the abolitionist campaign.

The church's interior is relatively unlike Hawksmoor's other
churches, overtly square in plan and likely based on Vitruvius' influential description of the Egyptian Hall or a perhaps simply a Roman
atrium.[74] It was altered quite considerably in the 1880s by William
Butterfield, who removed the galleries (mounting their sawn-off
fronts flush against the walls behind) and inserted a new, coloured
stone flooring. He also raised the reredos so that it sits too high into
the arch above it. Despite these alterations, walking into the church
today it is still hard not to be struck by its drama. The dark, brooding exterior gives way to a dazzlingly bright interior, lit from above
by four huge lunette windows, invisible from the outside.

Although St Mary Woolnoth has benefitted from its prominent
location by being, for a long time, Hawksmoor's best-known work, in
other ways it has suffered. From the 1860s to the 1920s, the church
was up for demolition numerous times. It survived on each occasion,
but often by the skin of its teeth and not without some surprising
alterations. This was, however, more than could be said for several
Wren churches that perished over these years – all before the Luftwaffe's
bombs would wreak their havoc.

More often than not, the enemies of the City churches were
actually the Church authorities themselves: the Bishop of London
and the Ecclesiastical Commissioners, driven, as they saw it, by the
necessities of practicality and efficiency. As the City of London's
population fell from mid-century, a consequence, largely, of London's
expansion and the advent of the railways, so congregation sizes
dwindled. Anxious to release funds to cater for the new populations of London's suburbs, the Church sought to free itself of the
burden of supporting so many underused City churches. That there
were also considerable financial advantage to be had by selling off
the valuable sites to railway builders or property developers also

played a considerable, if sometimes deliberately understated, part in the Church's thinking.

In 1860 the Union of Benefices Act legislated for the amalgamation of parishes and the demolition of the subsequently redundant churches. St Mary Woolnoth was one of those identified for removal, with the General Post Office behind it keen to expand. However, as the antiquary John Timbs described in his *Curiosities of London*:

> At a vestry meeting, The Lord Mayor (Alderman Rose) as a parishioner by his tenancy of the Mansion House, ably supported the opposition to the 'amalgamation' scheme, and an amendment rejecting it was carried unanimously. In the Report of the Ecclesiological Society, the committee recorded that the parishioners had successfully resisted a scheme put forward under the auspices of the Bishop of London's Act for the demolition of the remarkable church of St Mary Woolnoth (Hawksmoor's *chef-d'œuvre*), which it was proposed to destroy for the convenience of the General Post Office.[75]

The vocal opposition to the plans illustrated just how woven into the very fabric of the City of London's identity the City churches had become. This was, though, something that the Church authorities felt able to ignore, apparently little concerned with the City churches' social or cultural value.

By 1883 Arthur Mackmurdo was able to note that 'Happily the bill for their destruction is no longer before the House; yet there is nothing to prevent its being brought forward again at any time'.[76] Before long, St Mary's was again under threat. This time the enemy appeared, at first glance, to be the City & South London Railway (c&slr) company.

New challenges

London's first underground railway, running between Paddington and Farringdon, opened in 1863. It was immediately successful and soon other routes followed. All of the early underground lines were constructed using the 'cut and cover' method – essentially building a large trench that was then roofed over to create the tunnel. The first deep-level tunnels were built by the c&slr and ran between Stockwell and a station on King William Street, which had been laid out along the south side of St Mary Woolnoth in the 1830s. The line opened on 18 December 1890, with the trains running on it among the first to use electric traction.[77]

The configuration of the station at King William Street quickly proved inadequate and plans were, in any case, soon afoot for extending the line north to Moorgate. The c&slr proposed to replace King William Street station with a new larger station for which they identified the site of St Mary Woolnoth as the ideal location. Their first intention was to demolish the church and build a street-level station entrance and ticket hall in its place. To do this, however, the c&slr required parliamentary approval.

The 'City and South London Railway Bill' was put before Parliament in 1891 in order to clear the legal and physical obstacles to the railway's construction, which included St Mary Woolnoth, standing literally in the railway's way. The Bill's progress was slow and it was not until 24 April 1896 with its second reading in the House of Commons that the fate of St Mary Woolnoth was directly considered. An order was put to the Bill's committee to 'consider whether any, and, if any, what provisions can reasonably be made for the preservation of the church of St. Mary Woolnoth, without preventing the construction of the railway and station'.[78]

The House of Lords debated the issue several months later. Lord Dorchester reported that a 'protective clause', which would have saved the church, had been 'struck out' and in its place inserted a new clause that would 'facilitate the sale of the Church of St. Mary Woolnoth'.[79] The Earl of Meath agreed with Lord Dorchester's assessment, adding 'It would be a great pity if St. Mary Woolnoth's Church was destroyed . . . The clause authorising it had been inserted simply and solely at the request of the rector of the parish'. Meath proceeded to make some thinly veiled accusations as to the financial gains the rector would make upon the church's destruction. He concluded his statement noting the considerable support that existed for preserving the church, just as it had in the 1860s:

There was much feeling on the subject in the City, and amongst all interested in old churches ... a large meeting was held on the 22nd January at the Mansion House to protest against the destruction of the Church, with the result that, in the House of Commons a clause was inserted protecting the Church ... It was an extraordinary thing that, at the last moment, without warning to anyone, the Rector should come and ask for his own church to be destroyed.[80]

The chairman of the Bill's committee, the Earl of Morley, responded to these accusations, clearly hoping to clarify the situation. He explained how the first 'protective' clause had 'enabled a shaft 90 feet deep to be run through the bottom of the church, a hole to be made in the church wall to cart out rubbish, and there was to be a booking office in the crypt'. The second clause 'to enable the church and site to be sold' was inserted, Morley noted, trying to deflect the various accusations, 'not at the request of the Rector, but, because the Committee thought it right'. He concluded that he hoped the Bill be passed; even in its current state, it would provide the church greater protection than if no bill was passed and the C&SLR relied on existing powers, which apparently already allowed its removal. In the end, the second clause was left in the Bill, which was then returned to the Commons.

The Commons debated the Bill the following week.[81] Sir Joseph Savory (Member for Westmorland, Appleby) opened proceedings and, from the off, he attacked the Lords' amendments, citing the considerable public support for the church. 'In the City of London,' Savory reported, 'there was a very strong feeling that this church, which was the central parish church, ought to be preserved.' Shouts of 'Hear, hear!' reverberated around the chamber. 'Standing at the western end of Lombard Street,' Savory continued, 'facing the Mansion House, and within sight of the Bank of England and the Royal Exchange, it had a beautiful exterior'.[82]

Savory also drew attention to the 'the many remarkable men who had worshipped within its walls, and had been interred there in bygone centuries ... [and also those] who had ministered within its walls – men like the Rev. John Newton'. Savory hoped that, as in

1863, the 'Lord Mayor and citizens ... might again be successful in saving the church.' The rector was again accused of being an enemy of his church, despite his writing of a letter to *The Times* the previous day 'in which he stated that he was utterly opposed to the church being destroyed'. The rector had, however, 'failed to attend the meeting in January at the Mansion House'. It was also noted that he actually lived in Hendon and 'it was impossible for a clergyman living at such a distance adequately to minister to the flock whose spiritual care was intrusted to him'.[83]

Savory was followed by R. B. Martin (Member for Worcester, Droitwich), who stated that 'He had no hesitation in saying that there was no building in the City of London which was so completely suited to the position which it occupied, or was more universally admired for the fine character of its exterior than the Church of St. Mary Woolnoth.' He also added a further twist to the tale:

> A large Scotch banking firm wished to set up a high suite of offices over the railway, and in this way something might be done to reduce the cost incurred ... [A station on the site of the church] was, indeed, an excuse to get hold of the site for the contractors, who would be enabled to dig the soil out, and this, no doubt, would be a great convenience to them. Otherwise, there was no necessity for pulling down the church or destroying it.[84]

Arguments heard in reply reminded the House of the railway's necessity, as well as the simple fact that the C&SLR already possessed the legal right to demolish the church, which would surely have happened if the Bill was thrown out. The chairman of Ways and Means, J. W. Lowther (Member for Cumberland, Penrith), concluded 'that the House was anxious to retain this church. It was built by a famous pupil of Wren's, and was an object of some artistic, and he might almost say historical, value to the City. At any rate they would rather see this church on the site than a big block of buildings'. The 'protective' clause, which the Lords had noted had been removed, was reinserted and the House took their chances.[85]

Underground

That St Mary Woolnoth is still standing today is the indication that these attempts to demolish it ultimately failed. It is fascinating to read members of both Houses argue so passionately for the church's survival, both for its social and historic value and to some degree its architectural merits. In the latter, they were actually several decades ahead of architectural opinion.

In the end, the solution to church and station's coexistence was the one mentioned by Earl of Morley. A lift shaft was inserted underneath the church and a ticket hall created in what had previously been the crypt. The highly complex work of underpinning and excavating under the church was overseen by the engineers David Hay, Basil Mott and Sir Benjamin Baker, designer of the Forth Bridge, one of the most remarkable engineering feats of the nineteenth century. Steel girders were inserted underneath the body of the church; they can actually be seen protruding through the floor near the side walls. The contents of the crypt were removed and carried

A cross-section from the late 1890s showing St Mary Woolnoth with lifts beneath going all the way down to platform level.

Photograph taken by David Secombe in the late 1980s showing the entrance to Bank Station under St Mary Woolnoth.

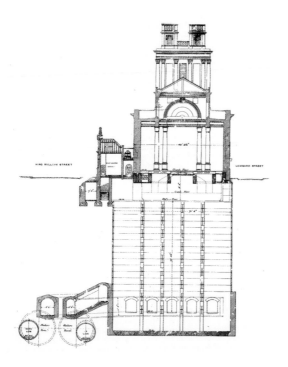

to the City of London Cemetery in northeast London, thus in a way finally reflecting the original recommendations of Wren and Vanbrugh that burials should not take place in or near the churches, but in large cemeteries on the outskirts of the city. The remains of John Newton and his wife were reinterred at Olney, Buckinghamshire, where he had begun his career in the ministry. To this day, the lifts to the Northern Line platforms at Bank Station still run immediately below St Mary Woolnoth and the underside of the crypt is still visible from within the lift shaft.

At street level, a neo-Baroque ticket hall entrance was built abutting St Mary's south side facing King William Street by Sidney R. J. Smith, the architect best known as the designer of the Tate Gallery at Millbank.[86] Smith's addition is but a pale imitation of Hawksmoor, but is certainly not as bad as Goodhart-Rendel described

Sidney R. J. Smith's entrance to Bank Station adjoining St Mary Woolnoth to the south and facing King William Street, 1899–1900.

The west front of
St Mary Woolnoth
photographed by
F. R. Yerbury in 1924.
A version of this
photograph was used
as the frontispiece for
Goodhart-Rendel's
book on Hawksmoor.

it: 'disgusting architecture erupted from the bowels of the earth by the tube-railway whose station now underlies it'.[87] 'Of this eruption little can fortunately be seen from the position from which this photograph is taken', he added, referring to the photograph of the church that was included on his book's frontispiece, in which he actually had the London Underground signs affixed to the church's railings scrubbed out.[88]

After so much time, effort and money was spent allowing St Mary's and Bank Station to coexist, it might have been reasonable to expect that the church was now safe. On the contrary, less than twenty years after the opening of Bank Station, St Mary's was again up for demolition – and as in the 1860s, the Church authorities were once again behind it. However, as we will see, the passions already stirred up in the 1890s had helped focus attention towards Hawksmoor's masterpiece, ensuring that the proposals were met with immediate and concerted opposition.

The Phillimore Report

In 1919 the bishop of London, Arthur Winnington-Ingram, established a commission under Lord Phillimore to look into the possible consolidation of London's churches and parishes. Phillimore was a prominent lawyer and judge who specialized in ecclesiastical matters, and on the surface appeared to be the ideal choice. He oversaw the commission's investigation of the sizes of congregations, parish populations and individual church's income and expenditure.

After the briefest of 'consultations' the commission submitted a series of unerringly practical recommendations. Heavily inspired by the 1860 Union of Benefices Act, the commission's main proposal was to create four new unified parishes or 'quarters'. Central to this idea was that 'No one of the Quarters will have a resident population above the size of an ordinary town parish.'[89]

As ever, this consolidation would necessitate the removal of several churches and Phillimore carefully spelled out the criteria by which the selections for removal were made: 'We have gone carefully into the question of the architectural merits, the historical associations and the topographical advantages of the several Churches, and we have come to the conclusion that those named in the list which follows might well be removed.'[90] St Mary Woolnoth was among the nineteen selected for demolition. There was some wavering over Hawksmoor's church, however, as a note in the report explained that 'the Commission was equally divided, and the recommendation for its removal was carried by the casting vote of the Chairman'.[91]

The reasons cited for the demolitions were rooted in supposed practicality, just as they had been in 1860 and, arguably, still are today when church buildings are scheduled for demolition. Reducing the number of churches would lower overall running costs and allow for the better care and funding of those that survived. The considerable capital released from the sale of the sites – the report stated that 'From our own knowledge we should anticipate keen competition for sites in the financial quarter of the City' – would go towards 'the building of mission rooms and parsonages, the endowment and the increase of endowment of benefices of the Metropolis'.[92]

This shifting of resources and capital from the City to the suburbs was a case of the church trying to follow the people – a tactic that Hawksmoor would probably have recognized. The report noted that 'we have not recommended the removal of any which we understand to have great architectural merit or antiquarian associations'. The proviso added, however, that 'In many cases the beauty and interest of the Church lies not in its shell, but in its fittings and furniture, especially carving, which can well be fitted into some future Church in the outer ring of London.' Here, we have a rather strange premonition of the new churches being erected in London's then suburbs fitted out with a Grinling Gibbons reredos stripped from a City church. Despite all the provisos, the simple fact remained that in the eyes of the commissioners, 'the Churches we propose to remove are not needed'.[93]

As soon as it appeared, the Phillimore Report sparked controversy. Indeed two commissioners, Hugh Cecil and William Collins, only signed it subject to attached notes in which they expressed their uneasiness with both the choice of the churches and the planned speed at which they were to be demolished.

The London County Council (LCC) prepared its own report on this 'drastic proposal', with a particular focus on the 'architectural and antiquarian features of the buildings'.[94] St Mary Woolnoth was found to be 'a fine example of monumental church architecture . . . [which] may be considered one of the best of Hawksmoor's efforts. It is in many respects unique in treatment and is certainly one which should be preserved'.[95] The LCC report also raised another important question: as churches built after the Great Fire had been paid for by a tax on coal – essentially public money – did the Church therefore have the moral and legal right to destroy what was in effect owned by the public?[96]

The press soon took note. A letter to the editor of *The Spectator* recounted the 'close shaves' of numerous city churches during the First World War and asked 'is it irrelevant to express a hope that historic fanes which have eluded the havoc of the Bomb may not after all fall victims to the zeal of the Bishop?'[97] In June 1920 *The Times* reported on an address to the City Livery Club by the architectural historian Sir Banister Fletcher, who passionately argued that

> the City churches were heirlooms, and not chattels that could be sold when they were hard up. The site of the Acropolis in Athens would make a first class site for an American hotel but no suggestion had yet been made that it should be sold . . . [The report] would go down to history as one of the most disgraceful documents ever put before the British public.[98]

Later that year *The Times* reported that the Lord Mayor had received 'a deputation which put before him arguments in favour of the preservation of the City churches threatened under the City of London Churches Commission Report'. It contained 900 signatures in support of St Magnus the Martyr alone.[99]

Despite the public protestations against it, the Phillimore Report was eventually approved by the National Assembly of the Church of England. Two years later, in 1926, its recommendations came before Parliament as the basis of what was essentially a new Union of Benefices and Disposal of Churches Act. The Bishop of London himself began the debate in the Lords, duly noting the opprobrium the report had stirred up:

> My Lords, the first thing I want to remove from your Lordships' mind is that this is a Bill for the destruction of a great many City churches. It is nothing of the kind. I myself have been lampooned in many magazines and newspapers on the subject, and your Lordships may have seen a picture of the Bishop of London, on the occasion of the bi-centenary of Wren, represented as saying: 'Good old Wren, let's pull down one of his churches to commemorate his memory.' There have been worse lampoons than that which have not come before the public eye. One is a picture of the Bishop of London leaning on a pick-axe drinking tea while the death beetle does its work.[100]

'I love these City churches,' the Bishop maintained, 'I have restored many of them, I have opened them, and I would not have one of these monuments of beauty destroyed.'[101] He then proceeded to list all the conditions that would need to be met before a church might be pulled down. The arguments for demolition still largely rested on the notion that funds could be better directed towards London's suburbs, but aesthetics did also come into it. The Bishop continued:

> Some City churches have been removed with advantage in the past. They had no architectural beauty. There was St. Martin Outwich, which was one of the most hideous churches and was removed some years ago. As the result there is now a church with £600 a year in poor Dalston and another church with £600 a year in poor Stepney.[102]

Considerable debate ensued as to the Bishop's rights to dispose of the churches. Perhaps having read the LCC report, Lord Marshall of Chipstead noted that their erection was paid for by coal taxes which 'were levied on every hearth and furnace in the City, and being a compulsory tax it was borne by Nonconformists, Roman Catholics and Jews, as well as by members of the Church of England'.[103] The churches were, this line of argument held, not just religious centres, but emblems of municipal identity.

Phillimore himself was in attendance, though in the first day made no contribution to the debate. This did not stop him being the subject of personal attack, especially regarding his conduct as to St Mary Woolnoth, as Lord Crawford remarked:

> The Report is accompanied by a map, and in a thoughtful way the doomed churches are marked on Lord Phillimore's map by black spots. What are they? ... St. Mary Woolnoth is in the condemned list. That church showed how great a man Nicholas Hawksmoor, the architect, was. He really deserves much credit for the work attributed to Vanbrugh at Blenheim, at Oxford, at Castle Howard and elsewhere ... St. Mary Woolnoth is one of the condemned churches and as to that church the Commission was equally divided and the recommendation for its removal was carried by the casting vote, of the Chairman, Lord Phillimore. There he sits, blithe, learned and debonair, and yet on his shoulders must rest the responsibility that as Chairman he voted for the destruction of this incomparable church.[104]

Despite the protestations, the Lords passed the motion and it was sent to the Commons, where, despite his earlier reservations, it was proposed by Hugh Cecil on 25 November. That morning an article appeared in *The Times* reporting that

> There remains only the House of Commons, and a great number of people, not only in the City, but in the country at large, are devoutly hoping that as the result of to-day's debate the Measure may be rejected and the seven years

old controversy on the fate of the City Churches finally settled.[105]

The article questioned both the need for a new law and the procedures it would create, should it be passed, for the removal of churches which, as the article's writer saw it, laid all power in the Bishop of London. The article concluded: 'These City churches, because of their unique beauty and the genius of the men who built them, are a possession of the City of London and of England without a rival in any country of the world'. To emphasize the point it included a full page of photographs of some of the threatened churches, including St Mary Woolnoth ('designed by Hawksmoor, a pupil of Wren').[106]

In his opening remarks to the house, Cecil was anxious to remove the impression that there was any kind of 'conspiracy' behind the proposals. He noted, in particular, the number of institutions and organizations that had to be consulted before the removal of church could take place. He cited the *Times* article referring to the 'amazing misstatements in that tissue of unreliable misrepresentations'.[107] As the debate continued, it became clear that while many members were generally in favour of the union of parishes, they were unable to support the bill because of the aspects that allowed the demolition of City churches. When finally put to the vote at 12.40 in the morning 'The House divided: Ayes, 27; Noes, 124'. The measure was thrown out.

Monuments

Reading these debates and imagining these proud men holding forth as to the quality or otherwise of the measures presented before each House, it is hard not to be struck by the passion of their arguments. Whether for or against, it is abundantly clear that the members of both houses were not driven by political expediency, simply following where they thought public opinion to be headed. These were deeply felt issues of conscience and morality – arguments over what was believed to be in the public good – and were approached with suitable seriousness. That the fate of the City churches merited so long and impassioned a debate in the highest chambers of the land indicates in just how high esteem they and their architects were held.

The rejection of the 'Union of Benefices and Disposal of Churches (Metropolis) Measure' in some ways marked a turning point in the way historic buildings were seen and valued. On one side were those who saw the City churches as purely functional buildings that were no longer required and could therefore be removed. On the other were those for whom the City churches had become something far more. They stood as tangible links to the past – markers of continuity while all around them the City was rapidly changing. In their walls were infused the very residues of history. Demolishing the City churches would be to destroy not only beautiful structures in their own right, but symbols of the City of London's ancestry, magnificence, and its very sense of identity. As Christopher Hussey observed in the pages of *Country Life* just over a week before the measure was debated in the Lords,

> Their sites are hallowed by antiquity and by the bones of men great and inspiring in their day. Their towers and walls, even if they do not speak to him of religion, are a contrast to his workaday surroundings. Though he may not have the faculties for appreciating them as works of art, they are symbols of history, romance, genius, the liberty to create. The mere walls of the City churches are potentials of inestimable spiritual, in contrast to material, welfare.[108]

In the years that followed, the City churches, together with the rest of the capital would face an even greater foe in the form of the Luftwaffe, but this only strengthened their hold over the national imagination.

If we are looking for a single marker or index, in which are distilled the different stages of Hawksmoor's neglect and rehabilitation during the course of the nineteenth and early twentieth centuries, we need look no further than the treatment of his grave. In *The Builder*, in 1862, under the heading of 'British Architects: New Materials for Their Lives', the writer, Peter Cunningham, who had written the first biography of Inigo Jones, described how,

During a year's residence in St. Alban's . . . I have made more than one pleasant pilgrimage to the graves of Hawksmoor and [Edward] Strong, – a pilgrimage, as my readers will see, not unmixed with pain; for the inhabitants of Hertfordshire would seem to care little or nothing about Wren's assistants or Wren himself.[109]

Cunningham 'found the 5-inch-thick blue ledger which covers his [Hawksmoor's] remains broken in two – wantonly broke, I suspect, during the recent reparations of the church'. The gravestone, he reported, 'lies buried . . . under a splendid yew of the Plantagenet and Robin Hood period. The grave of a man so eminent in his art calls for protection and restoration'.[110]

That 'protection' and 'restoration' went undone for nearly 60 years. A brief note in the RIBA Journal in June 1921 reported that, on a recommendation of its Art Standing Committee, RIBA's 'Council have arranged for the reparation of the tomb of Nicholas Hawksmoor in the churchyard of St Botolph's, Shenley'. This work was to consist of 'clearing away the overgrowth, filling up the crack in the slate slab and making the inscription more legible'.[111] This note solves the mystery of when this concrete repair was made.

It was also stated that the RIBA Librarian had prepared a brief account of Hawksmoor's career to hang in the church, which the Journal also printed. Interestingly, even at this date, the account largely followed that established in Walpole's *Anecdotes*. It did, however, add the following remark which is revealing of an already significant change in Hawksmoor's status:

His fame has been a little overshadowed by his great contemporaries, Sir Christopher Wren and Sir John Vanbrugh, for whom he worked. Appreciation of his influence on the architectural movement of his time has, however, grown; and although all the works which can be directly attributed to his own creation are not accepted with equal favour, he remains in the history of English architecture an outstanding figure and, at his best, a great architect.[112]

Fifteen years later, in 1936, a note appeared in *The Times* marking the exact date of Hawksmoor's death 250 years before. Later in the year, on 15 October, *The Times* carried another report stating that

> The two-hundredth anniversary of the death of Nicholas Hawksmoor, the architect who assisted Sir Christopher Wren throughout the building of St Paul's Cathedral and who was responsible for many of the best-known buildings erected in this country in his time, will be commemorated on Sunday (St Luke's Day) at Shenley, Hertfordshire.

After the 11 am service 'a wreath will be laid on his tomb on behalf of the Dean and Chapter of St Paul's'. This quaint little service would, the writer noted, be attended by RIBA representatives.

It is quite a transformation, which neatly reflects the one Hawksmoor's reputation underwent over the same period. For much of the nineteenth century Hawksmoor remained cloaked in obscurity. Though Soane, Turner and Cockerell were perhaps more aware of his work than most, even for them Hawksmoor remained a marginal figure. A light was, however, slowly being shone in Hawksmoor's direction. It is hard to know what effect, if any, Goodhart-Rendel's just published book and mission to establish Hawksmoor as one of the great figures of British architectural history had in the final round of debates concerning the fate of St Mary Woolnoth in the mid-1920s. But as so often happens, when a building comes under threat people suddenly see it with quite different eyes. The arguments over St Mary's survival not only focused attention towards its particular qualities, but were vital in drawing attention to those of its architect as well, paving the way for Hawksmoor to finally take his place in the light.

FIVE

INTO THE LIGHT

IN 1922, TWO YEARS BEFORE the publication of Goodhart-Rendel's book, a poem by T. S. Eliot that has since come to be seen as one of the greatest of the twentieth century appeared in print for the first time. *The Waste Land*, a complex composition of multiple voices, quotations, fragments, snatches of different times and other-worldly places, has an early passage titled 'Unreal City', which focuses readers' attentions on a precise location in the City of London:

> Under the brown fog of a winter dawn,
> A crowd flowed over London Bridge, so many,
> I had not thought death had undone so many.
> Sighs, short and infrequent, were exhaled,
> And each man fixed his eyes before his feet.
> Flowed up the hill and down King William Street,
> To where Saint Mary Woolnoth kept the hours
> With a dead sound on the final stroke of nine.[1]

This stands as undoubtedly the most famous mention of a Hawksmoor building in literature. It is clearly no mere passing reference, but deeply tied into the poem's web of ambiguity, symbolism and latent monumentality that emanated from the complex inter-relation of Eliot's psychological state and the broader dehumanizing 'unrealities' of the modern city.[2]

Having arrived in Britain three years earlier in March 1917 Eliot began working for Lloyds Bank, where he spent much of the next eight years. Lloyds' offices were located on Cornhill and Lombard Street, then and now the heart of the City of London.[3] Walking to his office at Lloyds, Eliot became acutely aware of how London was being transformed. The City of London's population had long been dwindling and by the 1910s its residents barely numbered more than 10,000. Meanwhile, the rise of grand commercial institutions, like Lloyds, had precipitated the daily influx of hundreds of thousands of office workers accommodated in new office buildings that now loomed over the City's historic fabric.[4] From a city where people had both lived and worked, London had transformed into one that, to Eliot's eyes, was haunted in the daytime by ghost-like figures, who then departed at night to leave its streets a deserted, eerie apparition. Eliot had such experiences in mind when he wrote *The Waste Land*.[5] In his notes to the poem, he remarked that the sound of the bells of St Mary Woolnoth, which was immediately adjacent to Lloyds' offices, was 'a phenomenon which I have often noticed'.[6]

The City churches stood as vital counterpoints to this unrelenting grey malaise. Commenting amid the threat to St Mary's and also the Wren church of St Magnus the Martyr just four years after the publication of *The Waste Land*, Eliot described how the City churches gave

> to the business quarter of London a beauty which its hideous banks and commercial houses have not quite defaced . . . the least precious redeems some vulgar street . . . The loss of these towers, to meet the eye down a grimy lane, and of these empty naves, to receive the solitary visitor at noon from the dust and tumult of Lombard Street, will be irreparable and unforgotten.[7]

While some, such as Harold Clunn in *The Face of London*, saw the demolition of such churches as St Mary Woolnoth as freeing up space for the building of the new banks that Eliot so loathed, *The Waste Land* can be seen in retrospect as signalling the important changes that had occurred in the ways architecture was seen and understood.[8] Eliot's reference to St Mary Woolnoth sets the scene for how over the next few decades the spotlight began to shine on

Hawksmoor like never before. This chapter charts that process: from the pioneering research which uncovered important new material that pulled Hawksmoor out the shadows, to the tenacious campaigns to preserve his buildings and establish him as one of Britain's greatest architects.

Eliot was not the only writer to refer to Hawksmoor's work around this time. In Evelyn Waugh's novel *Scoop* (1938) Algernon Stitch is said to live in a 'superb creation by Nicholas Hawksmoor', while the opium dens of Limehouse, still towered over by Hawksmoor's church of St Anne, were the setting for Sax Rohmer's books about the devilish master criminal Dr Fu Manchu.[9] But neither Waugh, Rohmer, nor, indeed, any other writer had referenced Hawksmoor's work with anything approaching the significance that St Mary Woolnoth held for Eliot.

Looking back, the 'Phillimore Report' in many ways constituted the last gasp of a school of thought that saw historic buildings primarily as functional structures, and which led to the destruction of many of Britain's great country houses on the basis of what was practical. With services rarely held and its doors mostly shut up, to Eliot's eyes St Mary Woolnoth had crossed over into the realm of the symbolic to become almost an emblem of another world. Despite his powerful Christian faith, Eliot's view of the building was essentially one divorced from its everyday functional reality as a space of congregation and worship. To him, it became a beacon of meaning amid the shifting sands of time, standing unchanging and eternal, while the world around it steadily marched towards an uncertain future.

The immediate aftermath of the Blitz saw much of the London that had fuelled Eliot's imagination reduced to a literal waste land. As the world emerged from another bloody and destructive war, many looked at this fundamentally altered landscape – physically and psychologically – with new eyes. New attitudes fed new research and for the first time scholarly interest was turned in a serious way towards Hawksmoor's architecture. This academic awareness culminated in the monograph by the young historian Kerry Downes, which has since paved the way for every subsequent scholar of Hawksmoor's work.

At the same time, attention was turning towards the plight of the buildings themselves, several of which had suffered decades of neglect and were in dire need of restoration. The tireless work of the 'Hawksmoor Committee' not only saved Christ Church, Spitalfields from possible demolition, but by raising public awareness it did much to bolster Hawksmoor's reputation and allowed his work to enter the public consciousness. As Hawksmoor's architecture achieved greater prominence – aided by two important exhibitions – it increasingly became an important cipher for the new: new ideas, new architectural outlooks and, fundamentally, new ways of seeing the past, real and imagined. For many observers, Hawksmoor's buildings were vital sources of meaning in a fast changing world.

Amid the ashes

Not since the Great Fire had London seen devastation on such a scale as that wrought by the Luftwaffe – and it was, of course, far from the only city to suffer significant damage. The ports of Portsmouth, Southampton, Liverpool, Cardiff and many others were hit hard, while industrial cities, particularly in the midlands, but also Glasgow and Belfast, suffered huge damage. One of the saddest architectural losses was the medieval centre of Coventry, which was almost entirely destroyed.

Art generally fared rather better than architecture. As soon as war was declared the National Gallery's paintings, to take one example, were evacuated to Wales, where they were safely stowed in a slate mine. It was recognized early on that culture had an important role to play in raising the nation's spirits and daytime concerts were quickly organized to animate the empty galleries. Some temporary exhibitions were also held despite repeated bomb damage. From 1942, when the bombing had somewhat relented, one painting each month was brought from Wales to hang in the Gallery.

Despite the almost daily frequency of bombing raids at the height of the Blitz, the National Gallery far from monopolized exhibitions of art and culture. The exhibitions held at the Warburg Institute, then temporarily housed in South Kensington, became vitally important for showing how, in the words of Sir Kenneth Clarke, then director of the National Gallery, 'human studies can be kept alive under the most difficult circumstances'.[10] The particular exhibition to which Clarke referred was *English Art and the Mediterranean*, opened in December 1941. Curated by the Institute's director, Fritz Saxl, and one of its leading scholars, Rudolf Wittkower, the exhibition explored the origins of English art and architecture in the classical world of the Mediterranean. A section on the 'Impact of the Baroque' focussed on the apparently Italianate components of St Paul's Cathedral; it was still a few more years before England was considered as having had its own Baroque period in the late seventeenth and early eighteenth centuries.

Mentions of Hawksmoor appeared in a part of the exhibition largely focused on Vanbrugh. The single inclusion of one of Hawksmoor's own works was a photograph of the spire of St George's, Bloomsbury. Its derivation from the Mausoleum at Halicarnassus was noted, along with a more fanciful link made via the depiction of a pyramid in Francesco Colonna's *Hypnerotomachia Poliphili*, first published in Venice in 1499. The exhibition struck a chord with the public and was subsequently shown in six other cities across England.[11]

The success of *English Art and the Mediterranean* derived both from its subject matter and how it was framed on a conceptual level. A wartime audience was naturally receptive to an exhibition that argued for English art's international significance, if not preeminence. But by making the link to the art of the Mediterranean, the exhibition aimed to reveal a set of broader historical continuities that, it asserted, had only been interrupted by the war. It was an inspiring and enlightened message – and an important one to be coming from an itinerant institution of European, mostly German, émigrés that had fled to Britain in 1933 amid the rise of Nazism.

English Art was far from 'exhibition-as-propaganda', but it was inescapable that what was on show would be viewed as the material manifestations of the increasingly threatened English way of life. Culture became a totem of national identity, and architecture figured so centrally in this because it was so visibly under attack. The visual confirmation of this was undoubtedly Herbert Mason's iconic photograph of 29 December 1941 showing St Paul's Cathedral rising

Herbert Mason's iconic photograph of St Paul's Cathedral standing defiant during the height of the Blitz. It was published in the *Daily Mail* on 31 December 1940.

above the clouds of the Blitz – in this image, architecture became the defining symbol of a defiant nation.

St Paul's did not escape the Luftwaffe's bombing campaigns, despite the popular myth that it had remained miraculously untouched. However, the damage it sustained was easily reparable, and work began on it even before the war's end. As the bombs rained down on the Square Mile from September 1940, many City churches were not so fortunate, not to mention the vast, devastated swathes of south and east London that were very heavily hit and in some areas almost totally destroyed. Several of Hawksmoor's churches suffered significant damage; others were luckier and escaped largely unscathed.

During the night of 11 January 1941, a huge bomb landed on the Bank interchange and ripped through the booking hall, escalators and tunnels, tragically killing 111 people sheltering there. The

vast crater visible the following morning revealed just how close St Mary Woolnoth had come to destruction. Legend has it that the church survived only because of the underpinning work in the 1890s; if it had still been standing on its original eighteenth-century foundations the blast may well have caused it to topple over. It is one of the many ironies of this desperate moment in London's history that had this church been then left as it was in the 1890s, as many advocated, it would not be here today.

The huge crater after an air raid that killed 111 people and caused extensive damage at Bank Underground station, January 1941.

'Air-view'

As the great burst of euphoria around the Allied victory died down and Britain's thoughts turned towards rebuilding the still smouldering ruins of its cities, a book appeared that acted as a clarion call for much of what was lost. *Georgian London*, a now seminal work by the great architectural historian John Summerson, was derived from a series of lectures he was to give to the Courtauld Institute in

1939, 'but not delivered owing to the turn of events'. The intervening period, Summerson noted, had 'been somewhat unpropitious for a book of this sort' and for that reason, it remained 'an outline' and a spur for future research. 'This research needs doing now,' Summerson urged, 'before the age of reconstruction blots out all that vast quantity of minor evidence which, battered and often derelict, cannot be expected to survive long'.[12] He was not wrong.

The book begins with a memorable passage entitled 'Airview'. 'I ask you to imagine yourself suspended a mile above London; and to imagine yourself staying up there for a period of time proportional to two centuries, with the years speeding past at one a second.' From this vantage point, the scene below would unfold rather like a time-lapse film of the growth of a plant, revealing, in Summerson's words, 'the same startling impression of automatic movement, of mindless growth'. For Summerson, 'a town, like a plant or ant-hill,

Aerial view of St George-in-the-East and surrounding area, which includes Christ Church, Spitalfields at the very top of the frame, from the 1960s.

is a product of a collective, unconscious will, and only to a very small extent of formulated intention.'[13] This characterization paved the way for the emphasis Summerson gave to the market forces driving London's development, and the roles played in it by figures like Nicholas Barbon.

Though indebted to Victor Hugo's 'bird's-eye' view of Paris from *Notre Dame de Paris* (1831), it is hard not to see Summerson's 'Air-view' passage as being decisively formed against the backdrop of the Blitz. As Londoners' eyes were turned towards the skies to witness the RAF's squadrons of Spitfires and Hurricanes fighting valiantly to beat back wave after wave of enemy bombers, many must have pondered what those pilots saw of the city unfolding below them.

Summerson devoted a whole chapter to '"Fifty New Churches" and Some Others'. It began with James Gibbs – 'an architect of very great ability but not of genius' – before devoting the pivotal, central section of the chapter to Hawksmoor. Summerson was glowing in his praise for Hawksmoor: 'a remarkable man – one of the most remarkable architects and (I am inclined to believe) one of the most admirable men, in the whole of 18th-century architectural practice ...a genius of the disposition of mass and volume unlike anything previously seen in English architecture'.[14] Of Hawksmoor's working relationship with Vanbrugh, Summerson wrote how 'It seems nobody can believe that *both* these men had genius ...The truth is, I believe, that the Vanbrugh-Hawksmore [*sic*] combination was that rare thing, a perfect marriage of minds.'[15]

Despite his at times conspicuous lack of first-hand research, Summerson's view of these architects was remarkably perceptive, as subsequent better-researched studies would reveal. He began his brief analysis of the churches with their plans. 'Every church', Summerson noted, 'was to be an essay in solid geometry ...[deriving] from a square, placed within another square'. 'Once the basic shape is found and its divisions expressed, the details of the plan resolve themselves quickly and architectural form grows out of the geometry.'[16] To confirm his point, on the adjacent page Summerson included an axonometric, 'cut-away' view of St Mary Woolnoth, intended to show how every element of the building derives from this basic geometrical concept. It is a jarringly modern view of such a building, not least because in reality St Mary's never does quite conform to the square within a square theory.

The emphasis on the plan as the main determinant of an architectural composition – elevations and all – betrayed Summerson's interests in modern architecture. Since the 1930s he had been a member of the MARS Group, an association of like-minded architects and critics who had come together to further the cause of architectural modernism in Britain. For modernists the plan was everything, with a building's sections and elevations all deriving from it. When it came to Hawksmoor's buildings, the plan was only half the story. As a consequence, Summerson's discussion of the 'detail' of Hawksmoor's churches went far beyond what one would normally assume the details to be:

> Hawksmore's [*sic*] detail is always exciting; and nowhere is it better than in the trio of elaborately recessed windows in the north and south walls of St. Mary Woolnoth – a piece of architectural eloquence unsurpassed in England. Sometimes he affected in his detail a gloomy grandeur which approaches the monstrous. At St. George's-in-the-East, there are tiny doors wrought about with architectural pomps so heavy and superabundant as to suggest the extravagance of dream-architecture.[17]

Turning of the tide

Georgian London was just one, albeit the most important, of a number of works published around this time that dealt with significant episodes in the nation's artistic history. Both highly focused academic research and more popular surveys began to take notice of Hawksmoor's work like never before. Of the latter, Sacheverell Sitwell's *British Architects and Craftsmen*, first published in 1945, in common with *Georgian London*, was among the most widely read. The presence of craftsmen in the title made it clear that the book's subject was not confined to the work of architects, but the many different crafts involved in constructing, fitting out and furnishing buildings of various types. But it also indicated, as confirmed in the book's introduction, that this was very much a paean for a lost age amid the upheavals of modernity and the horrors of war.[18]

Hawksmoor appeared quite prominently in Sitwell's self-proclaimed 'survey of taste, design and style' from 1600 to 1830. The book's title page included a small line-drawn elevation of the Mausoleum at Castle Howard, while a chapter entitled 'Hawksmoor and the Baroque' gave him equal weight to Wren, Vanbrugh and Inigo Jones, whose work was now increasingly being classed together as the 'English Baroque'. Sitwell discussed the various theories put forward for Hawksmoor's relationships to his peers; whether he was the 'ghost' architect for one or the other, or if Wren or Vanbrugh had in fact guided his hand. In the end Sitwell concluded with an insight belying the paucity of his research that 'a close degree of consultation between all three architects must be assumed, and is the true solution to the mystery'.[19]

Then followed a brief resumé of Hawksmoor's works – accorded the status of those of a fully-fledged 'Baroque architect'. St Mary Woolnoth, Sitwell noted, 'could be a fragment of Blenheim built again in Lombard Street', Christ Church, Spitalfields was 'a work of utmost originality' while the Mausoleum at Castle Howard was Hawksmoor's 'masterpiece' and which together with Vanbrugh's Temple of the Four Winds were 'greater works of art than many of our cathedrals'.[20]

At the more academic end of the spectrum several articles appeared in the late 1940s and 1950s unearthing previously unseen material that shed new light on several areas of Hawksmoor's architecture. Most notable was an article by Howard Colvin that appeared in the March 1950 edition of the *Architectural Review*, which detailed, for the first time, the circumstances surrounding the commissioning of the 'Fifty New Churches'.[21] Colvin delved into the archival material with gusto: from the *Commons Journal*, personal correspondence, building accounts, contemporary comments, both published and unpublished, to the drawings that now reside in the British Library. As his meticulous research so often did, Colvin helped chart the course for subsequent historians, establishing the facts of the situation and telling them where to look – all with even-handed academic restraint. The article contains barely a single statement that cannot be backed up with evidence.

Four years after Colvin's pioneering article appeared he published the first edition of his *A Biographical Dictionary of English Architects, 1660–1840*.[22] This monumental achievement soon became – and remains to this day – the first port of call and invaluable reference for historians working on any architect of the period. Colvin included a sizeable and still largely accurate entry on Hawksmoor. Here, he allowed himself the hint of an opinion on Hawksmoor, albeit by proxy, remarking how although 'in his earlier buildings (e.g. Easton Neston) he is, as Sir Reginald Blomfield put it, "incessantly trying to interpret Vanbrugh in terms of Wren", his mature works form a unique contribution to English architecture'.[23]

In the fourth revised edition that appeared in 2008, just after its author's death, Colvin's entry on Hawksmoor remained remarkably consistent with the first edition, though, of course, updated to reflect new research that had appeared in the interim. While in the first edition Colvin had, reading between the lines, perhaps deemed Hawksmoor a lesser talent than either Wren or Vanbrugh, by the fourth edition Colvin was able to describe Hawksmoor as

> one of the great masters of the English baroque, more assured in his command of the classical vocabulary than the untrained Vanbrugh, more imaginative in his vision than the intellectual Wren. No one understood better than Hawksmoor the dynamic deployment of architectural form or the dramatic possibilities of light and shade. The complex forms of the Queen Anne churches, whether in internal planning or in external embellishment, are as eloquent as anything by Borromini, the Italian architect with whom Hawksmoor most obviously invites comparison.[24]

Kerry Downes

Summerson's *Georgian London* and Sitwell's *British Architects and Craftsmen* were both widely read, in particular by one sixth-form student at the Benedictine Ealing Priory School in west London. A budding architectural historian from a young age, over his career Kerry Downes would go on to do more than anyone in explaining the mysteries of Hawksmoor's architecture.

Downes's interest in architecture had started early, a consequence of an apparently natural inquisitiveness.[25] 'Living in West London, [I] had acquired a considerable first-hand knowledge of London buildings, including the Hawksmoor churches'. On a number of these trips 'cycling around', Downes was accompanied by his father, Ralph, the renowned organist and organ designer.[26] A Catholic convert, Ralph was musical director and organist at the new chapel at Princeton in the u.s., before returning to England and to the Brompton Oratory, the great neo-Baroque Catholic church in west London. Ralph's interest in the Baroque – a style which found manifestations in music as well as art and architecture – no doubt fuelled similar passions for his son.[27]

At school Downes's background in Greek helped refine his architectural interests, which began to be shaped by the school curriculum: a 'School Certificate Art paper on the English parish church [and] Pevsner's *Outline*, set book for the Higher Cert [Higher School Certificate] 1947'. 'One of the H C exam questions was on the lines of "Was there any Baroque in England? Give your reasons", so of course I did', Downes recalls, but 'rather differently from Pevsner's version because in 1946 I had read Sitwell's *British Architects and Craftsmen*'. In his 1959 book on Hawksmoor, Downes credited Michael Franks, 'my art master after the war, and a self-taught historian', as the person 'who first suggested English Baroque to me'. Already, it seems, Downes was beginning to construct the historical and stylistic context for his later academic analysis of Hawksmoor's architecture.

From Ealing Priory School Downes headed, in October 1948, to the Courtauld Institute, the specialist art history college of the University of London. The Courtauld was then situated in the Robert Adam designed Home House on Portman Square. It was presided over by the great art historian Anthony Blunt, also Surveyor of the Queen's Pictures, but most famous, now, for his exposure as a Soviet spy in 1979. The Institute had first opened in 1932, founded as a result of the efforts of Viscount Lee of Fareham, Samuel Courtauld and Sir Robert Witt to improve the understanding of the visual arts in Britain.

At first its aims tended towards the training of museum or gallery professionals. But through the influence of the methods of those scholars attached to the Warburg Institute, the Courtauld soon widened its outlook and began working towards establishing art history as a valid subject within the humanities.

Following the methods expounded by the Warburg scholars, art and architecture were studied as part of and within the field of history, not as something detached or autonomous – a world away from the types of connoisseurship that had ruled the roost in Britain before the war. Downes recalls that

> All Courtauld students in those days studied 'English' art and architecture either pre- or post-1550 ... Everyone did art *and architecture* though most were most interested in painting and sculpture and a few found things like ground plans off-putting ... [But my] studies at the Courtauld taught me to look at architects' drawings in the same light, and with the same preoccupations, as those of the great Renaissance and 17th-century artists.

Margaret Whinney lectured on the English seventeenth century and at this time was working with Oliver Millar on a book which became *English Art, 1625–1714*, but 'there weren't any books to speak of on most subjects' – at least not of the rigorous historical variety that young scholars like Downes were yearning for.[28] It was perhaps this pervading sense that the surface had only been scratched, and that much of art and architectural history remained up for grabs, that made the Courtauld such an exciting place in the 1950s.

As for Hawksmoor, Downes remarks how 'The staff didn't consider an interest in Hawksmoor as at all *recherché* but (in Blunt's word) *germane* rather than central.' In an atmosphere where old assumptions were being overturned and light was shone for the first time on even the murkiest margins of art and architectural history, Hawksmoor was perhaps a natural choice of subject for an architectural historian who had already experienced some of his works first hand. And it was very much Downes' own choice: 'I remember asking my tutor if there was "enough on Hawksmoor for a thesis" and receiving the considered reply that there *might* be, because there were quite a lot of drawings.'[29]

One of the remarkable things about the Courtauld during the 1950s was how the students were essentially left to their own devices. Advice was imparted from time to time, but the topic and direction of their research were determined by the students.[30] It is for that reason that such a high proportion of the influential scholars of succeeding decades – Downes included – had studied at the Courtauld during this particularly fertile period, and why there was such a diversity in their interests and approaches. It was hugely to the benefit of Hawksmoor's subsequent reputation that his life and architecture became the focus of a mind as powerful and perceptive as that of Downes. As he recalls, 'My own good fortune lay in timing, hunch, obsession and obstinacy, the moral support of fellow students and the example and encouragement of elders and teachers.'[31]

From 1951, Downes's research into Hawksmoor became the subject of his PhD degree, supervised by Margaret Whinney.[32] Unusually for the time and, indeed, today, that research was published as a book, in 1959, before it was accepted for Downes's degree by the University of London in 1960. 'There was much talk in the 1950s of ultimately "making one's thesis into a book." As I had a living to earn, I thought I would save my limited and valuable time instead making a book into my thesis.' An opportunity came in about 1956 when, Downes recalls, Blunt 'was looking for authors and subjects' for a series of books he was editing with Rudolf Wittkower of the Warburg for the publisher A. Zwemmer Ltd.[33]

The instigator of the series was Desmond Zwemmer, son of Anton, the Dutch-born bookseller and publisher, whose initial adorned the company's name.[34] Zwemmer senior had established a well-known bookshop (with nearby gallery) on Charing Cross Road, the spiritual home of London booksellers. The publishing business was something of a sideline but it had a good reputation, having produced translations of books on Matisse and Picasso and the first work on Henry Moore. The bookshop, meanwhile, became an important champion of avant-garde artists working abroad, as well as those charting their careers at home. It was the only place in London one could buy copies of Surrealist publications like *Minotaure* and *Labyrinthe*.

With London's publishing scene beginning to prosper after the war, Desmond Zwemmer saw the opportunity of expanding his father's publishing business by commissioning a new series of books on major figures of art and architecture. Zwemmer had studied at the Courtauld before the war, knew Blunt and deemed him the natural choice as an editor; Wittkower, who would cater more towards the architecture side, was another. As a young scholar, Downes was fortunate to be in the right place at the right time, and his subject matter fitted well within the roll-call of canonical and more obscure or overlooked architects who were the subjects of the series: Bramante, Michelangelo, Bernini, but also Borromini, Philibert de l'Orme and Alessandro Galilei.

The huge amounts of new material that Downes unearthed allowed him, for the first time, to survey all of Hawksmoor's career with real depth and insight. Chapters focused on all the major projects with which Hawksmoor was involved, as well as some smaller, lesser-known ones. But perhaps the most interesting part of his book are the opening chapters, which, after a brief biographical outline, deal first with Wren as Hawksmoor's 'Teacher' and then with the 'claims' of the man himself. In these chapters, Downes charted the intellectual and architectural context from which Hawksmoor emerged and through reference to Hawksmoor's own comments in letters and a wide range of sources – from Hobbes to Dryden – offered a pioneering account of how and why Hawksmoor designed as he did. The book finally put to rest the notion that Hawksmoor was an inferior architect to Wren or Vanbrugh, and the idea that Hawksmoor was passively executing the ideas of others. Downes revealed Hawksmoor to be an extraordinary and independent architectural spirit – and one of Britain's finest.

Even after 50 years, Downes's book remains the best, most even-handed monograph on Hawksmoor. Its longevity is due in part to the real passion and intuitive understanding Downes brought to his descriptions of Hawksmoor's constructions of form and mass on paper and in stone. Though erudite and scholarly, the book was far from being a cold academic view. To truly understand Hawksmoor's architecture, Downes contended, the observer must allow oneself to be affected by it, to experience the buildings in the round, as he remarked in the book's closing lines:

The effects at which he aimed were the most directly forceful, emotive, even violent. It is to the buildings that we must always return. They must speak for themselves. They will repel us or fascinate us, but we cannot escape from their strange haunting power.[35]

Wayland and Elizabeth Young

Kerry Downes was far from the only observer to be struck around this time by the still relatively unknown delights of Hawksmoor's architecture. As Downes researched and wrote his book, Wayland and Elizabeth Young, later Lord and Lady Kennet, a couple of young architecture enthusiasts, also discovered Hawksmoor's East End churches, becoming both intrigued by their power and concerned by their current plight.

'When we started being interested in Hawksmoor,' Liz Young recalls, 'we'd been living in Rome some time and loved the Baroque there, particularly Borromini. We came back here and I spent a lot of time being pregnant and feeding babies. On Sunday mornings Wayland, my husband, would go on long walks in the East End and came back saying "it was absolutely astonishing – there are these wonderful white churches – as good as Borromini".' So, when the Youngs came to write their book *Old London Churches*, 'which covered all London's churches standing or no longer standing up to 1830, we praised the Hawksmoor churches like anything'.

Their book was published in 1956 and, Liz Young remembers, 'John Betjeman was kind enough to make it his book of the year'. It is an elegant, quite large volume, copiously illustrated with photographs mostly by the architectural photographer A. F. Kersting. The tone of the text is factual but richly layered with the Youngs' often rather quirky assessments and opinions of what they were surveying. St Mary Woolnoth is described as 'a work of the highest refinement and intelligence', but the most effusive and evocative praise is reserved for Hawksmoor's East End churches.[36]

St Anne, Limehouse, the Youngs wrote, 'rears like a startled horse at the appearance of London upstream'.[37] At St George-in-the-East, ruined by an incendiary bomb in 1941, they describe how

'In winter the river wind yells through the deep funereal arches in his mighty tower and past the ruthless keystones, each as big as a child's coffin . . . It is a waste of time describing such a building . . . the only thing is to go, and gape at what remains'.[38] Christ Church, Spitalfields was their 'hero-building', the subject of no fewer than four of the plates. Its entry contains the most extensive description of any of the Hawksmoor churches, which emanated from a sustained period of looking: 'With Hawksmoor one is always aware of the form of both the contained space and containing solid'; 'the tremendous spire which dominates Tower Hamlets' and the way 'As you move round the church outside the triumphal arches of the east and west aspects of the tower separate, show a hemi-cylindrical hollow, then join again'. 'This is difficult and entirely rewarding architecture'.[39]

For anyone else, that might have been the extent of one's 'dealings' with Hawksmoor; an interest established and then put to rest through the writing of these evocative entries and their ensuing publication. But the Youngs were tenacious campaigners on a variety of issues – from nuclear disarmament and foreign policy, to freedom of speech and conservation. Inheriting his father's title in 1960, Wayland entered the House of Lords and served as a junior minister in Harold Wilson's government until its fall in 1970.[40] Liz sat on numerous boards and advisory panels for a number of different institutions and organizations, all while raising six children. It was highly fortunate, therefore, for the fate of Hawksmoor's churches that such a well-connected and influential couple as the Youngs took on the cause of their preservation.

The Hawksmoor Committee

In December 1960 a call came through to the Youngs from Prebendary Stephan Hopkinson, a friend who sat on a Stepney diocesan committee. The news was grave. 'Look', he said, 'they can't afford to mend the roof of Christ Church, Spitalfields and are thinking of getting the faculty to pull it down – do something, girl!' 'I saluted smartly, as it were,' Liz Young remembers, 'and did something'.[41] The first thing was to telephone 'everyone who I could think of' in the architecture world: John Betjeman, John Summerson, the architect and planner Sir William Holford and Ivor Bulmer Thomas, the writer and former politician who had recently set up the Friends of Friendless Churches to help save redundant churches. Enquiries were quickly made and it was discovered that, in fact, the peril was not quite as imminent as Hopkinson had suggested. There was no immediate threat and the quick response saw the demolition idea dropped before it could be developed into any kind of plan.

Yet Christ Church and also St Anne, Limehouse remained in terrible states, with their architect still relatively unknown despite the publication of Downes's monograph the year before. 'For us,' Liz Young wrote much later, 'Hawksmoor's buildings were exhilaratingly unfamiliar and glorious, but this was a rare taste, we thought'.[42] The year 1961 marked possibly the tercentenary of Hawksmoor's birth and Liz Young was able to convince *The Guardian* to run a long article she had written arguing for his rightful place among the greats of British architectural history.[43]

> There is no end to rehearsing the skills and joys of Hawksmoor's buildings – that is what genius means. That our ancestors should have seen nothing but ponderousness in them is no more surprising than their distaste for Donne, say, or Caravaggio. We are luckier than they in having eyes and ears open to such things. The question now is how to keep and restore those of Hawksmoor's buildings that need it.

Young outlined some of the work that was required to return all the churches to order, which was estimated would come to something over £200,000. An address was given for individual contributions, but the primary purpose of the article was one of raising awareness of Hawksmoor's architecture and, in particular, those buildings in need of restoration. It was hugely helpful, therefore, that the article was accompanied by large caricature drawings of Christ Church and St Anne's by the cartoonist Papas.

The Hawksmoor Committee, as it became known, assembled over the course of 1961, with John Betjeman as its chairman. He was in many ways the obvious public face, though was much more than

Illustration by 'Papas' accompanying the article on Hawksmoor by Elizabeth Young in *The Guardian* on 1 April 1961.

a figurehead. By this time he was one of Britain's best-known poets and a leading voice in the growing architectural conservation movement. He was a founding member of the Victorian Society, which had formed three years earlier – demonstrating his fondness for the overlooked and unfashionable. The other members of the Hawksmoor Committee were Reverends W. S. Allam, C. G. Watts, and Denis Downham, all rectors of Hawksmoor churches; Ivor Bulmer-Thomas; Kerry Downes; Sylvester Gates; J.H.V. (Vaughan) Davies, the civil servant and architecture enthusiast who had published an appreciation of Hawksmoor in the March edition of *Architectural Design* as well as an article several years before on the history of Greenwich Hospital; Prebendary Stephan Hopkinson, of course; the critic Ian Nairn; and Wayland Young. Liz Young became the Committee's secretary. Much of the correspondence is preserved in her personal archive and provides a good deal of the source material of the following passages.

Even before the Committee's formation the possibility of an exhibition was mooted as a way of building awareness of Hawksmoor in his tercentenary year. The idea was raised by W. S. Allam, Guild Vicar at St Mary Woolnoth, writing to Liz Young, at the suggestion of 'Prebendary Stephan Hopkinson, who was my predecessor at St Mary Woolnoth'.[44] Young replied the following day: 'I think an exhibition would be an excellent idea'.[45] Investigations were made and Young wrote again to Allam in March:

> I have heard from our chum at the Whitefriars Press, [added in pencil is 'Theo Crosby', the architect and writer, who Liz Young recalls 'built us a large playroom at the back of our Wiltshire cottage'], who tells me this: 'As for an exhibition,

you might get something reasonable for £300, but not very much. The best way is to find a sponsor – like a stone producers federation, or a big firm with a social conscience. I can lay on a designer easily enough – either Edward Wright who now works here – or someone else – provided it's not wanted in a hurry or before July'.[46]

It seems that the initial thought of a venue was St Mary Woolnoth itself, though in replying to Young's letter Allam noted that 'an exhibition here looks very remote' because of the very limited space in the narthex.[47] In light of this and more generally because of how important an exhibition could be for their cause, the Committee decided to aim higher.

At the suggestion of Ivor Bulmer-Thomas, in early October Liz Young wrote to Sir William Emrys Williams, Secretary-General of the Arts Council, suggesting that they might like to hold the exhibition. The anniversary date was now deemed to be less important: 'We had originally intended to stage the exhibition in, if possible, December or January but in view of the doubt about Hawksmoor's date of birth it does not seem sensible to try to hurry to coincide with a tercentenary which may well be no such thing'.[48] Some urgency was, however, required as Christ Church, especially, was deteriorating.

Discussions ensued, with Bulmer-Thomas himself also writing a note to Williams. Finally, in January the following year, Gabriel White, Director of Art, wrote to Liz Young to report that the Arts Council 'would like to produce the exhibition for a London showing, to be followed by others in the provinces'. The London gallery was 'fully booked this year . . . but,' White added 'I think there is a doubtful starter for the period September 7th to October 6th'.[49] Two months later, David Thomas wrote to confirm the availability of the Arts Council's galleries at 4, St James's Square.[50] Funds were tight, with Thomas reporting to Young in June he had 'escaped a nasty financial crisis over Hawksmoor' by reusing some equipment from another exhibition.[51] He did add though one query: asking whether Kerry Downes and Vaughan Davies might work on the exhibition for just an honorarium, which both in fact agreed to do.[52] Downes and Davies each contributed to the small but handsome catalogue, the elegant grey cover of which was marked only with Hawksmoor's name in a stark sans-serif font.[53]

With the Committee up and running and plans for the exhibition moving apace, Liz Young set about soliciting signatories for a letter to *The Times* that would publicly launch the Hawksmoor Committee. Once signed-up, these eminent names would then sit on the Committee's 'masthead', lending the campaign prestige and weight. Young approached a diverse group of the wealthy, well-connected and prominent, both within and outside the architectural world; 'cheeringly, no-one refused to join'.[54]

The 'masthead' list would go on to include Sir Colin Anderson, Director of the Orient Line; Lord Crawford, who, as we saw in the last chapter, had argued so passionately for St Mary Woolnoth in the House of Lords in 1926; the media baron Sidney Bernstein; owners or incumbents of Hawksmoor buildings like George Howard (Castle Howard) and John Sparrow (Warden of All Souls College, Oxford); a broad range of architects, from traditionalists like Albert Richardson and Raymond Erith to the more progressive, like William Holford and Denys Lasdun, and even the avant-garde in the Brutalist couple Alison and Peter Smithson, friends of the Youngs who built an addition to their Bayswater home; and a group of leading critics and historians including John Summerson, Nikolaus Pevsner and Rudolf Wittkower.

For the initial letter to *The Times* the list of signatories was smaller. Kenneth Clark replied, saying, 'I know nothing of Hawksmoor by modern standards – I am an early admirer, but nothing more. But I will gladly sign the excellent draft letter, and will make a donation at the time of the exhibition', while Denys Lasdun replied to Liz Young's letter of 27 July, noting simply that he 'signed with pleasure'.[55]

Confident that Hawksmoor's fame was now extending beyond Britain's borders, Young also looked to America. For the masthead, though not for *The Times* letter, she was able to sign up the famous American architect Philip Johnson: 'I knew his name and I wrote to him asking whether he would like to join the masthead and he wrote back saying "yes, and here is $100 or something"'. Another major coup was securing the support of the American historian of modern architecture Henry-Russell Hitchcock. The influential American urbanist Lewis Mumford responded to Liz Young's speculative letter, saying that, if at least two others sign *The Times* letter, 'I will be happy to join them: but I feel it would [be] inappropriate – if not dishonest – for me to sign a statement I could not possible have written.'[56]

The content and composition of the letter passed without further comment. The one exception was T. S. Eliot, who by his seventies had become world famous and a recipient of the Nobel Prize for Literature. In reply to Young's letter, Eliot wrote:

> I should, of course, be very glad to sign an appeal together
> with other sponsors of the Hawksmoor appeal but I simply
> cannot sign a letter, especially when addressed to *The Times*,
> so badly written as the one you enclose. There is nothing
> in the contents of the letter to which I object; my objections
> are entirely to the phrasing.[57]

Eliot enclosed a copy of the letter with his annotations. Two exclamation marks in the margin drew attention to the eccentric phrasing, while the assertion that 'Hawksmoor's great white churches would be even better cynosures and scalemakers to the new open Stepney' drew the comment 'what's a scalemaker'?

Eliot concluded his letter in mischievous fashion, taking aim at a fellow poet: 'Why not ask John Betjeman, as he is the Chairman of the Committee, to produce a more polished and grammatical letter?' In the end, none of Eliot's changes were made to the letter – in any case it was too late to recirculate – and his name was not among the signatories when it appeared on 24 September.[58] He did, however, lend his name to the Committee's masthead.

Results

The exhibition opened on 8 September 1962 and garnered terrific coverage. Articles appeared in all the major broadsheets as well as the more specialist press – 'they seem to be saying extremely nice things about Hawksmoor in the papers', Liz Young wrote to David Thomas.[59]

To help build publicity in the run up to the exhibition, Vaughan Davies had given a talk on Hawksmoor at the RIBA chaired by John Summerson, while John Betjeman had done his best to stir up conversation and debate by including, in an article in the *Daily Express*, Christ Church, Spitalfields and St Anne, Limehouse among the ten buildings in England 'for which he was prepared to go to the stake'. 'Young and old', he claimed, 'are joined in a battle against grey men without eyes or heart, whose only literature is a cheque book and to whom beauty is an indecent word'.[60] As Liz Young later recalled, conservationist passions were running high; the Euston Arch had just been demolished and many were wondering what would be the wrecking ball's next victim.

One of the more surprising pieces of coverage to emerge from the exhibition was a feature in the fashion magazine *Vogue*. The 'line-up of shapes that'll be making the news this season ... [a] coat with a direct line on Paris via welted seams and a shawl collar' were shown against photographs of Christ Church and St Anne's.[61] The article even included the address to which readers could send contributions towards the Hawksmoor Committee's campaign.

Confirmation that Hawksmoor had finally 'arrived' came with the National Portrait Gallery's commissioning of a cast of the bust of him that looks out over the buttery he designed at All Souls. Made in the 1730s, probably by Sir Henry Cheere, the All Souls bust is the only known representation of Hawksmoor. The National Portrait Gallery's bronze cast of the plaster original saw Hawksmoor finally take his place among his peers in the rooms devoted to the leading artistic figures of the early eighteenth century. 'It seems extraordinary', exclaimed *The Guardian*, 'that an architect who worked on St Paul's Cathedral, Hampton Court Palace, Castle Howard and Blenheim and who built those curious neighbours, Queen's College and All Souls at Oxford, should so nearly be forgotten'.[62] For Liz Young, the satisfaction that Hawksmoor's renown now extended to the 'right people' was the inadvertent posthumous 'awarding' of a knighthood by Mr Boydell, an Office of Works Minister. In a speech to the House of Commons on 1 August 1966, Boydell justified repairs at St James's Palace on the grounds that 'The facade was very probably built by Sir Nicholas Hawksmoor'![63]

Hawksmoor's bust in the buttery at All Souls College, Oxford. It is usually attributed to Sir Henry Cheere and date to the 1730s.

Thanks to the exhibition and to the Committee's work, Hawksmoor's star was certainly on the rise – but what of the buildings they were fighting to save: St Anne's and especially Christ Church? At this stage there was no chance of public money. In 1912 the Church of England had secured what became known as the 'ecclesiastical exemption', allowing it freedom from planning law. The proviso was that it would forfeit state aid for the maintenance and repair of its vast number of historic buildings. Fortunately the Committee contained some resourceful and creative minds who had ideas where money could be found, notably Ivor Bulmer-Thomas.

Having set up the Friends of Friendless Churches, Bulmer-Thomas was familiar with the procedures and protocols that determined the fate of redundant churches and how funds might be found for their repair and return to ecclesiastical or, indeed, secular use. Important in this was the Report of the Archbishops' Commission on Redundant Churches, which appeared in 1960. The Report codified how the hundreds of redundant churches across the country might be disposed of. Sale was one viable means, which would both avoid demolition and hopefully raise funds that might be spent elsewhere. The report specified 'that all proceeds of sale, either of a site or a standing building, should be divided equally between the diocese and the proposed Redundant Churches Fund' – that is, to maintain churches for which no use could be found but which should remain as monuments.[64]

It just so happened that at the same moment that funds were being sought for Christ Church, Spitalfields, another of the churches built by the 1711 Commission – St John, Smith Square – was also in dire need of repair. Designed by Thomas Archer, the church's odd, four tower configuration was famously described by Charles Dickens in *Our Mutual Friend* as like 'some petrified monster, frightful and gigantic, on its back with its legs in the air'.[65] An incendiary bomb had gutted its interior in 1941 and it had remained open to the sky for the twenty years since. With little congregation to speak of, the idea was raised of the church being sold and restored for use as a concert hall. Following the recommendations of the Archbishops' Commission on Redundant Churches, Bulmer-Thomas saw a possibility that the proceeds from the sale of St John's might be used to pay not only for its own restoration, but also for the repair of the roof of Christ Church, Spitalfields. It was an ingeniously elegant solution – as Liz Young put it 'two excellent Baroque birds restored to life with one stone' – which, miraculously, Bulmer-Thomas was able to persuade the Diocese of London to take up.

Even with the promise of a significant sum from the sale of St John's, restoration funds remained in short supply. Surveys of both Christ Church and St Anne's had been conducted in the early 1960s by the architect Cecil Brown on behalf of the London Diocesan Fund, which outlined the extensive work that was needed to bring both back to a decent state of repair. The sum required was well out of reach at this stage. However, with the momentum generated by the exhibition and the Committee's campaigning, the Diocese of London was now minded to do what it could to safeguard the churches' futures, funds permitting.

In November 1964 Pamela Bennetts, Deputy Secretary to the London Diocesan Fund, wrote to Liz Young to report that even with the proceeds of the sale of St John's, plus £2,500 from a local brewery and £5,000 promised from the Historic Churches Preservation Trust, 'we are only in position to do the bare minimum of repairs to Christ Church, Spitalfields, and the immediately necessary works to St Anne, Limehouse'.[66] As to the Diocese undertaking fundraising, a letter of January the following year from The Ven. M. M. Hodgins, Archdeacon of Hackney, made clear that

> The point of view of the Diocese [of London] is that we are restoring these churches because of their architectural interest, and we do not think it right to appeal for money which would otherwise be available to help the pastoral work of the church, and will expect the money to be forthcoming from sympathetic people who wish to see notable churches preserved and restored.[67]

Work finally began in 1965. In November Liz Young wrote to Bulmer-Thomas to say 'I was along at Christchurch last week; it is very cheering to see the scaffolding all the way up to the top of the spire'.[68] The Committee itself raised over £2,000 from donations which had been sent in from as far (and near) afield as Huddersfield, Islington, Liverpool, Shropshire, Sidcup and Winchelsea – how widely the name of Hawksmoor had travelled. With the initial work to make both churches safe and dry nearing completion, that money was disbursed to the Diocese in June 1967.[69]

In March 1968 Pamela Bennetts reported that at St Anne's the 'more urgent repairs are now nearing completion, and the church is in use', while at Christ Church with the roof now safe, Denis Downham, the rector, was able to open up the crypt as a homeless shelter.[70] Much work still needed to be done, but in the space of less than ten years, the Hawksmoor Committee, under the tireless leadership of Liz

Young, had secured the future of two of London's greatest buildings and been instrumental in getting their architect the acknowledgement his achievements surely deserved.

Recognition

Over the 1960s as repairs were being made to two of his churches, Hawksmoor's reputation continued to rise. His architecture began to receive a level of recognition and renown far beyond what it had ever received before – and from a wide variety of places. One of those closest to home was in the writings of the critic Ian Nairn, whose own reputation has, in recent years, enjoyed something of a revival.[71] A former RAF pilot, Nairn began his career in architectural journalism with a bang. In *Outrage*, a special edition of the *Architectural Review*, published in June 1955, Nairn attacked the banality he saw in post-war architecture and planning, coining the term 'subtopia' to denote the draining out of a sense of place that had afflicted so many of Britain's cities and towns. Nairn's was an acute eye, sharpened perhaps by his years flying Gloster Meteors, and one who, at his best, could distil his observances into some of the sharpest, pithiest and most evocative comments on buildings and places of his period. His descriptions of Hawksmoor's churches are especially memorable.

Nairn became a familiar figure in the British architectural press during the late 1950s and 1960s, before becoming a television regular in the early 1970s. He was a natural topographer and in the early 1960s worked with Pevsner on both the Surrey and Sussex volumes of *The Buildings of England* series. Nairn's individual, emotionally charged, and often idiosyncratic observations, contrasted with Pevsner's more detached academicism. This was a clash of approaches to architecture: on the one hand, Nairn led by what he saw and what he felt; on the other, Pevsner concerned himself with questions of style and evidence. The collaboration lasted only two volumes and it must have been with some relish that Nairn began his series of personal views of London buildings for what became *Nairn's London*.

As he was a member of the Hawksmoor Committee, it comes as no surprise that Nairn gave Hawksmoor's buildings prominence in *Nairn's London* – though he went so far as to give them an almost central position. It is a small, highly selective book – very much a personal view – yet Nairn accorded space for good-sized entries on five of Hawksmoor's churches, excluding only St Alfege, Greenwich. For Nairn, St Mary Woolnoth was 'the one City church you must go in'. Being inside its top-lit square-within-a-square interior 'feels like being on the hot end of burning glass . . . Space, here, is made so tangible that you can experience, for the price of a bus ticket to the City, the super-reality of the mystics or mescalin'.[72] Mescalin is a hallucinogenic drug; and the possibility of an experience beyond that of normal reality, drug-induced or otherwise, was a feature of Nairn's descriptions of Hawksmoor's churches.

When it came to St Anne, Limehouse, Nairn's research, or rather his lack of it, tainted his view somewhat. This church was, in his view, 'a collection of disparate parts', indicative of Hawksmoor 'limbering up for his great London churches'.[73] The problem was Nairn had his dates wrong. He was following the long debunked convention that St Anne's was begun in 1712, the first of Hawksmoor's churches, rather than one of the three 'Stepney sisters', all started in 1714. Coming to Christ Church, Spitalfields, a few pages later Nairn began the entry with one word: 'mighty'. Though further descriptions and comments followed, they added little more beyond this simply arresting opening statement.[74]

The bombed-out shell of St George-in-the-East, itself surrounded, even in the 1960s, by acres and acres of desolate rubble, almost confounded Nairn. For once, one can sense him almost struggling for words to describe the experience of standing in front of this great hulking shell:

A ruin among ruins, in the lost part of Stepney, south of Commercial Road. The old life has gone or been deliberately killed, the new has not yet come up with any pattern of buildings worth twopence. It makes no difference to Hawksmoor's bizarre poetry. This is probably the hardest building to describe in London; it is an entity like a hand or a foot, total shape and total atmosphere.

Between St George's west tower and subsidiary 'pepper pots' Nairn saw 'a stage somewhere beyond fantasy, which is always comfortably related to common sense: it is the more-than-real world of the drug-addict's dream'.[75] This is a stage further even than the realm of 'dream-architecture' that John Summerson had so eloquently described St George as evoking in *Georgian London*.

It was only at St George's, Bloomsbury that Nairn saw Hawksmoor as perhaps going too far; here, 'Hawksmoor's prodigious invention ran away with him and produced such disparate elements that he simply could not call them to heel'.[76] Nevertheless, Nairn's was an enthusiastic endorsement of Hawksmoor. He was Nairn's sort of architect: an understated character, but one who produced buildings of extraordinary eloquence and emotion, which deeply affected an observer like Nairn, who let his intuition guide his head. Through Nairn's words Hawksmoor was finally getting his due: his buildings were being recognized as among London's finest.

As the 1960s wore on, Hawksmoor began to cross into mainstream public consciousness. The Arts Council exhibition of 1962 had ensured that many more people than before were aware of Hawksmoor. More broadly, though, it was clear that the architectural taste that had played a part in keeping Hawksmoor in the shadows for so long was changing. Baroque architecture was being rehabilitated. No longer was it viewed as over-wrought, overly intricate and distinctly alien to Britain; instead it was increasingly valued for its drama, the rawness of its forms, especially in Hawksmoor and Vanbrugh's work, and, for some observers, the variety of its sources.

In particular, Vanbrugh's work, and specifically his later, sterner and more martial phase, was a source of inspiration and interest for the similarly monomaniacal Brutalism of the architects Alison and Peter Smithson, who sat on the Hawksmoor Committee's masthead. The Smithsons enthused, albeit in a vague and characteristically pretentious way, over the 'magical emptiness' of the 'space between' at Blenheim, while they claimed that a late 1950s house they designed in Watford was 'intended to look like a blackish solid block pierced with windows in the manner of Vanbrugh Castle, Blackheath'.[77] For Brutalists like the Smithsons, who took the modernist tenet of truth to materials to an almost fetishistic level, there was much to admire in how Vanbrugh, and also Hawksmoor, used stone in a way that exaggerated its own materiality.

On a wider level, the spirit of renewed national self-confidence that marked the 1960s was steadily seeping into the ways the nation viewed its architectural past. Not only were St Paul's and the City churches symbols of national defiance, they were great architecture too. The work of Wren, Hawksmoor, Vanbrugh and Gibbs was increasingly celebrated because of its peculiar Englishness.

In academic circles until well into the twentieth century the Baroque was seen as a strictly continental and Catholic phenomenon. This was the view arguably first put forward by the German scholar Heinrich Wölfflin, in his hugely influential book *Renaissance and Baroque* (1888). Wölfflin saw the Baroque as the cultural manifestation of the Counter Reformation in which the qualities of illusion and drama superseded the order and rationalism that had marked the Renaissance. As younger German scholars emigrated to Britain under the spectre of Nazism, they brought these ideas and an interest and expertise in the Baroque arts with them. It was, in a way, really only a matter of time before thoughts turned to the question of whether England had had its own Baroque, and from the 1920s and 1930s the term began to be used with increasing frequency to describe the architecture of Wren, Vanbrugh, Hawksmoor, Thomas Archer, John James and others.

This had in many ways prepared the ground intellectually for Downes's study of Hawksmoor during the 1950s, but found fullest expression in his later book *English Baroque Architecture*, which placed these architects once and for all at the same level of those of the continent – Bernini, Borromini, et al. – with Hawksmoor at their centre.[78] Published coincidentally but also rather appropriately in 1966, the year of England's epoch-defining victory in the Football World Cup, Downes's book finally cemented the Baroque's place at the apogee of the nation's artistic achievements.

In 1969 Thames & Hudson published, as part of their World of Art series, a new book on Hawksmoor by Kerry Downes. Smaller, cheaper and more accessible than the earlier Zwemmer publication (by then out of print), Downes's new book was intended 'neither to summarise nor to supersede the earlier, though perhaps to supplement it in so far as research and thought have not stopped in the intervening decade'.[79] Rather than addressing the subject on a project by project basis as his earlier book had done, here Downes explored Hawksmoor's work thematically, creating a more rounded and integrated view of Hawksmoor's career, with copious illustrations in-tegrated with the text. Appropriately reflecting how views of the architect had changed in the interim, Downes dedicated the book to 'Nicholas Hawksmoor and to his many admirers in the present day'. It is still in print.

To sum up Hawksmoor's change in status over the 1960s, we really have to think about what was happening in urban terms in the city where he made his greatest mark. As London was steadily rebuilt after the war, just as it had been after the Great Fire of 1666, it emerged as a city reborn. Swathes of Georgian and Victorian London were replaced with modernist housing estates, offices and industrial buildings defined by geometry, abstraction and bare, unarticulated surfaces. The Hawksmoor Committee recognized the near unique capacity for Hawksmoor's architecture to survive, almost to revel in this new cityscape: 'Hawksmoor's churches, large and dramatic in outline, firm and humane in detail, can accept and use as few others can the background of simple shapes and regular surfaces that modern building techniques encourage.'[80] Amid this 'brave new world', Hawksmoor's buildings remained singular and proud counter-points, towering markers of meaning in the fast-changing cityscape.

To Whitechapel

Hawksmoor's renown continued to grow even as the optimism of the 1960s gave way to the economic and social realities of the 1970s. In 1975 Bassetlaw District Council organized a Hawksmoor exhib-ition in Retford Town Hall and the Worksop Museum as part of Architectural Heritage Year, a European-wide cultural endeavour.[81] The link was the proximity of Hawksmoor's place of birth in nearby East Drayton.

Kerry Downes, now at Reading University, had continued his studies into the English Baroque, as we have seen, and by the 1970s was researching Vanbrugh for a major book that appeared in 1977.

Together with the other members of the Hawksmoor Committee, Downes had hoped the 1962 exhibition would travel to other venues. However, this was something that the Arts Council was unable to support financially and, in any case, the timing was perhaps not quite right.[82] While the response to the exhibition held in a building in St James's Square, then thought (erroneously) to have been designed by Hawksmoor, had certainly been impressive, there was no guarantee the same success would be had elsewhere, especially with the national press having already covered the exhibition.

So, Downes must have been quite excited when he received a letter in mid-November 1976 from Nicholas Serota, recently appointed director of the Whitechapel Art Gallery, informing him that 'I would very much like to present a large exhibition of the work of Nicholas Hawksmoor and naturally thought of asking you to act as adviser'.[83] As Serota recalls, it was clear to him that Downes 'had wanted to do this show for a while and was quick out of the blocks'. This was fortunate, as Serota reported in his opening letter to Downes that 'owing to a change of plans there would now be an opportunity of presenting a Hawksmoor exhibition in the second half of March and April next year'.

Today, Serota is Director of the Tate and a major figure in the art world, but back in 1977 he was an ambitious young gallery director, keen to remake the slightly struggling East End gallery. A Hawksmoor exhibition was a way of reintroducing the occasional historical exhibition into the Whitechapel's established programme of contemporary art and, in his words, 'of rooting the gallery more firmly in its local community'.[84]

> Being that close to Christ Church, Spitalfields . . . made me wonder about the possibility of doing something to bring attention to those greats ships of state sailing throughout the East End . . . My interest was probably also sparked by the realisation that Hawksmoor was a figure of great importance for architects who were emerging into public consciousness, like James Stirling. The challenge was to organise it in six months; one would never do that now.

In a letter of 5 December addressed to 'Nick' (they had clearly met in the interim), Downes included a list of possible works. With the timeframe so short, they would be relying on lenders' goodwill, and fortunately all were very supportive. 'Given the churches were nearby', Serota remembers, 'there seemed little point of including . . . newly made models. We couldn't afford it anyway'. Drawings were, therefore, the exhibition's major focus, accompanied by small reference photographs, all displayed 'in a way [that] was to make the work tangible . . . [and to show how the] drawings themselves became the means by which these great sculptural forms were created, and to give a realisation . . . that light and shade played an important part in Hawksmoor's architecture'. The exhibition did, however, also include the National Portrait Gallery's bronze bust and, borrowed from Lord Hesketh, the model of Easton Neston.[85] There was a further notable three-dimensional inclusion, as Downes wrote to Serota at the time:

> Thinking further about large objects, there is one which could be copied with less difficulty than anything else and would make a splendid entry piece: one of the side doorways to St George-in-the-East. At least, it seems to me it could be made out of plywood once one had accurate drawings, and the mouldings are minimal in complication. If you haven't a tame scenery maker I would be prepared to make it in the Dept. workshop for the cost of the materials. If it were finished in Snowcem or similar it would pass for Portland stone on a dull day.

Downes was taken up on his offer and the monumental doorcase made it into the exhibition: all seventeen-by-seven feet of it.[86] An installation photograph shows just how striking it looked in the otherwise relatively spare display. Suddenly transposed into the gallery context, the sense of scale and proportion gave a far more tangible sense of the power of Hawksmoor's architecture than any photograph could engender.

With the exhibition predicated on it being easy to visit the actual buildings nearby, it was surely a welcome coincidence when

Nick Serota received a letter from London Transport, reporting that 'It just so happens that the next poster in our programme is also about Hawksmoor and just as soon as the accompanying leaflet is ready ... we shall be displaying it around our system'.[87] Hawksmoor had already, in 1961, featured as part of a London Transport poster on 'London Tercentenaries'.[88] This time, however, Hawksmoor had the whole poster to himself. Designed by Richard Beer, it showed three drawn views of the spire of St George's, Bloomsbury, one of Hawksmoor's 'six splendid churches, each in its way a masterpiece'. 'Read about them, and how to visit them by bus or underground, in the special London Transport Hawksmoor leaflet'.

With the exhibition's run coming to an end at the beginning of the month, Serota wrote to the lenders on 23 May to thank them and report that it had been 'an exceptional success and was visited by 15,328 people'.[89] Like the 1962 Hawksmoor exhibition, the press coverage was tremendous. Marina Vaizey, writing in the *Sunday Times*, called it 'one of the best architectural exhibitions (notoriously difficult to present) I have ever seen ... [and] makes the case for cherishing what has survived from the mind and energy of this obsessive, gouty, solemn, student and creator'.[90] 'Everyone knows about Hawksmoor

Installation view of the 'Nicholas Hawksmoor' exhibition at the Whitechapel Art Gallery (23 March– 1 May 1977).

these days', reported Barbara Wright in *Arts Review*, but in this exhibition 'the man and his ideas really come to life'.[91]

There was also coverage on BBC Radio Four's 'Kaleidoscope', which featured an interview with John Summerson talking about Hawksmoor and the exhibition. Summerson recalled his first experience of Hawksmoor, staying as a boy at a hotel in Bloomsbury which looked out across St George's, Bloomsbury and its remarkable spire.[92] What fundamentally differentiated Hawksmoor from Wren, Summerson noted for an audience for whom the younger architect was still much less known, was how 'He loved masonry with big chunks of it and that you know, has an appeal to anybody, there's something elemental about it, these stones quarried out of the rock and then hauled to a site and piled on each other, that comes across in Hawksmoor as in very few architects'.

After its showing at the Whitechapel Art Gallery, a version of the exhibition, consisting of photographs and the reconstructed doorcase, was shown at the University of Manchester until 3 June. The arrangement was made by the architect Trevor Dannatt, Professor of Architecture at the university.[93]

That the exhibition ended up at an architecture school was indicative of the attention Hawksmoor was now receiving from a number of contemporary architects, which was very much part of Serota's reasons for putting it on so early in his tenure at the Whitechapel. More broadly, though, the very fact the exhibition was held at the Whitechapel, a gallery known for its exhibitions of contemporary art and not, say, the more obvious venue of the RIBA, was vitally important for what it said about the relative worth of Hawksmoor and his work. Serota recalls:

> Artists and architects were excited about the presence of this show at the Whitechapel . . . It was a moment when a lot of the best art being made was of a very conceptual nature. The show preceding it was a pairing of two artists: Richard Long and a Dutch artist Stanley Brouwn – both of whom engaged in walking and making maps . . . the leading edge of the art world was very much about the concept, diagram, sketch and drawing at that moment. In that sense there

was probably a receptiveness to the notion of gallery which specialised in that sort of work then taking the works of an architect-draughtsman and then presenting them in that way.

On a practical level, Serota notes how the success of the Hawksmoor exhibition 'encouraged us to do the Wren show that was more elaborate and difficult to realise five years later.' ('It was interesting that I did Hawksmoor followed by Wren.') Yet for the still much lesser-known Hawksmoor, the very presence of a comprehensive exhibition of his work at the Whitechapel helped lift his reputation to a new level. This was not just as exhibition of the drawings of a late seventeenth and early eighteenth-century architect; this was an exhibition of a free creative spirit grappling with the essentials of form, mass and reference that had fundamental relevance in the present day.

Taking stock

Hawksmoor's reputation had come a long way over a few short decades: from an intriguing though rather oblique reference in *The Waste Land* to an exhibition at one of London's most important galleries of contemporary art. This rise would, undoubtedly, have been impossible without the pioneering academic research that opened up Hawksmoor's architecture to wider views and appreciation. More than anyone it was Kerry Downes who debunked the myths that had built up around Hawksmoor and revealed him as one of Britain's greatest ever architects, who rightfully sat on the same elevated plane as the more widely known and appreciated Wren and Vanbrugh.

Without the scholarly and academic attention that was now turned towards the architect for the first time, the Hawksmoor Committee – which comprised a group of enthusiastic though less knowledgeable amateurs – would have found their task harder still. It was a great benefit to Hawksmoor's reputation and the condition of his churches that this cause was taken on by such a couple as the Youngs. Their efforts, which culminated in the Arts Council exhibition and the securing of Christ Church, Spitalfields, were born from a deep emotional connection with Hawksmoor's architecture. Hawksmoor's churches were not just any eighteenth-century churches in remote parts of London; these were buildings with emotional pulls that sparked the imagination. A fellow Committee member, Ian Nairn, captured this rare quality most succinctly, and the popularity of *Nairn's London*, and the central place of Hawksmoor's churches within it, was a vital part of widening awareness of Hawksmoor's achievements.

One of the most intriguing aspects of how Hawksmoor's reputation rose over the period were the processes through which it occurred. Here, the extensive press coverage that greeted both the Arts Council exhibition of 1962 and the Whitechapel one, fifteen years later, was vital. Given how newspaper circulations are generally several orders of magnitude greater than exhibition attendances, many more people would have read reviews and associated articles than would ever see the exhibition. Thinking purely about the effect on Hawksmoor's reputation, the very fact that the Arts Council and, especially, the Whitechapel Art Gallery would both see fit to put on exhibitions about Hawksmoor was of arguably greater significance than the content of the exhibitions themselves.

Beyond simply widening awareness, however, exhibitions have the capacity, beyond a book or even a TV programme, to change dramatically our perception of an artist or architect and their work. We might think of the seminal exhibition *Modern Architecture: International Exhibition*, organized by Henry-Russell Hitchcock and architect Philip Johnson – later both included on the Hawksmoor Committee's masthead – that took place at New York's Museum of Modern Art in 1932 and thrust modernism onto the global stage. While nearer to home and on a smaller scale, the major retrospective on Edwin Lutyens at the Hayward in 1981–2 engendered a major popular reappraisal of his work.

Hawksmoor's exhibition at the Whitechapel Art Gallery, though even smaller, we can look back on as having had a similar effect. The Whitechapel exhibition had the further advantage of being put on in close geographical proximity to some of Hawksmoor's greatest works, and came at a time when Whitechapel, Spitalfields and Limehouse were being colonized by artists and writers attracted there by the cheap rents and the alluring sense of the unknown. Increasing numbers of people, including architects, were becoming entranced by Hawksmoor's buildings, which stood proud and singular over the surrounding cityscape, especially with several now subject to renewed restoration campaigns, as we will shortly see. For several artists and writers, Hawksmoor's churches became a part of their visual imagination in which the real and mythological freely played – and it was from this context that Hawksmoor was to be reborn.

SIX
REBIRTH

EVEN TODAY, walking along Bishopsgate, past the steel and glass and polished granite office buildings, it is hard not to be startled when you turn right onto Brushfield Street. Looming at the end of the long street, that runs west to east, sits the great hulking mass of Hawksmoor's Christ Church, Spitalfields. The way the church confronts you as it suddenly rises into view is one of the most striking architectural experiences in London – and having made the short walk many times before, I still always find myself surprised by its power.

Heading down Brushfield Street towards Hawksmoor's Baroque masterpiece feels almost like stepping into a whole other city. There's a change of scale but also a discernible change in mood and atmosphere. The cascading glass oblongs of Foster & Partners' Bishops Square development, which replaced part of Old Spitalfields Market, serve now to soften the effect (as do the ubiquitous outlets of Starbucks and All Bar One). But for all its high-tech polish and refinement, Foster's building cannot, it seems, quite escape where it's situated. Soon, the remnants of the old market come into view, faced on the other side of the street by a row of Georgian terraces and then the old Fruit and Wool Exchange. By now Christ Church's magnificent west front is completely dominating the scene. It's a building whose looming presence is hard to escape even when out of sight, as if it's casting an invisible shadow all around it.

A left turn takes you into the surviving part of the old market. Today, one is conscious of the peculiarly twenty-first century

Christ Church,
Spitalfields, at the end
of Brushfield Street.

conjunction of stalls selling hats, scarfs and other knick-knacks in an old Victorian fruit and vegetable market. As if dressed for a film set, the building has been reborn as the setting of vintage fantasies – all available for the price of a cup of designer coffee while sitting on an artfully distressed Chesterfield armchair. During a weekday it's busy with City office workers spilling east in search of a lunchtime sandwich or some of the more exotic culinary experiences on offer. At the weekend, it's the first stop for those on the way to Brick Lane's trendy markets and food stalls.

Across Commercial Street, on the corner with Fournier Street, adjacent to Christ Church, is the Ten Bells. Although the pub can be traced back earlier, the present building and site date from the mid-nineteenth century when Commercial Street was cut through this area to provide a better thoroughfare for goods coming from the docks. The pub has a colourful tiled interior of the sort that the Victorians were so fond of and which adorned similar establishments all over London. It was here, back in the 1880s, that two of Jack the Ripper's unfortunate victims were purported regulars, with one – Annie Chapman – having possibly drunk at the pub on the very evening of her grisly demise. A mural in the pub, by the artist Ian Harper, commemorates the more recent past, depicting the view from outside the pub down Fournier Street and showing some of the area's characters going about their business. Most immediately recognizable are the artist-duo Gilbert and George, who have since 1968 lived and worked at a house further down Fournier Street.

Compared to Commercial Street, which is always busy with traffic and people, Fournier Street is a haven of tranquility. The sheer north face of Christ Church appears like an ocean liner, the smooth white stone punched through with circular port-hole windows. The other side of the street remains much as it would have been in Hawksmoor's day. House after house repeats the formula of a plain yet elegant red brick frontage with polite sash windows and sometimes an elaborately carved wooden door case. Fournier and surrounding streets are mostly restored and relatively smart, exuding an air of rugged gentility (with the prices to match). Yet just a few decades ago most of these now sought-after houses were terribly dilapidated, some even derelict. Such is this area's resurgence over that short time, it is now once again possible to purchase a pint of Truman's ale at pubs across London, including the Ten Bells – an experience that had been lost since the Brick Lane brewery's closure in 1989.

Spitalfields has undergone a remarkable transformation, which is continuing unabated as new housing developments sprout up at every turn. But despite this intrusion, it seems that what makes the area special will never quite be lost. It is that sense of somehow being at London's frontier, of an area in a constant state of flux, of continually being reborn.

On the surface it appears something of an anomaly for Hawksmoor's Christ Church to stand sentinel over such an ever-changing area. It is a building, perhaps even more so than Hawksmoor's other churches, that appears curiously timeless, born from and very much rooted in the past, yet also irrefutably contemporary in its capacities to entrance and inspire in the current moment. Peering at just the top half of its spire from the elevated garden roof of Bishops Square might make Hawksmoor's great creation seem baseless and distended – a curiously surreal apparition in London's skyline. But somehow it's one's own position that appears groundless, rendering the very idea of looking towards the church from such an elevated vantage point utterly absurd. Christ Church, it seems, will outlive all around; at the end of the world, a ruin and a wreck, its stone will remain gleaming and proud.

Despite its appearance of eternity today, Christ Church's present state is a far cry from even a few years ago. The Hawksmoor Committee was able to secure its roof in the 1960s, but the church remained locked and shut up for years afterwards, and unrestored until the completion of long-running restoration campaigns in 2004. Like the area in which it sits, over the last few decades Christ Church has itself been reborn. Hawksmoor's other churches, too, have in different ways been subject to restorers' attentions over this time, though Christ Church remains the pre-eminent example. Against this backdrop, their architect has himself also undergone a rebirth, from which, I argue, no single Hawksmoor has emerged, but many.

This chapter is about the numerous Hawksmoors that came to exist in the latter part of the twentieth century. Having charted Hawksmoor's rise to prominence, we now examine the different ways and different reasons people were drawn to his architecture and how they recast it and its creator. It is remarkable to consider the extent to which Hawksmoor's architecture has become a magnet for those seeking creative inspiration: architects, of course, but also artists and even writers. What unites the disparate results of this phenomenon is the way many saw in Hawksmoor's work what they wanted to see – what, in fact, they were already predisposed to seeing. Hawksmoor's architecture became a frame from which to build new meanings and new ideas that had powerful resonances in the contemporary moment.

During the immediate post-war decades, architects began for the first time to take note of Hawksmoor's work in a concerted way, especially his churches. For several artists, who began, mainly from the 1970s, to take studios in the East End, Hawksmoor's churches were important markers in an often grim and desolate urban landscape. Writers, too – and here stand tall the names of Iain Sinclair and Peter Ackroyd, both lovers of mysteries – became fascinated by the East End's murky histories and the strange events that had taken place around Hawksmoor's churches. Yet another Hawksmoor was born: the occultist figure synonymous with myth and mysticism. The result was to drive a wedge between how people saw the buildings and how people saw their architect; for the first time, their fates were no longer tied together. This has allowed the churches to exist in a different realm, casting shadows from this world into another and vice versa, that ensures even as their surrounding areas undergo even more considerable changes, they will never lose their transitory character. We begin, though, with the fates of the buildings themselves.

Modern Hawksmoor

In November 1941 an obituary notice appeared in the *Architectural Review*, not for a person, but for a building. The subject of the note, written by John Summerson, was Hawksmoor's St George-in-the-East:

> Incendiary bombs clattered down . . . in one of the biggest
> air raids of this year. Some were put out, but a fire started in
> the tower. The vast timbering of the roof caught alight, fell

into the church, burned up every vestige of the wood-work and calcined the columns. Only the sturdy shell remains.[1]

It was fortuitous that just a few days before the destruction of its interior, the church had been visited by photographers from the National Buildings Record, a project with which Summerson was involved. The photographs they took, a number of which illustrated the article, are the main surviving record we have of the building's interior. 'Few will remember the interior of St George's', Summerson continued, 'for the church was very generally locked. Standing in a district where three-quarters of the inhabitants are Jews and many of the remainder Roman Catholics, it was one of London's unwanted churches . . . its last days were days of melancholy padlocked silence, as if its doom was understood and patiently expected'.[2]

Wayland and Liz Young saw the ruins when researching their book *Old London Churches* in the early 1950s and mentioned the 'tiny tabernacle inside' the shell of Hawksmoor's church.[3] This prefabricated shed – dubbed 'St George-in-the-Ruins' – had been erected even before the end of the war so that worship could carry on exactly where it had until the incendiary bombs had wrought their destruction. The church remained largely unchanged until 1957 when an architect, Arthur Bailey, of Ansell & Bailey, began working on designs for its rebuilding. Bailey worked on the rebuilding of a number of bomb-damaged churches, and during the war had been involved in the Mulberry harbours that had allowed the Allies to quickly establish ports on the Normandy coast soon after D-Day. Reconstructing Hawksmoor's interior was out of the question. There was no chance of the war damage funds being able to support such an ambition, even if the size of the congregation had warranted it. The idea, then, was to construct a modern church within the walls of Hawksmoor's burned-out shell.[4]

Bailey initially toyed with the idea of roofing over the whole of Hawksmoor's shell.[5] However, given the small congregation, there was no need for such a large church, and space could therefore be allocated for other parish functions. Soon, Bailey arrived upon the idea of constructing a smaller church centred around the east end of Hawksmoor's shell with an open courtyard between it and the west tower. Four flats were inserted in the sides of the church where Hawksmoor's galleries had originally stood. The crypt became a large parish hall. Satisfyingly, Bailey was able to preserve a sense of the scale of Hawksmoor's interior. A large geometric west window preserved the view from Hawksmoor's great tower through to the apse at the east end, where the Victorian mosaics had survived the fire surprisingly intact.

Bailey and his team had developed more adventurous designs, right up until construction began. These included variations on angular layouts and complex geometric rooflines that were reminiscent of the more adventurous end of contemporary church design. One particularly striking drawing shows a bird-like reredos suspended above the church floor, reminiscent of Ansell & Bailey's more overtly modernist work at Sheffield Cathedral or their Holy Trinity church at Twydall in Kent.

This was not the only example of a modernist flirtation in the context of a Hawksmoor building. In the late 1930s, soon after the dissolution of his short-lived partnership with Walter Gropius of Bauhaus fame, Maxwell Fry was invited to propose designs for a new building in the Warden's garden at All Souls College, Oxford. Fry's design was avowedly modernist: a reinforced concrete frame, pilotis, sweeping ribbon windows, and a roof terrace 'commanding one of the loveliest prospects in Europe'.[6] Anticipating the college fellows' disapproval for such a radical departure from the college's existing buildings, Fry cited the precedent of Hawksmoor's interventions at the college: 'in my report I showed them how easily they had accepted the quite violent change from the medieval to the early Georgian'. In fact Fry's scheme was not quite as dramatic an imposition as he suggested, with a number of concessions to the site revealed by a striking perspective of the proposed scheme. The building would be clad in honey-coloured Headington stone, while its complex form could be seen as bordering on the picturesque; Fry had perhaps learned from the rejection of his and Gropius's radical proposal for Christ's College, Cambridge a few years earlier.[7]

Fry's scheme for All Souls still proved too alien an intervention at this moment and for this particularly sensitive site. At St George-in-the-East the overriding rationale behind the small, relatively conservative modern church was ultimately one of money. Bailey's

more ambitious ideas were confined to paper and the built scheme remained very low key, with the great west window its most striking feature.

For anyone looking through this window today, the effect is perhaps even more striking, as the window functions as a literal and symbolic lens on this period of the church's history. An even more tangible reminder were the two fire-damaged cornice stones Bailey left visible in the interior of his church, faintly echoing Basil Spence's Coventry Cathedral. Incorporating space for worship, living quarters for the priest and parish workers, with a multi-purpose parish hall, the rebuilt church became a kind of spiritual community centre, which for the incumbent, Father Alex Solomon, was the embodiment of his ideal mission.[8]

Maxwell Fry's perspective view of his proposed new building for All Souls College, 1938.

Ruins and reconstitutions

Despite its success, the modern rebuilding of St George-in-the-East remains, for some, only a temporary measure, dictated by the climate of post-war austerity. A proposal to modernize the crypt and roof over the courtyard, to designs by Stanton Williams, was in fact put forward in the early 1990s, but went unbuilt, leaving Bailey's work largely intact.[9] In any case, St George had actually fared much better than other Hawksmoor churches damaged during the Blitz. St John, Horsleydown was similarly gutted, but when rebuilding plans fell through, the ruins, including Hawksmoor's infamous tapering column spire, were demolished. The site was sold to the London City Mission, who built their headquarters on top of the church's surviving base. St Luke, Old Street, the other church co-designed by Hawksmoor and John James, was also very badly damaged, and remained a ruin for 40 years before being converted into a rehearsal space for the London Symphony Orchestra in the mid-1990s.

From demolition to modern reconstruction and faithful restoration, one can actually chart the full range of responses to war-damaged churches through the few of Hawksmoor's that were hit. At St Alfege, Greenwich, incendiary bombs had, again, destroyed much of the interior, including woodcarving by Grinling Gibbons. What could be salvaged was painstakingly conserved as part of a restoration campaign led by the architect Albert Richardson, who would later sit on the Hawksmoor Committee's masthead. The bulk of the work was complete by the early 1950s and the church, restored to a state that Hawksmoor would have recognized, was dedicated in 1953.

Christ Church, Spitalfields escaped the war unscathed. This was doubly fortunate because its crypt was frequently used as an air-raid shelter. A number of photographs by Bill Brandt, who otherwise more famously depicted those sheltering in London Underground stations, show the Spitalfields residents installed within Hawksmoor's hauntingly magnificent vaults. (One memorable photograph includes a man actually sleeping inside a stone coffin.)

One can also see from the photographs what a sorry state the crypt was then in. The church had been subject to several quite major campaigns during the nineteenth century, which had taken their toll on the integrity of Hawksmoor's original fabric.[10] The entrance steps on the north and south sides of the church were removed in the mid-eighteenth century. In the 1830s the dormer windows that punctuated

Hawksmoor's spire were taken off. Its appearance before this event can be seen in a print by Rudolf Ackermann of 1815. The various alterations carried out around this time, which included many to the interior, were mired by financial mismanagement and scandal, a situation compounded in 1836 when a fire took hold in the spire causing major damage to the masonry, bells and woodwork. In 1841 yet another disaster befell the spire when it was struck by lightning, though, fortunately, the damage was less severe.

One of a series of photographs by Bill Brandt of people sheltering during the Blitz, here in the crypt of Christ Church, Spitalfields in November 1940.

Etching and coloured
aquatint of Christ
Church, Spitalfields
by Rudolf Ackermann,
1815.

A further round of modifications was made to the church's
interior in 1851, but the most extensive and lasting came in 1866,
the work of Ewan Christian, the architect of the National Portrait
Gallery. Christian's most significant interventions were the removal
of the side galleries and the changes to the side windows of the
central body of the nave. The upper windows were lengthened by
reducing the height of the lower ones, thus fundamentally altering the
character of Hawksmoor's elevations.

The fire at St Anne, Limehouse, which destroyed the interior on 29 March 1850, was depicted in the *Illustrated London News* the following week on 6 April.

Christian's major alterations at Christ Church make an interesting comparison to the near-contemporary work at St Anne, Limehouse.[11] Gutted by fire in 1850, St Anne's was restored by Philip Hardwick, the architect best known as the designer of the demolished Euston Arch. The restoration was carried on by Hardwick's son, P. C. Hardwick, and his pupil Arthur Blomfield, who later remodelled the chancel in the 1890s. All involved kept to Hawksmoor's original remarkably closely, with Blomfield taking the unusual step at this point in time of designing a new pulpit in an eighteenth-century style. Two notable additions to the otherwise faithfully restored fabric were the organ, which had won first prize at the Great Exhibition of 1851, and the stained glass in the east window, a scene from the Crucifixion in lustrous enamel by Charles Clutterbuck.

Drawn to Hawksmoor

For the group of architects who at various times altered, restored or rebuilt Hawksmoor's churches, their interventions derived from either the changing demands of parishioners or the need to rebuild after major damage – and sometimes a combination of the two. From Ewan Christian and Philip Hardwick to Albert Richardson and Arthur Bailey, each architect brought their own ideas to bear, shaped by the realities of the particular historical contexts in which they worked. Although Hawksmoor 'aimed at eternity', it was inevitable that his buildings, like any others, would be subject to alteration and intervention, even demolition, over their history. Some of Hawksmoor's churches were recast, others were reborn; and it is testament to their strength that what made them so special and singular was rarely lost.

It is intriguing in retrospect to observe that at the very moment the state of Hawksmoor's churches had reached a nadir in the aftermath of the war, a new generation of architects began to take notice of them for the first time. Most notable were Denys Lasdun, Robert Venturi and James Stirling – architects of wide and varying backgrounds and interests, but united by a resistance to the conventions and ever increasing clichés of mainstream modernism. All had grown up with modernism; its abstract forms, plain surfaces, fidelity to materials and refusal of decoration were all part of their visual imagination. So when they discovered Hawksmoor they saw his work in similar terms. For a generation growing increasingly restless by the bounds of modernist convention, Hawksmoor's churches were proof that instead of rejecting the past, modernist architecture could be powerfully enriched by it. Here was a group of buildings in which the presence of the past was far from literal, but conjured through allusion, effect and by an almost sculptural handling of abstract form that, they saw, had much to offer the contemporary moment.

The common factor between these architects who were drawn to Hawksmoor of their own accord, and those who at earlier moments had been professionally engaged in making interventions to his buildings, was the direct and insistent focus on the buildings themselves.[12] As both raw sculptural objects and containers of ideas, it was as if everything one needed to know could be found in the buildings, which were seen as hardly, if at all, in thrall to such considerations of time, place and even function. For Lasdun, Venturi, Stirling and many lesser names who followed in their footsteps, Hawksmoor became a powerful totem of a creative spirit unbound by rules or strictures – something that had considerable resonance for their own time.

Sculptural modernist

Lasdun's discovery of Hawksmoor came while studying at the Architectural Association in the 1930s, where he was taught by, among others, Rowland Pierce, the architect best known for Norwich City Hall. While Le Corbusier was a constant touchstone for the young Lasdun, Pierce opened his eyes to a broad stroke of classical architecture, from Lutyens to Hawksmoor. In his third year Lasdun chose Hawksmoor's Kensington Orangery for a building measuring project and recalled the effect it had had on him at that formative moment:

> I remember ... how the act of measuring a building, of being close to the building, gave me a great understanding of the forces of structure and a sense of the weight of materials. This started a life-long interest in an architect so singular and so profoundly concerned with the roots of architecture and the nature of space.[13]

If anything, Lasdun's interest in Hawksmoor grew over his career as he established a reputation as one of Britain's leading modernist architects. Lasdun's preferred material was concrete, which allowed him to create rich, sculptural architecture most often composed of layered horizontal planes, whose deep recesses and projections engendered powerful effects of shadow and light. For someone who conceived architecture in these terms, there was much to admire in Hawksmoor's buildings, especially as he similarly often built in a single material that enhanced the architectonic values of his designs.

Looking at the startling arrangement of forms of Lasdun's great National Theatre, it is possible to see in it something of Hawksmoor, abstracted and recast for the modern age. If one looks up from ground level at the complex concrete geometry of the National Theatre's river side, one sees a view that is remarkably similar to catching a glimpse of the tower at St Anne, Limehouse from its base. Stripping off the imprint of the shuttering on one, and the classical adornments from the other, we are left with the same elemental effects of light and shadow falling on geometrical masses.

Denys Lasdun's National Theatre, opened in 1976.

By the 1960s Lasdun was working mainly for institutions, including several universities, including the newly established University of East Anglia, the Royal College of Physicians, for whom he created probably his best building, at Regent's Park, and, of course, the National Theatre. It is interesting to wonder to what extent Lasdun looked to Hawksmoor for how to present an idealized image of an institution through architecture.[14] If Hawksmoor's churches are an image of anything, it is the institution of the established Anglican church. Yet their complex synthesis of historical reference and allusion allows them, on another level, to transcend that kind of fixed interpretation. Lasdun was fascinated by the ways Hawksmoor achieved this, particularly how he

> used elements of classical and gothic . . . in a free, unprejudiced manner not just quoting them but reconstituting them in a new and original whole which is neither classical or gothic but is wholly original and wholly convincing. He took elements, metabolised them with a concentration on the thing itself, the apotheosis of the single architectural element taken out of its normally humdrum context and exposed for what it really is.[15]

For Lasdun, this process of 'metabolising' architectural elements was the answer to the question he posed in a lecture in 1991 on Hawksmoor, on 'how to break with [the] past [but] not ignore'. Lasdun saw ancient Rome as Hawksmoor's point of departure. For Lasdun it was modernism, which became the starting points for an architecture that, like Hawksmoor's, was full of resonance and allusion.

Proto-postmodernist

As architects looked to move beyond the bounds of mainstream modernism in the 1950s and 1960s, the issue of the past, which modernism had aimed to negate, became an important one. Central to this was the work of the American architect and thinker Robert Venturi, for whom Hawksmoor was a vital figure.

Trained at Princeton University in the late 1940s before being awarded a fellowship at the American Academy in Rome, by the early

1960s Venturi was teaching at the University of Pennsylvania alongside Louis Kahn. The lectures Venturi gave at Pennsylvania formed the basis for his hugely influential book *Complexity and Contradiction in Architecture* (1966). The book acted as a manifesto for Venturi's idea of an architecture that was 'hybrid rather than "pure," compromising rather than "clean," distorted rather than "straightforward", ambiguous rather "articulated," perverse as well as impersonal'. The fundamental challenges Venturi posed to the tenets of mainstream modernism soon saw his ideas described as 'post' modernism.

'Architects', Venturi urged, 'can no longer afford to be intimidated by the puritanically moral language of orthodox Modern architecture'.[16] Instead, he argued, they should be free to explore architecture's communicative possibilities through mining the past for forms, signs and symbols. What followed over the course of the book was an exploration of the phenomenon of complexity in architecture over history, with English architects, particularly those of a Baroque persuasion, playing an important part; Venturi had in fact visited Blenheim on his first day in Europe.[17] Lutyens, Butterfield, Soane, Vanbrugh and, of course, Hawksmoor were all notable, particularly in the section on the 'phenomenon of "Both-And" in Architecture'. This challenged the modernist idea of the 'either-or', which ensured, in Venturi's words, that 'a sunscreen is probably nothing else; a support is seldom an enclosure'.[18] One of Venturi's first examples of 'both-and' was Hawksmoor's St George-in-the-East where

> the exaggerated keystones over the aisle windows are wrong in relation to the part: when seen close-up they are too big in relation to the opening they span. When seen farther back, however, in the context of the whole composition, they are expressively right in size and scale.[19]

This was just one example – from Michelangelo and Borromini to Lutyens – that Venturi cited of an architectural device being 'wrong' on one level but 'right' on another; it is interesting as far as Hawksmoor's standing is concerned that his architecture was referred to by Venturi in the same light as that of Michelangelo. The effect of 'both-and' also accounted for the competing cross-axes at St George's, Bloomsbury, which are signalled externally by the counter pressures of both the south portico and west tower. Venturi noted how 'These contradictions, which resulted from particular site and orientation conditions, support a richness and tension lacking in many purer compositions.'[20]

Venturi's interest was mainly in the buildings themselves and their spatial and formal complexity. But when addressing Christ Church, Spitalfields this opened out to a discussion of its impact on an urban scale. Its tower 'is a manifestation of both – and at the scale of the the city . . . [it] is both a wall and a tower'.[21] Looking from the west, 'the vista is terminated' by the side walls extending to the left and right of the huge Venetian arch, which Venturi saw as acting as 'buttresses', giving the frontage wall-like qualities. Meanwhile the spire 'is seen from all sides, spatially and symbolically dominating the skyline of the parish'.

Venturi's analysis here is strikingly similar to Hawksmoor's intentions, and it is interesting, furthermore, to see the emphasis Venturi places on the extent to which 'a perceptual rather than a formal kind of change in meaning is possible'. The very act of moving, in Venturi's words, 'through or around a building, and by extension through a city' itself brings new complexities and contradictions to bear in a way that immediately recalls Hawksmoor's allusive pen and wash drawings we saw in chapter Two.[22]

Vigorous architecture

Venturi's teaching at Philadelphia and the extraordinary influence of his ideas, encapsulated in *Complexity and Contradiction in Architecture*, introduced Hawksmoor for the first time to a new audience on the other side of the Atlantic. Detached from the urban realities of London's East End, Hawksmoor's buildings were seen largely in isolation as the work of an architect who designed with startling freedom and originality. Something of a 'cult of Hawksmoor' developed as he became a major figure for the postmodern architects who rose to prominence in the 1980s, among them Charles Moore, Robert A. M. Stern and Michael Graves. When the last was asked in 2011 'Which architect have you learnt the most from?' His first reply was 'Hawksmoor'.[23]

It is strange, in retrospect, to see Hawksmoor become so important for such a diverse range of architects. Though similarly informed by the architecture of the past, there is little more in common between Lasdun's powerful sculptural modernism and the playfully self-conscious architectural reference games of the postmodernists. Quite simply, the richness, abstraction and sheer vigour of Hawksmoor's architecture allowed different architects to see different things in his work, and, in effect, each remade Hawksmoor according to their own ideas and dispositions. This was no truer than for James Stirling, arguably the most significant figure in British architecture of the second half of the twentieth century.

Born in Scotland, Stirling studied at the University of Liverpool's School of Architecture in the late 1940s, where he met the theorist Colin Rowe, whose writings became hugely influential for the generation of architects who came of age over the 1950s, 1960s and 1970s. Rowe's approach was encapsulated in his famous essay 'The Mathematics of the Ideal Villa', first published in 1947, in which he compared villa designs by Palladio and Le Corbusier in order to identify common compositional ideals. Rowe's mission was to reinvigorate architecture with the presence of the past – from the individual building right up to the urban scale. In Stirling, Rowe found a kindred spirit, an architect with an intense feel for how the forms of modernism could be powerfully infused with the ideals and language of classical architecture.

Stirling came to London in the autumn of 1950. After working for the planning department of the LCC, he joined, as an assistant, the office of Lyons Israel Ellis. He began to find his niche in London's architectural social circles and soon became good friends with fellow architect Colin St John (Sandy) Wilson. Together they visited Sir John Soane's Dulwich Picture Gallery and Hawksmoor's St George-in-the-East, then still a burned-out shell.[24] Wilson's own admiration for Hawksmoor showed through when in the early 1960s he was working, together with Leslie Martin, on designs for a new British Library to be built south of the British Museum. Their intention was to create an open vista from the British Museum running south to New Oxford Street, flanked on either side by massive new reading rooms and facilities for prints and drawings. Wilson and Martin were actually given the option of demolishing Hawksmoor's St George's, Bloomsbury, but instead decided to make it the incongruous centre-piece of this radical urban plan – which, of course, ultimately went unrealized.[25]

Both Stirling and Wilson belonged to the generation who not only discovered Hawksmoor, but also Soane, the French Neoclassicist Claude Ledoux and the Elizabethan Robert Smythson, architect of Hardwick Hall; and looked with fresh eyes at architects as wide ranging as Palladio and Giuseppe Terragni, the Italian architect who worked under Mussolini's regime. But Stirling's early work apparently owed little to this legacy. The flats he designed at Ham Common with his architectural partner, James Gowan, seemed to owe most to Le Corbusier's Maisons Jaoul and the prevailing climate of Brutalism. Similarly, Stirling's 'Red Trilogy' – the Engineering Building at the University of Leicester (1963), designed with Gowan; the History Faculty Library for Cambridge University (1967); and the Florey Building, Queen's College, Oxford (1971) – comprised highly inventive additive structures informed by intersecting geometries that seemed above all to point towards a technological future, rather than the past.

The fame and critical acclaim these works received established Stirling as one of Britain's leading architects, and during the 1970s, working now in partnership with Michael Wilford, he won major projects in Europe and the USA. During this time aspects of his work began to tend increasingly towards the classical. Most important was the Neue Staatsgalerie in Stuttgart, a conscious response to the adjacent neoclassical Alte Staatsgalerie, in which Stirling created a complex composition of forms, plans and materials infused with a variety of classical references.

There was little, if anything, in the composition of the Neue Staatsgalerie that linked directly to Hawksmoor, but, as Michael Wilford recalls, in the process of 'stacking and collaging of elements to make buildings that were quite complex geometric compositions, one can trace similarities in compositions to Hawksmoor'.[26] Hawksmoor, Wilford remembers, was never far from Stirling's mind:

Stirling often expressed great interest in Hawksmoor, particularly the churches . . . the spires, the west fronts of the classic Hawksmoor churches. He had great admiration for the way elements were piled one on top of the other, the increase of scale, using strong clear sculptural elements to do that.

Stirling's actual pronouncements on the subject of Hawksmoor are surprisingly rare, but around the time the Staatsgalerie was nearing completion, he himself remarked how 'As soon as I graduated and got to London in 1950, I set about visiting the bombed out churches of Hawksmoor. I was intrigued by English Baroque architects such as Archer, Vanbrugh and Hawksmoor and admired the ad-hoc technique which allowed them to design with elements of Roman, French and Gothic etc. – sometimes in the same building'.[27] Stirling brought this same freedom to his own later designs.

While one can detect some 'Hawksmoorian' elements in Lasdun's architecture, in Stirling's they are far more elusive, if present at all. Stirling idealized Hawksmoor's architecture for being eclectic, rule-breaking and above all 'vigorous' in composition and effect. 'Hawksmoor and Vanbrugh were very prominent in our minds', Wilford notes.

In terms of the sculptural forms of their building massing they produced something that Stirling and I felt very strongly is part of architectural design, the buildings should be as vigorous as possible and express the parts that comprise them . . . [They] were shining examples of vigorous architecture.

'But', Wilford is keen to point out 'we didn't really talk about this. There wasn't any kind of conscious reference'. This was even the case when Stirling and Wilford landed the commission for No. 1 Poultry that looked east across the Bank interchange towards Hawksmoor's St Mary Woolnoth.

The commission had come to Stirling and Wilford after the developer Peter Palumbo's first plans for the site fell through. Palumbo had intended to replace the Victorian Mappin & Webb building with a Seagram Building-like tower to a design by Mies van der Rohe himself. This scheme was shouted down by the conservation lobby;

No. 1 Poultry by James Stirling and Michael Wilford, completed after Stirling's death in 1997.

but despite the interventions of his old polo-playing friend Prince Charles, Palumbo was in the end able to secure the removal of the Mappin & Webb building.

Stirling's scheme was the antithesis of Mies's twenty-storey tower – low-rise; stone rather than glass-clad; eclectic in its references and allusions – though perhaps no less visually affronting. It contains all the qualities of 'vigorous' architecture Stirling advocated: complex geometries that allow it to inhabit the wedge-shaped corner site in a sophisticated way; stacking of elements and forms; and dynamic contrasts between glazed elements and the building's two-tone stone veneer. In this, the design appears to draw from Lutyens's adjacent Midland Bank, while in an odd way its rounded frontage also looks back to the Mappin & Webb building, its predecessor on the site. There are also intriguing similarities with St Mary Woolnoth: the use of the arch to define the first stage of the facade; the horizontal banding, white Portland stone in the case of Hawksmoor's building, polychromatic in the case of Stirling's; and, more abstractly, the way that neither facade diminishes in scale as they get higher – if anything both seem to get wider.

As one of a group of buildings that address the Bank interchange – quite aside from being a church by Hawksmoor – St Mary Woolnoth had, of course, not escaped Stirling's attention. But any allusions to it in the design for No. 1 Poultry were, Wilford cautions, unintended. Stirling's references at No. 1 Poultry, as in his other buildings, were rarely ever direct, but

> from the back of the mind, not a straight lift or copy. The example tends to become modified and nuanced to suit the particular circumstances . . . I believe associations that are subsequently made are not conscious evocations . . . Sometimes you design an element and you make a connection back to something you've seen somewhere. But it's only afterwards that you make that connection.

It is perhaps in this idea that Stirling and Hawksmoor came closest. Both created buildings that looked to the past, but both reconstituted those references in the language of their present moments. Hawksmoor was emblematic of an architecture that was intuitive, born from rich experience, and, above all, vigorous in composition and effect – qualities which he himself continually aimed towards.

In his biography of Stirling, Mark Girouard asked 'What was Jim's influence?' and replied: 'I am tempted to draw an analogy between him and the eighteenth-century architect Nicholas Hawksmoor, with a side look at Hawksmoor's contemporary James Gibbs.'[28] To Girouard's eyes, the latter's work was 'civilised' but rarely challenging, designed in many ways to be copied, which it was. 'Hawksmoor's buildings',

Girouard contrasted, '. . . can catch and haunt the imagination in a way that Gibbs's buildings never can.' Just as there was 'no school of Hawksmoor', there is no school of Stirling – though both in different ways cast long, strong shadows over British architectural culture.

Stirling died unexpectedly in 1992, with No. 1 Poultry uncompleted. It was finished by Michael Wilford, along with several other projects. Stirling's premature death had also left a career uncompleted. For someone whose energy had burned so bright, he slipped from view remarkably quickly, a consequence in many ways of the emphatic turn away from the postmodernism with which he had become so associated. Had he lived longer, his architecture would have surely evolved once again. In recent years there has, however, been something of a revival of interest in Stirling's work, spurred by a major exhibition held in 2011 at Tate Britain in the Clore Gallery, which Stirling himself designed.[29] It is a strikingly familiar tale of rebirth to that of Hawksmoor, though one with a much shorter gestation. As a final reflection of the ties that bind these two architects, a small memorial plaque to Stirling was installed just inside the entrance of Christ Church, Spitalfields, a building he so loved.[30]

The pull of the East

London's East End has always had an attractive, magnetic pull. From the Huguenots in the late seventeenth century and the diaspora of Jews escaping persecution in Russia and Eastern Europe in the nineteenth, to the Bangladeshi communities who began to arrive in the 1950s and the middle-class gentrifiers of today, the East End, and Spitalfields in particular, has never remained the province of one particular group of people for long, yet has always, it seems, been of fascination for artists.

In the 1920s and 1930s the East London Group, which included the artists John Cooper, Phyllis Bray and William Coldstream, achieved considerable success, capturing both the character and mood of the East End in urban scenes loosely inspired by the work of Walter Sickert.[31] The paths worn by these artists were soon trod by others. The painter Roland Collins was one such artist who became intrigued with the East End, and particularly by its architecture.[32] As a nineteen-year-old he had a painting accepted by the Royal Academy for the Summer Exhibition of 1937 and, after attending St Martin's School of Art on Charing Cross Road, he took a job in the studio of the London Press Exchange before beginning a career in advertising after the war. Painting always remained close to his heart and he retained a studio on Percy Street in Fitzrovia for over 40 years. Collins's love of the areas between river and city, sea and land, frequently drew him east and in particular to Hawksmoor's churches. His block colour gouache views of Christ Church, St Anne's and especially St George-in-the-East wonderfully capture the spirit of these great hulking masses of stone standing in the largely forgotten working areas of London.

Collins's views provide interesting counterpoints to the near-contemporary works of John Piper, another artist fascinated by recording the world around him. Piper made his name as an Official War Artist working on Kenneth Clark's 'Recording Britain' initiative, which sought to preserve in watercolour views of British building and countries at risk of destruction. Piper's view of Coventry Cathedral the morning after its destruction brought him particular attention and he went on to design a window as part of the rebuilt cathedral. Though he dabbled in abstraction early in his career, and in some of his stained glass designs, Piper was committed above all to painting

Roland Collins,
*St George-in-the-East,
Wapping*, 1958,
gouache on paper.

architecture and its settings. His subjects were far and wide, but notably included Vanbrugh's Seaton Delaval Hall and a composite view of the Temple of the Four Winds and Mausoleum at Castle Howard, painted before the end of the war.

Lithographs of St Anne, Limehouse and Christ Church, Spitalfields appeared later, in 1964, in Piper's *A Retrospect of Churches*. The view of Christ Church's west front is particularly striking, appearing to emerge from the shadows. Piper described how he came about this mode of depicting buildings before a dark background in an interview in 1983 for the BBC radio show Desert Island Discs.[33] He had prepared drawings of Windsor Castle and was invited to show them to the king and queen. 'The King', Piper recalled, 'didn't really speak until we got to the end and said, "You seem to have been very unlucky with the weather".' He was, of course, referring to the dark, menacing skies that framed the buildings. Looking back, Piper reflected how 'It seemed to me perfectly natural to show up the rather pale coloured buildings in fleeting sunlight by putting black skies behind them . . . nothing seemed to be more natural'.

Both Piper and Collins's views of the East End were as itinerant artists – and the freshness, particularly of Collins's work, surely derives from that fact. Increasingly artists were finding studios in the east, attracted by the cheap rents, but also the creative possibilities these hidden places offered. One such artist, the painter Anthony Eyton, took an attic studio high on Hanbury Street from 1968 to 1982, where he worked surrounded, as he puts it, by

> That biggest strangest world, that whirlpool at Spitalfields, and all the several colours of the sweatshops, and the other colours of the degradation and of the beautiful antique houses derelict – I think the quality of colour was what struck me most.[34]

To Eyton's eyes, Hawksmoor's spire that stood over this scene 'is form and matter in stone . . . more Roman than English', and he was fascinated by the contrast of its gleaming white geometry as it rose up from the cacophonous cityscape he observed from his studio window.[35]

Anthony Eyton,
*Christ Church,
Spitalfields*,
July–October 1972,
oil on board.

The power of Eyton's paintings looking out from his window across Spitalfields derives from the oscillation between the grit of the real world of the street and the mystical, ethereal vision rising above. Hawksmoor's spire acts as an urban marker, locating Spitalfields to viewers from miles around, but through its sheer concentration of ideas and energy, stands as a symbol of something even more elemental. It is this duality, exhibited by all three of Hawksmoor's Stepney churches, that forced something of a double take for one intrigued observer, the poet Iain Sinclair, when he first set his eyes upon them.

Born in Wales, and having spent the 1960s in Dublin as a student, playwright and filmmaker, Sinclair and his wife moved to a condemned house in Hackney in 1969, where they have remained ever since. After time teaching, Sinclair 'made a strategic decision to get out. Jobs were easy to find'.[36] He worked as a bookseller and publisher of his own work, at the Truman's Brewery and even as a cigar packer, but it was a job he got, with the help of the artist Brian Catling, as a council gardener in 1974, which has arguably left its greatest mark on Sinclair's imagination.

'We travelled round in a Land Rover,' Sinclair recalls,

but my excitement grew as I found that, included in our repertoire was St Anne's Limehouse and St George-in-the-East . . . We wrecked a series of motor-mowers immediately which seemed to be some sort of strange, occult refusal to cut. You know you'd bring these things in, and there would be some sort of horrible smouldering noise, and smoke would go up and the machines would be ruined. So we were left sat, contemplating the buildings, and it was at that time that I began . . . to consider that there was some kind of pattern or alignment between the various churches, because they so dominated what was then a very derelict landscape.[37]

Unlike Eyton's elevated view from the safe confines of his studio, Sinclair's impressions of Hawksmoor's churches were shaped by literally digging down into the very matter – the mud, filth and detritus – of East London. Beneath the jagged surface of London's past, Sinclair could not help but find layer upon layer of myth, intrigue and forgotten history.[38] He was struck profoundly by the confluence of the material and metaphorical, the physical and psychic, the rational and irrational, and became acutely aware of the extra-ordinary visual dichotomy between these monumental churches and their surroundings. This had always existed, but in the mid-1970s it seemed particularly pertinent, with Hawksmoor's churches left to stand over a scene of grim, windswept desolation following the closing down of the docks and the still very visible destruction of the Blitz.

Why had such grand and strangely affecting churches come to have been built in this inauspicious area, Sinclair wondered. He was struck in particular by the ways these churches appeared to exist outside of the usual orbits of power – the City and Westminster. This was in stark contrast to the architecture of Wren, which on one level, and especially in his post-Fire plan for London, was always about the rational consolidation of power in the centre.

> I thought that St Anne's, Limehouse, Christchurch Spital-fields and St George-in-the-East were outside the official nexus. Hawksmoor became for me like a mockery of the high culture of Wren and the rational sweep of London. I became interested in why each church was where it was, and how this connected with Blake and other mythologies.[39]

Raking through the mud

From these initial fascinations with Hawksmoor's churches Sinclair produced a book entitled *Lud Heat*, which appeared in 1975. Part poem, part prose essay, *Lud Heat* comprises a number of the strange incidents, curious phenomena and dark episodes that Hawksmoor's churches had, in Sinclair's eyes, appeared to attract – all brought together into a loose constellation of quotations and references, with the mystical poems and imagery of William Blake a continual undercurrent.

Lud Heat is a strange, deeply heterodox work; at times it conforms to linear narrative, such as the diary of Sinclair's time working as a gardener, yet at others, fragmented and entirely free form in structure, it recalls poems of the modernist tradition, such as those of T. S. Eliot. It begins with a composition that comes the closest to an essay in form of any in the book, entitled, 'Nicholas Hawksmoor, His Churches'. The essay is prefaced by a quotation from Thomas De Quincey's *On Murder Considered as One of the Fine Arts* – 'All perils, specially malignant, are recurrent' – which points the way and acts as a constant reference for Sinclair's investigation. He begins by describing how 'the churches of Nicholas Hawksmoor soon invade the consciousness . . . built for early century optimism, erected over a fen of undisclosed horrors, white stones laid upon the mud & dust. In this air certain hungers were activated that have yet to be pacified'.[40] Here, the importance of De Quincey's quote becomes apparent. It is the idea that the sites of Hawksmoor's churches have a kind of magnetic pull that over time repeatedly draws people to them – often in dark ways.

Crossing time and place with dizzying frequency, Sinclair references events both familiar and less known. Among the former were, of course, the Ripper murders of 1888, and here Sinclair notes 'the ritual slaying of Marie Jeanette Kelly in the ground floor room of Miller's Court, Dorset Street, directly opposite Christ Church'.[41] He dwells more, though, on the Ratcliffe Highway murders of 1811, chillingly described by De Quincey, in a quote that Sinclair includes, as 'a work more lasting than brass . . . the most superb of the century by many degrees . . . the sublimest & most entire in their excellence that ever were committed'. Like De Quincey, Sinclair was captivated by the exacting, almost elegant, brutality of the attacks on the Marr and Williamson families, purportedly by the seaman John Williams. However, he was doubly interested in the nature of De Quincey's account, 'obviously assembled at a distance, by purely psychic connection . . . so that the major visual clue was missed' – that, in Sinclair's eyes, being St George-in-the-East, which appears in the backdrop of engravings produced around the time of the murders, but goes unmentioned by De Quincey.

Like the stars circling around the black hole at the centre of a galaxy, the incidences and events multiply and coalesce: 'St Luke's obelisk...stands over Bunhill fields, plague pit, burial place of William Blake, Daniel Defoe, John Bunyan'.[42] In Bloomsbury: 'Yeats in the British Museum, at the time of the Ripper murders, researching into Blake... Milton; his early-morning walks over the ground where St George's was to be built'. Some of the references become more tenuous, such as the example of Swedish scientist and theologian Emanuel Swedenborg, the 'feeder & source for Blake, was buried in Wellclose Square, alongside the Ratcliffe Highway, the immediate neighbour of St George's'. Sinclair was also fascinated by the way, for him, 'The Hawksmoor Churches have a close connection with burial sites, Roman & pre-Roman'. Mainly, this was due to the fact that they stood outside the walls of the City of London, where the Romans buried their dead. 'Ratcliffe,' though, 'which lies to the south of St George's, is an even earlier burial ground...[where] an ornate sarcophagus was removed from...during building work in the 17th century'.

The mention of a sarcophagus is just one example of the constant references Sinclair makes to Egyptian architecture. He talks repeatedly of the 'sphinx-form', the 'pyramid' and the 'fire obelisks: St Luke's, Old Street, & St John, Horsleydown', which stood with 'London's true obelisk – "Cleopatra's Needle"'. In Sinclair's analysis, Hawksmoor's churches derive from a complex 'admix of Egyptian and Greek source matter',which comes to a crescendo at St Anne's, Limehouse, a church that seems to have had a particular hold over his mind, as he describes when recalling an episode of 4 February 1974:

> I endure an apocalyptic dream of the moon disc growing, crashing down on the city, burying itself in the tower of St Anne's, Limehouse... I had not then seen the church by daylight, but recognized it immediately on my first day as a gardener.[43]

The church features in Dickens's *Our Mutual Friend*, with the author describing how its 'high tower' stands 'spectrally resisting the wind' as the story unfolds in Limehouse below.[44] It was also in this area that Sax Rohmer set his fantasy stories about Dr Fu Manchu and the opium dens that arose following the influx of Chinese immigrants in the nineteenth century. The pyramid in the churchyard, sometimes said to have been intended to the top the east end of the church, had, Sinclair notes, particular significance in the Fu Manchu stories, as 'access to a subterranean London, that you went down through there and entered into a criminal underworld, where everything was hidden away'.[45] In *Lud Heat* Sinclair brings these past incidences to bear with the St Anne's pyramid germinating an elaborately conceived view of the church as a kind of reincarnated Egyptian ritualistic shrine or temple.

Sinclair's analysis of St Anne's is, course, highly fanciful – and, to be sure, here and elsewhere in *Lud Heat* he plays pretty fast and loose with the facts – but to quibble over factual accuracy is to bely the driving forces of Sinclair's project. Again and again, we see the same strategy of Sinclair taking what he knew of Hawksmoor's intentions and intensifying them so that the results soon border on the fantastical. What, I would argue, prevents this complex collection of disparate incidents and references from collapsing under its own weight is the suggestion Sinclair raises early on in his account: that the churches are in some ways linked across the cityscape – an idea figured in Brian Catling's famous map that accompanies Sinclair's text.

'A triangle is formed between Christ Church, St George-in-the-East & St Anne, Limehouse. These are centres of power for those territories: sentinel, sphinx-form, slack dynamos abandoned as the culture they supported goes into retreat ... St George, Bloomsbury, and St Alfege, Greenwich, make up the major pentacle-star.'[46] Into this literal constellation Sinclair wraps in other seeming 'centres of power' – Blake's house in Lambeth, Cleopatra's Needle, the Tower of London, Bunhill Fields, Parliament Hill and several others – linked together by ley-lines. Hawksmoor's churches hold, as we have seen, special significance: 'Each church is an enclosure of force, a trap, a sight-block, a raised place with an unacknowledged influence on events enacted within their nome-lines.'

In a surprising way, this part of Sinclair's interpretation comes remarkably close to the 1711 Commission's original intentions for the churches: that they would stand apart from the surrounding cityscape, acting as beacons of political and moral authority. Similarly, the idea of churches being joined by lines or axes – if not ley-lines, as Sinclair would have it – was something that Hawksmoor was himself deeply interested in and tried to implement in various schemes for Oxford, Cambridge and parts of London.

It is a remarkable testament to the lasting power of Hawksmoor's churches that so long after their completion the outlandish interpretations of an observer like Sinclair can be so fundamentally shaped by the ideas that drove their creation. Sinclair had read Kerry Downes's book and makes reference to its insights in *Lud Heat*. He clearly understood the history, but takes it onto another level of interpretation shaped by his experience and impressions of the buildings themselves. One has to wonder if there are another set of buildings or another architect for whom someone such as Sinclair could have devised such theories. The answer is surely a resounding 'no'. Few if any other architects have produced work that is so singular, so obviously out of the ordinary, so dominant over their murky and overlooked locations. The richness of reference and quotation contained within Hawksmoor's churches, the way they appear almost to vibrate in changing light, combined importantly with how relatively little is known about their architect as a person, created a unique plane for the projection of meaning – one on which Sinclair constructed his beguiling edifices of myth and mysticism.

Why might Sinclair's theories have arisen at this moment, beyond the sheer coincidence of him then discovering Hawksmoor's churches? London, indeed the whole country, was changing as the post-war social and economic settlement unravelled to be replaced by the free market doctrines advocated by Margaret Thatcher. As the writer and broadcaster Patrick Wright has remarked, 'what was and is fascinating for me is that these systems of geometry and meaning are brought up by Iain just when the city is coming to the end of the enlightenment project, when the welfare state is being destroyed and the dream of London's municipal socialism is being crushed by Thatcher'.[47]

These transformations, which would see the old London docks re-emerge to provide upmarket housing for the office workers at the new Canary Wharf, irrefutably shaped the lens through which

Sinclair saw London and Hawksmoor's churches within it. They were markers of an older world being buried under the sheen of the new. Little has changed in Sinclair's thinking over the intervening period, as attested by a recent remark on the coincidence of St Anne's being built on a site known as 'Westfield' with the Australian shopping centre company of the same name having today so radically reinvented nearby Stratford. Hawksmoor's churches stand out, then and now, because they seem to resist those changes, in Sinclair's words:

> I think that Hawksmoor is forward looking by being backward looking, by not putting a ceiling on it. He goes back almost beyond the beginnings of ecclesiastical architecture. He's going to energies that are almost like drawings in caves . . . He's pushing it both ways to create something that is unbelievably eternal.[48]

The Hawksmoor mythology

T. S. Eliot had alluded to certain mystical qualities in his mention of St Mary Woolnoth in *The Waste Land* and Sinclair has been sure to note the latent affinities between Eliot's fragmented form and the 'slightly similar feeling from a Hawksmoor church – that so much material is having to be assembled, and synthesised into this single unit'.[49] But the association of Hawksmoor and his architecture with the occult – what we might call the 'Hawksmoor mythology' – was undoubtedly inaugurated by Sinclair's work. Sinclair's Hawksmoor is an extension of the real man, like a caricature, but ultimately rooted in the historical figure. In the work of Peter Ackroyd, another writer similarly intrigued by the mysteries of London, the real and imagined Hawksmoor became entirely separate entities.

Although the Hawksmoor mythology began with Sinclair, its fame and popularity derive largely from Peter Ackroyd's novel *Hawksmoor* (1985). Ackroyd had first become acquainted with Hawksmoor's architecture after reading *Lud Heat* and it was this work, he notes, that 'first directed my attention to the stranger characteristics of the London churches'.[50] With this seed planted, and already deeply connected to various mystical undercurrents of London's history, 'I went to a number of contemporary sources . . . and I came across a very powerful strand of radical thinking . . . which embraced theories of evil and darkness as central tenets of their philosophy. So I decided that I would for the purposes of a fantasy bring them all together and create this malign figure'.

The result was a novel that won both the Whitbread and Guardian awards and, today, remains the frequent subject of scholarly interest as an important example of a postmodern novel. *Hawksmoor* is simultaneously set in early eighteenth-century and late twentieth-century London and revolves around the parallel tales of the mysterious architect of seven London churches, recast as Nicholas Dyer, and a Metropolitan police detective, the eponymous Nicholas Hawksmoor. Renaming the architect as Dyer 'gave me the freedom', Ackroyd recalls, 'to experiment with some of the devices of the narrative. I used Hawksmoor for the detective in order to remind people that the narrative was loosely based upon the situation of the time'. The swapping of the names also signals the main structural and thematic devices of the book, the constant interweaving of two time periods, of hero and anti-hero, fact and fiction, reality and the imagination, and perhaps ultimately, of good and evil. It is this avoidance of such opposing binary distinctions – which also appears in an equivalent way in Robert Venturi's writing on architecture – that decisively marks it as a postmodern novel.

The book begins in Dyer's world where he soon emerges as something of a composite character, one whose mysticism is continually cast against the rational and Enlightenment ideals of his master 'Sir Chris' (Wren). Dyer's goal is to create an architecture that 'aims at Eternity' but, departing from Wren's dictum, 'must contain the Eternal Powers'.[51] Meanwhile in 1980s London, Hawksmoor is charged with investigating a series of mysterious murders around Dyer's churches. In charting these parallel stories, Ackroyd elegantly alternates between early eighteenth- and late twentieth-century prose. 'I trained myself . . . to be able to write early eighteenth-century prose with the same facility as what was then late twentieth-century prose to the extent that I would not have to look up words, I would just be able to write it all down'. As the book proceeds these parallel worlds become ever closer, so that by its end they become almost one, with Hawksmoor finally falling under Dyer's spell.

Hawksmoor is not a comfortable read. The sudden shifts in time, Ackroyd's carefully contrived early eighteenth-century phrasing, its grim, eerie atmosphere – all conspire to make reading the book a mesmerizing, intense process. It is gripping, but in an unconventionally haunting way; it is a book one cannot possibly ignore. The echoes from Eliot in theme and tone recur, and it is interesting in retrospect that Ackroyd was working on his famous biography of the poet while he wrote *Hawksmoor*.[52] The churches of the real Hawksmoor, plus the fictional addition of Little St Hugh, become almost active agents in the events – as scenes of the action and recurring motifs on whose haunting abstract geometry could be projected all manner of myths. 'I don't think there is any architect who has the potential Nicholas Hawksmoor had in terms of [there] being so little known about him, his churches are so striking and in some cases weird that he was the perfect subject . . . I'm sure Mr Hawksmoor will have forgiven me by now.'

Ackroyd himself was not, however, easily forgiven by architectural historians. The architectural writer Gavin Stamp, who had taken Ackroyd round Spitalfields and lent him a copy of Downes's book, admits 'he shares some of the blame'. Stamp's friend John Summerson sent him a letter around the time *Hawksmoor* was published in which he accused Ackroyd of 'defiling the wells of truth' in such a way that 'will permanently disfigure the historical image'. 'It's up for the Booker,' Summerson added, 'if it wins I shall be sick.'[53] For his part, Stamp wrote an article for *The Spectator* offering a factual rebuttal to Ackroyd's insinuations upon Hawksmoor's character. Stamp noted how Hawksmoor had only recently 'emerged from obscurity as one of the most sympathetic and interesting characters in architectural history, a modest and remarkable man'. That is, until Ackroyd's novel, the publication of which Stamp lamented: 'I profoundly wish he had not done so: obscurity would now be a mercy compared with the sensational and mendacious notoriety this harmless, unassuming architect now enjoys'.[54]

Nevertheless, Ackroyd's book was highly popular, despite some initial reservations about a project so original; 'I remember my agent telling me this would never sell because it was so weird'.[55] The book was enthusiastically reviewed in Britain and the U.S., and was even the subject of a short dramatization on Melvyn Bragg's *The South Bank Show*. The effect of the book's popularity for Hawksmoor's churches was dramatic. Ackroyd recalls how

> I went to a public house in Limehouse and the publican told me that parties of tourists were being taken around in search of Hawksmoor as it were . . . I was suddenly aware of the effect that fiction can have on the world in the ways that one could never expect. I assumed it would be taken as a mild fantasy tale . . . in the old fashioned gothic tradition, but in fact it seemed to impinge upon the world . . . people were literally going around Hawksmoor churches as they would go around Hampton Court or Kew Palace.

Despite this new mainstream interest in his architecture, it remains undoubtedly the case that Hawksmoor's reputation has subsequently been unable to shrug off the association of the occult; it will forever be part of the lens through which people view his buildings. But it has also seen Hawksmoor and his architecture reach a level of public prominence never before achieved, with important implications for the restoration campaigns of several of his churches. More immediately, Ackroyd's book also caused some observers for whom these were apparently familiar structures to see them with fresh eyes. This was the case for a painter, Jock McFadyen.

Looking again

Born in Scotland, McFadyen came to London to study at the Chelsea School of Art in the mid-1970s. After graduating he lived for a while at Butler's Wharf, but after 'They demolished my squat on top of my Morris Traveller!', he ended up in an Acme house on Salmon Lane, just to the north of St Anne, Limehouse.[56] 'A friend said I could stay three weeks, I ended up staying eighteen years'. Acme had begun in 1972 to provide affordable studios for artists and Salmon Lane had some of the first live-work units. It was a vibrant artistic community, McFadyen remembers, 'A whole street, every single person was an artist'.

'I used to go on bicycle, down Salmon Lane, across Commercial Road into the gate [of St Anne's churchyard] to the right of the bus stop and there's a diagonal path, worn by people shortcutting through to another gate that faced the door of the pub on Three Colts Lane. Then of course, I must have read *Hawksmoor* and thought bloody hell!'[57] In a roundabout and unexpected way Hawksmoor was to prove pivotal as McFadyen's work underwent a marked change of direction.

'My early work was very self-referential', McFadyen notes, 'it was influenced by Pop Art and it was schematic . . . and did that thing of appropriating bits of styles and stitching them together in an ironic way.' After a residency at the National Gallery in 1981 and an unsuccessful exhibition at a gallery on Sackville Street, McFadyen reached a point where, he remembers, 'I couldn't cheerfully carry on with this witty ironic work, so I decided to start drawing things and painting things that I'd seen'. By this time McFadyen was living in a flat he had bought in Hackney, where he decided,

> what I'm going to do is go out the front door, the first person I see I'm going to do a painting of them; and I did that. It was an old black man walking up towards Burdett Road with his stick and trilby and I thought, 'Right, I promised myself I was going to do this', so I followed and looked at him and tried to get a picture of him in my mind. I stalked him; he didn't notice me actually. I tried to retain the visual memory before it went away.

Reading Ackroyd's book had, it seems, induced something of a transformation in McFadyen's awareness of Hawksmoor's churches, because 'the next thing I did I went and drew that Hawksmoor church of St Anne's, Limehouse'. Having focused up to this point on intellectual games, McFadyen suddenly found himself 'drawing the buttresses, the windows and everything like a foundation course or sixth form student. I'd gone back to the drawing board, to the beginning. I was drawing cigarette packets, Rothmans King Size, that had been thrown

Photomontage by Jock McFadyen, most likely created as an aide-memoire while working on his painting *Hawksmoor and Golden Wonder*, 1988.

in the gutter, lager cans and things like that, because I wanted . . . this intrusion of the real into things I was essentially making up.'

McFadyen made several Hawksmoor paintings around this time: *Tesco and Hawksmoor* ('because of the Tesco bag which I'd never have put in a painting before'); *Pepsi and Hawksmoor* ('someone had put a cola tin on top of the bus shelter' in front of the church); and *Golden Wonder and Hawksmoor* – which 'had a crisp packet . . . [in a cityscape still] totally windswept, really, really grim, burnt out cars upside down in front of it, a waste land'. McFadyen soon moved onto other urban subjects, but the 'Hawksmoor pictures I did were the beginning of . . . my way into painting the real world' – a project with which he has been concerned ever since.

St Anne's and St George-in-the-East provided McFadyen with a timely bridge to a different way of seeing and representing the

Jock McFadyen in
his studio inspecting
one of his 'Hawksmoor'
paintings made in the
late 1980s.

world around him. For the painter Leon Kossoff, Christ Church, Spitalfields, assumed an even greater totemic significance. Born in London to Ukrainian-Jewish immigrant parents, Kossoff grew up in the streets around Hawksmoor's mighty church. His parents ran a bakery on Wentworth Street ('even I remember that place', McFadyen recalls) and there was no artistic side to his family. Nevertheless after life-drawing classes at Toynbee Hall, Kossoff made it to St Martin's and then studied with David Bomberg at Borough Polytechnic.[58] London became Kossoff's subject: the city which, 'like the paint I use, seems to be in my bloodstream. It's always moving – the skies, the streets, the buildings'.[59]

In the late 1980s Kossoff began a series of paintings of the west front of Christ Church, Spitalfields, their thick, swirling impasto encapsulating this idea of the city as a constantly moving body. Painted from street level looking up, Kossoff transmuted the bold confrontation the church makes looking down Brushfield Street into a kind of contorted, tense movement. The church teeters, appearing to be simultaneously falling away and advancing upon the viewer. Towering over part of the city that since its creation had become mainly Jewish, Kossoff depicted it as if the Church itself

Leon Kossoff, *Christ Church, Spitalfields, Morning*, 1990, oil on board.

were the outsider, symbolically and literally – an alien imposition on the city.

Though he had long known the church – growing up in Spitalfields its presence was hard to escape – Kossoff was drawn back to it by Ackroyd's *Hawksmoor*.[60] In many ways, though, Ackroyd's book was merely providing a fresh impetus for a force that had long attracted people to Hawksmoor's Spitalfields masterwork. In his book *People of the Abyss* (1903), the American novelist Jack London had described the poor who congregated in the churchyard:

> On the pavement, by the portico of Christ's Church, where the stone pillars rise towards the sky in a stately row, were whole rows of men asleep or drowsing, and all too deep sunk in a torpor to rouse or be made curious by our intrusion.[61]

By the 1980s a steady stream of artists, writers and bohemian intellectuals had, for different reasons, found themselves drawn to Spitalfields and the surrounding areas of East London. Ackroyd's book was not necessarily a revelation but rather a confirmation of what had attracted them to these areas. It served as vivid confirmation that just beneath its surface the East End was bubbling with myth and forgotten history, lending the whole area a kind of mystical glamour, fertile for creativity. As Sinclair recalls, 'Every Georgian house I went into that was reclaimed had at least three or four copies of *Hawksmoor*, because it gave a myth that underwrote the whole business, the idea that these churches had a mystery connected to them ... fitted the time perfectly'.[62]

Real and imagined pasts

The resonance of Ackroyd's novel extended well beyond Spitalfields, however, and emerged into a broader climate increasingly fascinated by looking back to Britain's real and imagined pasts. In many ways pre-empting *Hawksmoor*, Peter Greenaway's film *The Draughtsman's Contract* (1982) conjured a similar tale of mystical intrigue around a historical artistic figure. In this case, an artist is brought in to record a country estate that soon becomes the setting for a series of mysterious murders. The postmodern references similarly abounded with deliberate anachronisms, exaggerated costumes and Michael Nyman's pulsating score, which drew motifs from Henry Purcell – all amid the setting of the seventeenth-century Groombridge Place in Kent.

Indeed, by the early 1980s, the English Country House had become an important focus of the growing conservation movement. In 1974 the Victoria & Albert Museum had staged a popular exhibition – 'The Destruction of the Country House, 1875–1975' – that did much to galvanize public opinion and aid moves to protect this aspect of England's architectural heritage. As arguably the nation's greatest contribution to the visual arts, the English Country House became a site for sometimes rather bleary-eyed nostalgia, perhaps best exemplified in the popularity of the ITV adaptation of Evelyn Waugh's *Brideshead Revisited* in 1981, which was mostly filmed at Castle Howard.

A few years earlier Castle Howard had interestingly also featured in an experimental film by Derek Jarman called *In the Shadow of the Sun*. Among its various superimpositions and re-filmings is footage of the Victorian Atlas Fountain, which subsequently became the setting for a pivotal scene in ITV's version of *Brideshead Revisited*. But Vanbrugh and Hawksmoor's Baroque house and garden were the real backdrop to the series. Early on, Charles Ryder talks of how 'this was my conversion to the Baroque. Here under that high and insolent dome . . . I felt a whole new system of nerves alive within me.'[63] Later, at the close of one episode, Lady Marchmain's funeral procession is shown making the walk up to the Mausoleum – which for the first time put the Baroque grandeur of Hawksmoor's masterwork in front of a mass television audience.

The early Georgian period in particular had become something of a focus and repository of memory – and for some of the most committed this found a home in Spitalfields. From the lone cries of Nairn's *Outrage*, by the 1970s the conservation movement, whose concerns extended well beyond the English Country House, was growing in prominence just as the attacks on Britain's heritage had become greater and more daring. The hubris of post-war planning in Britain that saw fit to drive a motorway through the centre of Glasgow and propose the same for eighteenth-century Bath and

London's historic Covent Garden market north of the Strand was being increasingly undone by the very opposition its arrogance provoked. Colin Amery and Dan Cruickshank, two writers then working at the *Architectural Review*, soon emerged as some of the most vocal critics of this erosion of Britain's architectural heritage. The passion of their arguments and the urgency with which they made them was exemplified in the title of their book *The Rape of Britain* that appeared in 1975, European Architectural Heritage Year. As for Spitalfields, it was an area under threat like many others, but was also a place where resistance had begun to take root.

As early as the 1960s, artists as varying as Anthony Eyton and Gilbert and George were establishing themselves in Spitalfields, and were soon joined by other people, attracted particularly by the area's remarkably preserved – if rather run-down – early eighteenth-century architecture. One such person was Mariga Guinness, who set up home with Hugh O'Neill, later Lord Rathcavan, in a house on Elder Street, after the breakdown of her marriage to Desmond Guinness. Mariga's great passion was Georgian architecture, and houses in particular, and having set up the Irish Georgian Society she had become a pioneer in rescuing them from dereliction and destruction. It was in such a guise that Amery and Cruickshank ran into her while walking around Spitalfields in the mid-1970s.

'We didn't know her at all', Amery points out.[64] But after ascertaining that they were both 'interested in Georgian buildings . . . she took us into her house, which she had rescued . . . [and] said, "you know there are several houses in the street about to be demolished – what can we do about it?"' 'So', Amery recounts, 'we decided we would like to try to buy them.' The immediate problem was that the houses 'belonged to British Land who were planning a big redevelopment at Spitalfields and so we decided the only thing to do was to squat in the . . . two little houses on Elder Street. We had a sort of rota of people to sleep there and we had rockets to fire if there was going to be trouble.' For sustenance the squatters were 'fed by the market people who would bring us bacon rolls in the morning'.

After a while the small but committed band of conservationists decided to 'go and squat in the offices of British Land, not stay the night, but refuse to move on until they agreed to sell us the houses'.

This was probably the most effective tactic, Amery notes, and 'they eventually agreed to sell the houses to us. We bought them for £4,000 with a loan from [the eye surgeon] Patrick Trevor-Roper, who was the brother of the historian [Hugh].' Other than saving the houses themselves, the result of this piece of 'direct action' was the creation of the Spitalfields Trust, with the mission 'to buy houses, restore them, do them up and sell them on, with the profits to buy more houses, a kind of rolling fund'. This idea of conservation via ownership and occupation was, Amery recalls, 'quite an original thing at the time' – and one that has endured as the Trust's work has continued to this day.

Christ Church reborn

Towering over Spitalfields, the presence of Hawksmoor's Christ Church was not one that could be easily ignored, even if it remained mostly shut up and locked. Although it had been made safe with the re-roofing secured by the Hawksmoor Committee in the 1960s, while the crypt had become a centre for the area's populations of drunks and vagrants, the nave remained unused for anything other than storage. In 1972 two maisonettes were inserted for use by parish staff in the church's eastern corners.[65] But the photos taken around this time show an interior looking, in Amery's words, rather like a 'Roman ruin', though one littered with piles of mattresses (for use in the crypt), the dismantled Victorian pews and bundles of newspapers.[66] The exterior was stained and soot-blackened in places, the patina of history literally dripping from its walls.

In 1970 Denis Downham was succeeded as rector by Eddy Stride, who arrived, with his wife, Irene, from St Mary's, Dagenham. Having expected to become missionaries in Africa and then ending up in Spitalfields rather by surprise, their principal concerns were with evangelical ministry and not the church building.[67] Stride did, however, develop plans for horizontally partitioning the nave to create office space and a small church underneath. In a way, this idea reflected how among many of the clergy there existed a tension between the work of the Church and the need to preserve church buildings. This came to a head in 1975 in a letter to *The Times* from Trevor Huddleston, the Bishop of Stepney, responding to the historians Suzanne Lang and

Alan Colquhoun, who had written concerning the 'deplorable state of Hawksmoor's masterpiece, Christchurch, Spitalfields'.[68] Huddleston wished 'to make it clear that the state of disrepair of Christchurch, Spitalfields is in no sense due to the failure of the local Christian community, nor, in my opinion, to neglect by the authorities of the Church of England'.[69] The building was an 'appalling responsibility for the Church', and with there so few Christians in the area there was no need for a building of 'cathedral-like proportions'.

A subsequent flurry of letters ensued, including ones from Liz Young, Colin Amery and Mark Girouard. Despite Huddleston's

Mattresses, bundles of papers, broken pews and furniture stacked in the nave of Christ Church, Spitalfields. Photographed in 1974 by Bill Toomey.

equivocation, the groundswell of concern for Hawksmoor's church was building quickly; Amery remembers that he and Dan Cruickshank actually squatted in the church for a few nights to help raise awareness of its plight.

In August 1976 at Eddy Stride's invitation, the recently founded conservation group Save Britain's Heritage organized a meeting in the church to discuss its future. One of the speakers at the meeting was Jonathan Balkind, who was part of the Greater London Council's Historic Buildings Division. He had the brilliant idea of holding concerts in the atmospheric setting of the church's near-derelict interior, with the first held in November of that year.[70] Soon after, a charitable trust – the Friends of Christ Church Spitalfields – was formed to help kick-start the nascent restoration campaign. Balkind became the established secretary with local residents Eric Elstob (a city financier and the Friends' treasurer for over 25 years) and Michael Gillingham (an antique dealer very interested in music and in particular Christ Church's organ) playing leading roles. John Betjeman was the first president, while Hawksmoor stalwarts Liz and Wayland Young (now Lord and Lady Kennet) and Ivor Bulmer-Thomas were also involved.

The road to restoring the church must have seemed a long one in those days even to as committed a group as the Friends. Yet few of them could have imagined then that the undertaking would become a near 30-year project of fundraising, conservation and restoration. The architect throughout this process was Red Mason, and in many ways the story of the church's restoration is his.

Mason became involved at Christ Church as a young architect working for Whitfield & Partners. He had 'joined William Whitfield when he was doing the Institute of Chartered Accountants in the City', working on the famous John Belcher building and extension by John James Joass. This and work on the Hunterian Gallery in Glasgow perhaps qualified Mason within Whitfields for working at Christ Church, but, as he notes, 'we were a modern architecture practice [and] not a conservation practice and there were quite a lot of raised eyebrows at one of our first meetings'. Mason did, however, know Hawksmoor well. While at school in York, he frequently visited Castle Howard and was familiar with the Mausoleum. At the AA in the 1950s, Mason also remembers being taken on a bus trip to see the Hawksmoor churches – 'we stood outside Christ Church but they wouldn't let us in.'[71]

Beginning with a weekend working party to clear gutters and undertake a quick assessment of the building, 'our aim as architects was always to do a full restoration, if possible, [and] to do it based on as thorough an investigation of all the evidence that was there'. For Mason, 'thorough' meant an almost forensic level of examination of the surviving fabric, meticulously cross-checked against Hawksmoor's surviving drawings and the building accounts in the Lambeth Palace Library. 'I started this when I was thirty or whatever ... I had an associate above me and a partner above that, so I was the general dogsbody which was why I was able to do it. I spent so much time on my hands and knees. I annoyed the rector [Eddy Stride] once by telling him I thought I spent more time on my knees in his church than he had!'

In the early days, the restoration work proceeded slowly and piecemeal through a succession of small contracts. When a bit of money became available a bit more work was done, and so on. This was the cause of frustration for some members of the Friends who were keen to move quickly, but for Mason, looking back with hindsight, 'there is an argument that doing it in small bits was in fact very good, because it did allow you to unpick the building.'

The slow pace proved very helpful when it came to reinstating the galleries, perhaps the single greatest achievement of the project. Through careful inspection of all the surviving timbers in the church, Mason deduced that 'Ewan Christian simply took out all the galleries, put the timber in a pile and put it all back again – on the floor instead of up in the air.' Spending huge amounts of time looking through the books of works in Lambeth Palace Library, Mason was able to ascertain the sizes of timbers and basic structure of the galleries. Though it was long and sometimes tedious work there was the small thrill, Mason recalls, in 'turning the pages of the bills that have Hawksmoor's initials'. This documentary evidence was corroborated by what was left in the building: the timbers that Christian's carpenters had recut; the pockets in the wall that had been patched up; and where it was still possible to see where the ends of the gallery abutted the stonework. All this allowed Mason to 'build up an archaeological picture'.

Over time Mason restored the portico, rebuilt the stairs to the entrance in the middle of the church's south facade and returned the side windows to the original configuration. Back inside, Mason became very interested in the west end. It had been postulated up to this point that the two tiers of galleries were to Hawksmoor's design, a suggestion based on a surviving drawing. However, on closer inspection, Mason discovered that they were in fact installed by Christian: 'a hodgepodge of the eighteenth-century galleries ... we found mouldings that were upside down, mouldings that had been cut out of other mouldings'. This was just one example of numerous instances where Mason's archaeological examination of the building provided a clearer picture of Hawksmoor and his workmen's original intentions.[72] Many of the techniques during the restoration were little changed to those Hawksmoor had employed nearly three centuries before. For those working on the restoration, it must have been hard not to imagine those who had built the church and, in Mason's words, gain 'increasing respect for what they achieved, increasing respect for that moment'.

Transformations

As the restoration work continued in sporadic fashion, concerts continued to be held. 'Those concerts were very powerful', Amery notes, 'because they brought people there who had never seen the church ... [who experienced it] as a kind of Roman ruin with great music. It was all very, very romantic.' The concerts became the Spitalfields Festival, which continues now in the rather more comfortable surroundings of the restored church. In those early days, it was a different matter. Mason recalls one early concert during which the Soviet cellist Mstislav Rostropovich and his wife, the soprano Galina Vishnevskaya 'did a recital in a church with no proper floor and metal seats that came from Tower Hamlets baths: those awful early fifties metal and canvas seats'.

Funds to keep the restoration moving forward were secured from a variety of sources: trusts, foundations and the GLC, as well as individual donations. Indicative of the way the area around Christ Church was changing, money was also secured via a 'planning gain' arrangement, whereby a developer was granted planning permission for nearby offices on the condition they provided a contribution to the church's restoration fund.

There was, of course, the occasional setback and delay, as there always is when dealing with such a large and complex restoration project. One of the more intriguing came in 1984 during the crypt clearance, on which Mason worked in a close and quite pioneering collaboration with archaeologists. There was a general concern that some of those buried in the crypt may have succumbed to smallpox and all involved were instructed to be observant of any signs; Mason remembers that they were 'provided with very, very graphic photographs by Porton Down'. During the work, a suspicious pustule was spotted on one of the exhumed bodies, which caused, in Mason's phrase, a 'white-suit moment'. The crypt was shut down and a team of biohazard specialists extracted the sample which was then carried 'triple flask, with two vehicles in a convoy in case one of them breaks down, [and] flown to Atlanta'.[73] Fortunately, the test came back negative and work was able to continue.

By the mid-1990s, the already long-running project was gaining momentum thanks to major grant donations, notably from English Heritage, the National Heritage Memorial Fund, and from the Sainsbury family through the Monuments Trust. The exterior was completed in 2001, with the interior, with restored plasterwork, new floor and reinstated galleries, following in 2004, an occasion marked by a visit from the Prince of Wales. Intriguingly, 2004 also saw the completion of the nearby Bishop's Square and the redevelopment of old Spitalfields Market. This, too, had been a long-running project, but for rather different reasons.

The Spitalfields Development Group acquired the site in 1987 with the intention of building a new trading complex for the London International Financial Futures Exchange (LIFFE) – a weirdly ironic replacement for the old fruit and vegetable market. Amid vocal opposition, several redesigns, and with LIFFE actually dropping out, construction finally began in 2001.[74] The development became a powerful lightning rod for objectors because of not only its size but also the symbolic appearance of the City of London encroaching on the East End. Yet, the changes that many saw the redevelopment of Spitalfields Market as bringing were in fact already happening and would have carried on with or without it. The more appropriate index of Spitalfields's change in fortunes over the last few decades is actually Christ Church itself – a building whose transformation heralded that of its surrounding area.

In retrospect it is really no surprise that Hawksmoor's rebirth coincided with that of the East End of London. With eyes and thoughts turned towards these forgotten areas, they could not avoid being struck by the rare power of Hawksmoor's churches. Views of his buildings oscillated between those who considered them almost autonomous works of architecture-sculpture, and others who saw them as utterly inseparable from their locations and historical contexts. The result of all this was to irredeemably fragment Hawksmoor's image, so that he existed in people's minds as everything from the real historical figure, to a devil-worshipping architect of the occult, the latter largely thanks to Peter Ackroyd. At the same time, though, this fragmentation has also resulted in many more people being introduced to Hawksmoor's work, while also causing several artists to look again at a group of buildings with which they thought they were familiar.

It is impossible to say whether the restoration campaign at Christ Church, Spitalfields was hampered or, indeed, assisted by the popularizing effects of Ackroyd's *Hawksmoor*. However, it does not seem unreasonable to postulate that the novel's role in carrying the name Hawksmoor far and wide did have positive effects, certainly in terms of drawing attention to the project, even if it did sully the historical record. Such is the haunting power of Hawksmoor's architecture, it was perhaps inevitable that the fantastical interpretations of Sinclair and Ackroyd would appear at some point in time. Nevertheless, these theories never come close to overshadowing the buildings, so striking and powerful is their presence even today, with London trying to close in around them. So, if we want to find the real Hawksmoor, we really need look no further than the buildings themselves, and in particular the reborn Christ Church, Spitalfields. It is fitting, therefore, that over the project's long gestation its surrounding area changed just as radically as it had in the early eighteenth century, when the church first rose from the ground.

SEVEN

HAWKSMOOR TODAY

AS THE RESTORATION WORK at Christ Church, Spitalfields, was nearing completion, a project to restore another of Hawksmoor's churches was just beginning. St George's, Bloomsbury had never suffered neglect on the scale of its Spitalfields cousin and had similarly escaped the Blitz undamaged. By the late 1990s, however, the years were taking their toll. The horse and unicorn sculpture at the feet of George I that Hogarth had depicted in *Gin Lane* and which had so bemused Soane and Turner had long since become unsafe and been removed. Other bits of stonework were deteriorating and the roof in particular was in urgent need of repair.

While it had taken nearly a century before serious interventions were made to Christ Church's interior, Hawksmoor's internal configuration of St George's had lasted only 50 years. In 1780 the interior was reorientated, with the altar and reredos moved from the eastern apse and placed at the north end of the church, the north gallery having been ripped out. Half a century later, the overriding significance of the east–west orientation, which had determined Hawksmoor's complex interior layout, was of considerably less importance than the need to accommodate more people in the church and thus cater for Bloomsbury's growing population. It was this reorientated church that was the setting for 'The Bloomsbury Christening' in Charles Dickens's *Sketches by Boz*.[1]

In 2002 the church was placed on the World Monuments Fund (WMF) 'watch list' of the 100 most endangered buildings or sites, as well as English Heritage's Buildings at Risk Register. It was likely that without significant funds to restore the church, it would be deemed redundant and sold for secular use. But with Hawksmoor now widely considered one of the great figures of British architectural history, and St George's being an obvious masterpiece, support was much quicker in coming forward than it had been at Christ Church a quarter of a century earlier. Colin Amery was by now director of the WMF in Britain and set about marshalling support. The WMF had been a left a considerable discretionary fund by Paul Mellon, the 'galloping anglophile' American philanthropist who was a great lover of Britain's racehorses and its art and architecture. Deeming St George's a fitting cause, the Mellon Estate allocated £5.4 million to its restoration, while just under £3 million was provided by the Heritage Lottery Fund.

It was, according to Amery, an easy decision to reorientate the church's interior back to what Hawksmoor had intended. However, on the face of it the restoration of St George's was actually far more radical than that of Christ Church. St George's had existed for much more of its history in the north–south configuration than it had in the original east–west. The decision to reinstate the galleries at Christ Church was not immediately clear-cut and had taken quite some time to be reached. Yet several decades later at St George's, such was Hawksmoor's stature that his original vision was deemed to be of far greater significance than any subsequent alterations.

Along with the restoration and rearranging of the interior, and various essential repairs to the building's fabric, notably the roof, led by the architectural practice Molyneux Kerr, the opportunity was also taken to reinstate the lion and unicorn sculptures that had once adorned St George's spire. The WMF held a competition, which was won by the sculptor Tim Crawley, who had created the 'Modern Martyrs' sculptures for the front of Westminster Abbey a few years before. The results are sometimes said to be slightly too large, but any quibbles are surely overridden by the sheer joy of seeing Hawksmoor's strangest and most delightful spire restored to something approaching its original condition.

Only St Anne, Limehouse is today awaiting restoration, though it is safe and dry. Its roof was strengthened in the 1980s through an ingenious solution by Julian Harrap Architects, while more recently the chancel was reconfigured. The rest of its interior is described on the parish website as exhibiting 'derelict chic' and 'great for film-ing gritty dramas but less useful for the church and local community'.[2] Looking towards the other churches, a case might be made for re-instating the galleries at St Mary Woolnoth, in a similar way to both Christ Church and St George's, though a whole lot easier given that their sawn-off fronts survive, and thus recreate Hawksmoor's original space. However, more immediately pressing demands for increasingly limited conservation funds mean that this is unlikely to happen in the near future. Elsewhere, Hawksmoor's work is all mostly looked after and in good repair, though at Castle Howard, the costs associated with conserving the Mausoleum, especially, are sizeable.

Although 2004 marked the formal completion of the restor-ation at Christ Church, Spitalfields, work is continuing on the organ and also in reworking the crypt. Both projects are being led by Dow Jones Architects in close dialogue with the church's management team and the still active Friends of Christ Church Spitalfields. Dow Jones won the commission for the crypt after an invited competition in 2008, with it due to be completed in 2015. The project involves the clearing out of the crypt in order to create a café, gallery, performance space and small chapel, not to mention a commercial kitchen and the requisite wcs. It is a complex project for a space that was, of course, never intended to be used – at least by the living – despite the fact that over its history it has been everything from an air-raid shelter to homeless refuge.

Dow Jones's response to the brief is, therefore, quite complex, but will be realized with comparatively subtle means. Their approach, as practice director Alun Jones describes, stems from their conceiv-ing the church's western facade as a kind of 'gateway . . . [either] literally because it was a gateway to London from the east and the north, or whether metaphorically, it was a gateway to heaven'.[3] The 'role of the city gate', as they see it, is 'about reconciling the centre with the edge, a place of representation of the centre at the edge'. In terms of the way this translates into how they will organize the crypt, Jones continues: 'rather than divide it up as a bunch of rooms, what we did was to take the two or three key elements of the programme and . . . we made those the spaces and then everything in between dealt

Computer rendering of part of Dow Jones Architects' renovation and reworking of the crypt at Christ Church, Spitalfields.

with all the rest of the brief. This would be expressed spatially and also in their choice of materials: 'we used oak in the way that Hawksmoor used oak upstairs to create the space of human habitation . . . and the spaces in between we would just leave'.

So often in these sorts of interventions in historic buildings, the choice of material is about distinguishing between what is existing and what is new. It is an intriguing idea, therefore, to use the same material as Hawksmoor and, furthermore, in the same way, to define the positive, habitable space. The consideration of both the meaning and experience of material also extends to the flooring and means of access. As Biba Dow notes: 'we wanted the space of the crypt to feel part of the urban world. The idea of the ramp as the one way of entering the building felt like an appropriately direct and solid way of connecting the space of the crypt to the outside'. 'Crucially,' Jones adds, 'it's the same material, so the York stone of the pavement flows down the ramp and then fills the whole of the church; the underneath of the building is very much the ground of the city.' 'So when you go in there you will find these three realms: the ground of the city, the timber boxes and then Hawksmoor.'

Responding to Hawksmoor

Attending architecture school in the late 1980s, both Alun Jones and Biba Dow had grown up with Hawksmoor; as Dow notes: 'I remember going to see Christ Church on a year one trip to London'. Their first studio was just around the corner from Christ Church and, Jones remembers: 'we knew the building before it was renovated, when it was dark and dirty and peeling paint, it was incredibly atmospheric. Hawksmoor has always been part of the conversation.' While their project for the crypt is informed by this long-standing and personal connection with the church, it also reflects an interpretation of Hawksmoor that is entirely of the current moment.

As this book's story comes up to the present, and therefore to its close, it is fascinating to observe the ways architects are still finding intriguing concepts in Hawksmoor's work, and using it as a basis for new ideas. Hawksmoor remains an architect seen to be doing something different and special, even as he has been assimilated into the canon of British architectural history. It is, though, no longer the case that by identifying with Hawksmoor and his work, architects might position themselves as going against the grain of mainstream thinking in the way that Lasdun, Venturi and Stirling

Alun Jones and Biba Dow with a model of the Christ Church crypt, in their own 'crypt' in the cellar of their office in south London.

were able to do. Moreover, what those architects and their peers took from Hawksmoor, in terms of his form making and use of architectural quotations, is quite different to what today's generation see in his work.

Dow Jones's creative engagement with the materiality of Hawksmoor's spaces is just one example of the different ways architects working today are still drawing from his work – and this looks set to continue. One of the courses taught by the architect Sam Jacob, formally of FAT, at the University of Illinois at Chicago, uses Hawksmoor as a case study for an 'exploration of how one form of architecture is made out of combinations of others'.[4] Entitled 'Hawksmoor Undone', the course encourages students to think about Hawksmoor's work as a kind of 'rhetorical architecture', in which the spires were created using 'the imagery of many different kinds of buildings'. Bringing this 'tactic up to date', Jacob asks his students to create their own rhetorical spire, but 'unlike Hawksmoor's classical references, you should plug in things that are from ordinary, everyday contemporary life. Supermarkets, sheds, houses, lampposts . . . the kind of architectural stuff that surrounds our everyday lives'. The next stage for students is to take apart and reassemble these references using another set of rules deriving from contemporary culture, so as 'to subject the Baroque to a shuddering, ghosting, post-digital kind of arrangement'.

Hawksmoor's spires are also of interest, though in a quite different way, for the architect, Alex Scott-Whitby. In 2011 he won the RIBA 'Forgotten Spaces' competition with (IN)Spires, a project that aims to turn the belfries of a number of City church spires into low-rent creative studios. Conceived from the off to take 30 years, (IN)Spires hopes to bring together new creative networks within the City of London – the pulsating heart of London's economy – giving new civic meaning to these historic spaces.

The epiphany moment for the project came when Scott-Whitby stepped foot inside St Mary Woolnoth for the first time since being led around the City as a child by his father fifteen years years earlier.

> I walked back into that space and it hit me like a freight
> train. I had been in most of the Wren churches and some

Contemporary reworking
of St Mary oolnoth by
Don Kalant of the UIC
School of Architecture
Advanced Studio, 2013.

of the medieval ones . . . [but when]
you walk through the door at Bank
and you go into the nave [of St Mary
Woolnoth,] there's something so
spiritual . . . in how the light hits you
. . . you feel protected from the noise
and the sound of the city. The space
becomes almost a courtyard within
the city.[5]

It was this experience that gave Scott-Whitby
the idea for the (IN)Spires project – 'It all
started there' – and where he himself tested
out the idea, using a room in the tower as a
studio for several years. During that time, he
has pondered the building at length and even
discovered the letters 'ww' carved into a window
frame in the belfry, the initials perhaps of
William Wilberforce, who was among the
congregations that listened to John Newton's
sermons in the late eighteenth century.

'After spending five years in that space',
Scott-Whitby concludes, 'Hawksmoor will
always have an influence over the architecture
I find myself designing. He gets under your
skin.' Coming from a generation of architects, Scott-Whitby is particularly fascinated
by why Hawksmoor has been such a draw for
architects in recent decades. Unlike Wren,
'we don't hear about Hawksmoor doing anything other than architecture. We don't hear
about him solving equations of elasticity, and
all the rest . . . He was purely an architect.
Maybe that's why he has this magnetic pull.'

Reflection

The position Hawksmoor occupies for the generation of architects trained since the 1980s can be seen as the culmination of his rehabilitation since the Second World War. Although in many architecture schools, architectural history is still very often deemed for all intents and purposes to begin with the Modern movement, Hawksmoor is among a select number of figures to appeal well beyond their own epochs.

Architects' education always and irrevocably shapes their particular outlook. Even if they then subsequently move in quite a different direction, that choice can always be traced, consciously or unconsciously, back to one aspect or another of their education. Assessing Hawksmoor's own career, it was his great fortune to have been apprenticed to Wren and then begin a partnership with Vanbrugh. While some observers in the early twentieth century especially saw in these relationships evidence of Hawksmoor's lesser talents, we might in contrast see Hawksmoor's qualities as actually exceeding both his peers, being more original in his ideas than Wren, more rigorous in how he applied them than Vanbrugh, to echo the description of Howard Colvin. Yet architects always need the right commissions to show off their talents and in this Hawksmoor was both lucky and unlucky. Unlucky because he never had the opportunity to realize a single building of the scale or prominence of either Wren or Vanbrugh. But he was also lucky by becoming involved in the 1711 Commission whose aims so aligned with his own architectural interests, and having a patron in the Earl of Carlisle who stuck with him during thick and thin.

While the opportunities presented to architects both in terms of their education and the commissions they receive are determined to some degree by chance, there are always ways of improving the odds. Hawksmoor certainly made the most of the opportunities on offer in Wren's office, but outside that environment often appeared reticent about putting forward his own talents in the way that might have allowed him to get ahead professionally. So, in a way, we can actually trace the decline in his posthumous reputation to the character of the man himself. Reading the leaflet produced by the Hawksmoor

Committee in 1962, where they briefly outline the reasons for Hawksmoor's 'fame [being] not commensurate with his worth', one can almost detect a slight undercurrent of frustration as they cite the 'retiring nature' of the architect they were now championing.

Yet when it came to the changes in taste and fashion that sabotaged his later career, there was little Hawksmoor could have done to improve his lot, short of acquiescing to the strictures of his Palladian rivals. That he did not do so, but stuck firmly to his own principles in the face of sometimes concerted opposition, has clouded the lenses through which he was seen for most of the two centuries after his death. But when he finally began his ascent to prominence after the Second World War, Hawksmoor's obstinate belief in the powers of his imagination and intuition in creating architecture was, conversely, part of what attracted so many to his work. For those working in the 1950s and 1960s who looked at architecture through the lens of the failures and increasing banalities of post-war modernism, Hawksmoor appeared as a free creative spirit, with the reaction against his work and the opposition it aroused nothing more than confirmation of its power. As Jonathan Meades has observed, 'because they create what is unfamiliar, what was previously never thought or revealed, the greatest artists incite the greatest contempt, most furious denigration'.[6] If one judges an architect by these criteria, then Hawksmoor is surely one of the greatest.

But because it challenges existing sensibilities, the greatest art and architecture often needs champions and Hawksmoor has benefitted from the efforts of several over the years: from Batty Langley, who took on the vitriolic attacks of James Ralph, to Goodhart-Rendel in the 1920s and Elizabeth and Wayland Young after the Second World War. However, the figure of Kerry Downes stands tall among the rest. It was his research more than anything that brought Hawksmoor in from the shadows, by revealing the context and processes through which he designed, defending Hawksmoor's case with hard facts and persuasive arguments. Downes's work also paved the way for practising architects of a range of outlooks and sensibilities to be drawn to Hawksmoor's architecture. With hindsight we might consider this simply a case of Hawksmoor and his work being co-opted to bolster a new set of agendas in the 1950s and 1960s. Yet as much as his architecture was used to reinforce a range of ideas, it never sat easy with one interpretation, and thereby posed challenges to these ideas too.

In all of this, the main recurring element is the potency and inescapability of the architecture itself. Downes's books decoded just enough of its complex language to tantalize and intrigue a wide range of observers. This, combined with the comparative absence of biographical information about Hawksmoor, opened up a space for the mystical imaginings of Sinclair and Ackroyd. It is testament to the enduring strength of Hawksmoor's vision that his buildings are able to channel such interpretations, but at the same time not be subsumed or overcome by them. Despite their increasing familiarity, they are constantly offering fresh challenges, as the architect and long-time Spitalfields resident Richard MacCormac observed:

> Walking past Christ Church, as I have done daily for many years, has not made Hawksmoor's masterwork familiar to me. Its great architectural gestures retain their strange potency and continue to astonish and invite my curiosity.[7]

In Oxford, where the two towers of All Souls peer at a distance behind a locked gate across the quadrangle, Hawksmoor's is part of that city's broader story. But in the East End of London beyond the old City walls where Hawksmoor's ambitions were for once truly met, his churches are, in contrast, the main event, decisively shaping the character of that part of London. These buildings have been active players in both Hawksmoor's story and the story of the East End, which continues to enthral – whether in Alan Moore's graphic novel *From Hell*, in which Sir William Gull marvels with the impressionable Netley at the haunting power of Hawksmoor's churches, born from the ancient and malevolent practices of the 'Dionysiac architects' – or in the recent BBC television series *Ripper Street*, in which Christ Church is a constant motif of a place in a series that is actually filmed in Ireland.[8]

Ever present

Today, with Hawksmoor more widely known than at any point in history, the buildings themselves stand as their architect's champion; and this, finally, is as it should be.[9] Although this book is essentially one of two halves – the first on the creation of Hawksmoor's work, the second on its reception – one of the most striking things about the story are the strands that tie these two halves together. Time and again we have seen fascinating continuities between creation and reception: from Turner's watercolours of Westminster Abbey eerily reminiscent of Hawksmoor's own technique, to Venturi's 'both-and' spatial analysis of St George's, Bloomsbury and Sinclair's map and its 'nome-lines'. These are, of course, just a few examples where what we have seen is actually a much broader picture. While taste and fashion have, of course, irrefutably shaped views of Hawksmoor's architecture, the extraordinary presence of his buildings has always maintained a special power in how people have responded to them over history. His buildings are the ever present in this story.

Iain Sinclair has, typically, encapsulated this idea most evocatively. While researching a book on the poet John Clare, Sinclair visited Whittlesea Mere, a huge lake that used to exist in the Fens before it was drained in the mid-nineteenth century. He remembers being startled by the story of how on 'a country farm on the edge of the Fens out of the ground appeared these white huge stone blocks. [The explanation was] there were quarries nearby and they were taking the stones to build Ely Cathedral and they came off at the bottom of this lake.' Intriguingly the stones were already marked according to where they were planned go in the cathedral and, as Sinclair continues, 'as the ground dropped away they seemed to rise to the surface as if to anticipate a building. One always felt the Hawksmoor buildings were like this kind of submarine that emerged already pre-created.'[10]

The book has explored how Hawksmoor's architecture crosses time – in Sinclair's view drawing from energies from the very beginnings of architecture – but it also crosses place, with his eclecticism having particular importance for the postmodern generation of architects in 1960s and 1970s America. In contrast to these purely architectural interests, the spiritual and social significance of Hawksmoor's churches has also always remained close to the surface. The South African architect Jo Noero, who was appointed in 1982 by Desmond Tutu as Diocesan Architect to the Anglican Church of the Transvaal Diocese, recalls how

> Tutu's instruction to me was to design and build churches in the so-called Black Townships as beacons of hope in otherwise desolate places. He likened his vision to the work done by English Architects like Hawksmoor . . . who built wonderful churches in the slums of London which acted as beacons of hope for the poor and dispossessed.[11]

Though his work has been an inspiration for many, Hawksmoor had no direct architectural followers. It is, moreover, difficult to think of an architect working now who is so preoccupied, in both theory and practice, with the sculptural and symbolic aspects of architecture in the way that Hawksmoor was. Lasdun, the American architect Louis Kahn, and above all Stirling might have had a claim, but the changes in architectural practice today mean that they may be the last.

Even with the richness of the digital form-making and image rendering tools now available, it hard to imagine many buildings created in the immediate future that might offer the same unexpected jolt you receive when first confronted by one of Hawksmoor's masterpieces. His works are unique in the history of architecture – and will continue to be. Amid its ebbs and flows, peaks and troughs, and the great crescendo towards its end, never in this story have taste and fashion fully overshadowed the enigmatic capacity of Hawksmoor's buildings to capture and enthral the imagination. For that reason I feel this story is far from over.

Following his master's dictum, Hawksmoor's architecture aimed at eternity – and has now finally achieved it. Transcending stone and timber, plaster and brick, indeed matter itself, it is, though, no small irony that only in Hawksmoor's afterlife has his architecture come truly alive.

REFERENCES

INTRODUCTION: THE MAN AND THE MYTH

1 Kerry Downes, *Hawksmoor* (London, 1959), p. 6. Kerry Downes suggests that the slab, which was cut in 1736 by Andrews Jelfe, may have been underground at one time.

2 Ibid., p. 6.

3 For this and following references, see Iain Sinclair, *London Orbital* (London, 2003), pp. 158–61.

4 Temple Bar is the spot on Fleet Street where the City of London ends and Westminster begins. A gateway designed by Christopher Wren acted as the symbolic and regulatory threshold between the two jurisdictions until the late 1870s when it was removed as an impediment to traffic. It was re-erected and stood for over 100 years at Theobalds Park, Hertfordshire, where Sinclair saw it, before it returned to London to form part of the regenerated Paternoster Square, north of St Paul's Cathedral, in 2004.

5 According to Downes, Hawksmoor's will was made in January 1730. See Downes, *Hawksmoor*, p. 6, n. 13.

6 Peter Ackroyd, *Hawksmoor* (London, 1985), p. 5.

7 The exhibition was entitled *Nicholas Hawksmoor: Methodical Imaginings*, curated by Mohsen Mostafavi, Dean of Harvard University Graduate School of Design. After the Biennale it was shown at Somerset House, London (15 May–1 September 2013). A book deriving from the exhibition, *Nicholas Hawksmoor: Seven Churches for London*, was published by Lars Müller Publishers, Zurich, in Spring 2014.

8 *Bunkers, Brutalism and Bloodymindedness: Concrete Poetry with Jonathan Meades*, episode One, first broadcast on BBC Four, 9 pm, 16 February 2014.

1 Emergence

1 In Hawksmoor's entry in the *Oxford Dictionary of National Biography* (Oxford, 2004), Kerry Downes notes that the baptismal records for this period are incomplete; the assumption of 1662 is based on a calculation Hawksmoor made on the back of a drawing from 1707 which is now in the British Library; online edn, www.oxforddnb.com, accessed 6 July 2014. Some observers have favoured 1666 as the date of Hawksmoor's birth for the occultist connotations of the number and perhaps also the momentousness of the year that saw the Great Fire of London.

2 In the ODNB entry on Hawksmoor, Downes suggests the local grammar school in Dunham as a possible place of Hawksmoor's early schooling. The obituary appeared in *Read's Weekly Journal*, no. 603 (27 March 1736) and notices also appeared in the *Old Whig*, no. 56 (1 April 1736) and the *Gentleman's Magazine*, VI (1736), p. 168. See Kerry Downes, *Hawksmoor* (London, 1959), p. 7, n. 15.

3 Mellish owned property near East Drayton, indicating that Hawksmoor almost certainly still resided there at this time. Hawksmoor's connection with Gouge is suggested by George Vertue. See Downes, *Hawksmoor*, p. 1, where he quotes from George Vertue's 'Notebooks', *Walpole Society*, XXII (1933–4), p. 51.

4 Lisa Jardine, *On a Grander Scale: The Outstanding Career of Sir Christopher Wren* (London, 2003), p. 328.

5 Ibid., p. 280.

6 Wren was also knighted in the same year and this, together with his resignation of his position as Savilian Professor of Astronomy at Oxford, marked the completion of his transition from scientist to architect. See Jardine, *On a Grander Scale*, pp. 283, 289.

7 Hooke also served as one of the City Surveyors while also largely taking care of the day-to-day running of Wren's architectural office. See Jardine, *On a Grander Scale*, pp. 297–8.

8 Faith was the daughter of Sir Thomas Coghill of Bletchingdon. See Jardine, *On a Grander Scale*, p. 281.

9 Ibid., p. 283.

10 Downes, 'Hawksmoor, Nicholas', ODNB.

11 Anthony Geraghty, 'Nicholas Hawksmoor and the Wren City Church Steeples', *The Georgian Group Journal*, X (2000), p. 1; and also more generally, Anthony Geraghty, 'Introducing Thomas Laine: Draughtsman to Sir Christopher Wren', *Architectural History*, XLII (1999), pp. 240–45.

12 Geraghty, 'Hawksmoor and the Wren City Church Steeples', p. 2.

13   Gordon Higgott, 'Wren and his Draughtsmen', *St Paul's Cathedral Wren Office Drawings catalogue* (2013), www.stpauls.co.uk, accessed 6 July 2014. Higgott cites *Wren Society*, XIV (Oxford, 1939), pp. 84–5; and *Wren Society*, XVI (Oxford, 1937), p. 67.

14   For a good overview of the history of the cathedral, see *St Paul's: The Cathedral Church of London, 604–2004*, ed. Derek Keene, Arthur Burns and Andrew Saint (New Haven, CT, and London, 2004), particularly the following essays: Gordon Higgott, 'The Fabric to 1670', pp. 171–90; and James W. P. Campbell and Robert Bowles, 'The Construction of the New Cathedral', pp. 207–19.

15   Jardine, *On a Grander Scale*, pp. 286–7.

16   Lydia Soo suggests Wren worked on the Tracts early in his architectural career, with much of the work dating from the 1670s, as accorded by several sources, notably Hooke's diary. See Lydia M. Soo, *Wren's 'Tracts' on Architecture and Other Writings* (Cambridge, 1998), pp. 119–21.

17   Wren, 'Tract 1', in Christopher Wren the younger, *Parentalia: or Memoirs of the Family of the Wrens viz. of Mathew Bishop of Ely, Christopher Dean of Windsor, &c. but chiefly of Sir Christopher Wren, Late Surveyor-General of the Royal Buildings, President of the Royal Society, &c . . .* (London, 1750), p. 351.

18   Wren the younger, *Parentalia*, p. 351.

19   Despite his aversion to 'Fancy', Wren's work was itself criticized harshly by the Earl of Shaftesbury for its 'deformity' – essentially for its overabundance of 'Fancy' – indicating just how relative a concept it often was. See Anthony Ashley Cooper, 3rd Earl of Shaftesbury, 'A Letter Concerning Design', in *Characteristicks of Men, Manners, Opinions, Times: Miscellaneous Reflections on the Preceding Treatises, and other Critical Subjects*, III (London, 1732), pp. 401–2.

20   Gordon Higgott 'The Revised Design for St Paul's Cathedral, 1685–90: Wren, Hawksmoor and Les Invalides', *Burlington Magazine*, CXLVI (2004), p. 534, quoting Wren the younger, *Parentalia*, p. 283.

21   This is the view put forward by Gordon Higgott in an important article in which he argues a particular drawing for the dome, attributed by Anthony Geraghty to Hawksmoor, shows inspiration from Jules Hardouin-Mansart's church of Les Invalides in Paris, which was first published in 1683. See Higgott, 'The Revised Design for St Paul's Cathedral', pp. 534–47. This argument is refuted in Kerry Downes, 'Wren, Hawksmoor and Les Invalides Revisited', *Burlington Magazine*, CL (2008), pp. 250–52.

22   Anthony Geraghty, *The Architectural Drawings of Sir Christopher Wren at All Souls College, Oxford: A Complete Catalogue* (London, 2007), pp. 11–12.

23 Higgott, 'Wren and his Draughtsmen'. See also Anthony Gerbino and Stephen Johnston, *Compass and Rule: Architecture as Mathematical Practice in England, 1500–1750* (London and New York, 2009), pp. 86–91.

24 Higgott, 'Wren and his Draughtsmen'.

25 Interview with Gordon Higgott, 5 November 2013.

26 Ibid.

27 Geraghty has interestingly suggested John Locke's *Essay Concerning Human Understanding* (first published in 1689) as a kind of a contemporary 'conceptual framework' for what Hawksmoor was trying to achieve. See Geraghty, 'Nicholas Hawksmoor's Drawing Technique' of the 1690s and John Locke's "Essay Concerning Human Understanding"', in *Rethinking the Baroque*, ed. Helen Hills (Aldershot, 2011), pp. 125–41.

28 Louis Kahn, 'Form and Design', *Architectural Design*, xxxi/4 (April 1961), p. 149.

29 Geraghty, 'Hawksmoor's Drawing Technique', p. 2.

30 Nicholas Hawksmoor, 'Letter to the Dean of Westminster (1734–5)', in Downes, *Hawksmoor*, pp. 255–8.

31 See, for example, Cedric Reverand, 'Christopher Wren's Stylistic Development', *Eighteenth-Century Life*, xxiv/2 (2001), pp. 81–115.

32 Geraghty, 'Hawksmoor's Drawing Technique', p. 5.

33 Ibid., p. 5.

34 Ibid., pp. 3, 5, 7, 10–11.

35 For more on the King's Gallery and Orangery, see Downes, *Hawksmoor*, pp. 65, 81–2.

36 Downes, *Hawksmoor*, p. 53 quoting E. H. Pearce, *Annals of Christ's Hospital*, 2nd edn (Cambridge, 1908), p. 151.

37 For more on these drawings, see Downes, *Hawksmoor*, p. 280; Geraghty, *The Architectural Drawings of Sir Christopher Wren*, p. 274.

38 For an important discussion, focusing in particular on the relationship between Wren and Hooke, see Matthew F. Walker, 'The Limits of Collaboration: Robert Hooke, Christopher Wren and the Designing of the Monument to the Great Fire of London', *Notes and Records of the Royal Society*, lxv (2011), pp. 121–43.

39 Gordon Higgott, 'Introduction [to Greenwich Royal Hospital]', *Sir John Soane's Museum English Baroque Drawings catalogue* (2009), www.jeromeonline.co.uk/drawings, accessed 6 July 2014.

40 Downes, *Hawksmoor*, pp. 84–5.

41 For a commentary on the evolution of its design, see Gordon Higgott, 'Greenwich Royal Hospital', *Sir John Soane's Museum English Baroque Drawings Catalogue* (2009), www.jeromeonline.co.uk/drawings,

accessed 6 July 2014. The first enlargement plan is catalogued as SM volume CIX/1.

42 The plan is catalogued as SM volume CIX/64.

43 Downes, *Hawksmoor*, p. 86.

44 Shaftesbury, 'A Letter Concerning Design', p. 400.

45 Nicholas Hawksmoor, Letter to the third Earl of Carlisle, 4 October 1731, in Geoffrey Webb, 'The Letters and Drawings of Nicholas Hawksmoor Relating to the Building of the Mausoleum at Castle Howard, 1726–1742', *Walpole Society*, XIX (1930–31), p. 126. Downes goes into detail assessing the available evidence in Kerry Downes, 'Hawksmoor's House at Easton Neston', *Architectural History*, XXX (1987), pp. 50–76.

46 Downes, 'Easton Neston', p. 50.

47 For a description of the interior arrangement, see Downes, *Hawksmoor*, pp. 59–63; and also Downes, *Hawksmoor*, (1969), pp. 31–42.

48 Robert Williams, 'Vanbrugh's Lost Years', *TLS* (3 September 1999), and in more detail in Williams, 'Vanbrugh's India and his Mausolea for England', in *Sir John Vanbrugh and Landscape Architecture in Baroque England, 1690–1730*, ed. Christopher Ridgway and Robert Williams (Stroud, 2000), pp. 114–30.

49 For a discussion of Hawksmoor's role, see Downes, *Hawksmoor*, pp. 72–3.

50 For a full and entertaining account of the building process, and in particular the considerations of the patron, see Charles Saumarez Smith, *The Building of Castle Howard* (London, 1990).

51 Jonathan Swift, 'The History of Vanbrug's House' (1706), in *The Poems of Jonathan Swift*, vol. I, ed. Harold Williams (Oxford, 1958), p. 86.

52 See Jonathan Swift, 'Vanbrug's House' (1703), in *The Poems*, ed. Williams, pp. 79–81.

53 Swift, 'The History of Vanbrug's House', *The Poems*, ed. Williams, p. 97.

54 Kerry Downes, 'Vanbrugh, Sir John (1664–1726)', *ODNB*.

55 For a brief discussion of the nature of their collaboration, see Downes, *Hawksmoor*, pp. 76–7.

56 Nicholas Hawksmoor, Letter to the Duchess of Marlborough of 1722, in Downes, 'Easton Neston', p. 55, quoting David Green, *Blenheim Palace* (London, 1951), p. 309. The letter is held by the British Library (MS 61353, fol. 239).

57 John Vanbrugh, Letter to Lord Manchester, 18 July 1707, in *The Complete Works of Sir John Vanbrugh*, vol. IV: *The Letters*, ed. Geoffrey Webb (London, 1928), p. 14.

58 John Vanbrugh, Letter to Lord Manchester, 9 September 1707, in *Complete Works*, IV: *The Letters*, p. 15.

59 John Vanbrugh, Letter to the Duchess of Marlborough, 11 June 1709, quoted in Kerry Downes, *Sir John Vanbrugh: A Biography* (New York, 1987), pp. 347–8. Vanbrugh's proto-Picturesque justification for preserving Woodstock Manor was also ostensibly about economy too: it was 'One of the most agreeable Objects that the Best of Landskip Painters can invent'.

60 Wren the younger, *Parentalia*, p. 351.

61 For a wider discussion of the idea of association and the related concept of 'fancy', see David Cast, 'Seeing Vanbrugh and Hawksmoor', *Journal of the Society of Architectural Historians*, XLIII (1984) pp. 315–17.

62 For broader, though at times speculative, discussions, see Timothy Mowl, 'Antiquaries, Theatre and Early Medievalism', in *Sir John Vanbrugh and Landscape Architecture in Baroque England*, ed. Ridgway and Williams, pp. 71–92; and Giles Worsley, 'Sir John Vanbrugh and the Search for a National Style', in *Gothic Architecture and its Meanings, 1550–1830*, ed. Michael Hall (Reading, 2002), pp. 99–132.

63 See Downes, *Hawksmoor*, pp. 44–8.

64 Ibid., p. 45, quoting Thomas Hobbes, *Answer to Davenant*, in J. E. Springarn, *Critical Essays of the Seventeenth Century*, II (Oxford, 1908), p. 59.

65 For a fuller version of the relevance of these ideas to Hawksmoor and Vanbrugh's work, see Cast, 'Seeing Vanbrugh and Hawksmoor', pp. 310–27.

2 Achievement

1 For more on the Commission itself, see H. M. Colvin, 'Fifty New Churches', *Architectural Review*, CVII (1950), pp. 189–96; and Michael Port, *The Commissions for Building Fifty New Churches: The Minute Books, 1711–27, A Calendar* (London, 1986).

2 See Elizabeth McKellar, *The Birth of Modern London: The Development and Design of the City, 1660–1720* (Manchester and New York, 1999), p. 13, noting Roger Finlay and Beatrice Shearer, 'Population Growth and Suburban Expansion', in *London, 1500–1700: The Making of the Metropolis*, ed. A. L. Beier and Roger Finlay (London and New York, 1986), pp. 37–59; and also Vanessa Harding, 'The Population of London, 1550–1700', *London Journal*, XV/ 2 (1990), pp. 111–28.

3 McKellar, *The Birth of Modern London*, p. 14, noted from Finlay and Shearer, 'Population Growth and Suburban Expansion', p. 38.

4 Quoted by McKellar, *The Birth of Modern London*, p. 13, from Edward Hatton, *A New View of London* (London, 1708), preface, p. i.

5 Nicholas Hawksmoor, *Remarks on the Founding and Carrying on the Building of the Royal Hospital Greenwich* (London, 1728), pp. 8–9.

6 McKellar, *The Birth of Modern London*, p. 14.

7 Pierre de la Ruffinière du Prey, *Hawksmoor's London Churches: Architecture and Theology* (London, 2000), p. 49.

8 Kerry Downes, *Hawksmoor* (London, 1959), p. 156.

9 Du Prey, *Hawksmoor's London Churches*, p. 50.

10 Downes, *Hawksmoor*, pp. 156–7.

11 For more detailed accounts of the particulars of the Commission's formation, see Downes, *Hawksmoor*; Du Prey, *Hawksmoor's London Churches*; and Vaughan Hart, *Nicholas Hawksmoor: Rebuilding Ancient Wonders* (New Haven, CT, and London, 2002).

12 Downes, *Hawksmoor*, pp. 157–8. Dickinson left in 1713 without having a material impact on any subsequently built churches.

13 Hart, *Rebuilding Ancient Wonders*, p. 132, quoting Daniel Defoe, *A Tour Through the Whole Island of Great Britain* (London, 1725), p. 327.

14 Du Prey, *Hawksmoor's London Churches*, p. 49, quoting *Journal of the House of Commons*, XVI/581 (1708–11), meeting of 6 April 1711.

15 Judi Loach, 'Architecture and Urban Space in London', in *Urban Achievement in Early Modern Europe*, ed. Patrick O'Brien, et al. (Cambridge, 2008), p. 152, n. 2, quoting Jonathan Swift, *Examiner*, no. 42 (24 May 1711).

16 See McKellar, *The Birth of Modern London*, p. 26.

17 Ibid., p. 27.

18 For a full and excellent outline of London's expansion in the late seventeenth and early eighteenth centuries, and attitudes towards its growth, see McKellar, *The Birth of Modern London*, pp. 17–34.

19 Nicholas Hawksmoor, Letter to Dr George Clarke, 17 February 1714/15, in *All Souls: A College and its Buildings*, ed. Howard Colvin and J.S.G. Simmons (Oxford, 1986), pp. 86–90 (p. 89).

20 A discussion of the more immediately cultural aspects of this phenomenon, as well as the conception of the notion of politeness, can be found in David Solkin, *Painting for Money: The Visual Arts and the Public Sphere in Eighteenth-century England* (New Haven, CT, and London, 1993), pp. 27–47. Solkin's account is informed by the influential notion of the 'public sphere' developed by the German social philosopher Jürgen Habermas. See Jürgen Habermas, *The Structural Transformation of the Public Sphere: An Inquiry into a Category of Bourgeois Society*, trans. Thomas Burger and Frederick Lawrence (Cambridge, MA, 1989).

21 John Summerson, *Georgian London* (London, 1945), p. 28.

22 Ibid., pp. 28–9. This quotation is one of many comments and observations made on Barbon. See Roger North, *The Autobiography of the Hon. Roger North,* ed. Augustus Jessopp (London, 1887).

23 For a more detailed outline of Barbon's tactics, see McKellar, *The Birth of Modern London*, pp. 43–6. Both as a pioneer in his methods of property speculation and as the founder of the first Fire Insurance Office, Barbon was a notable economic thinker. It was to Barbon, before any other economic theorist, that Karl Marx turned in the first pages of *Das Kapital* in order to define commodities and use-value. See Karl Marx, *Capital*, vol. 1: *Der Produktionsprozess des Kapitals,* trans. Eden and Cedar Paul (London, 1974), p. 3.

24 Summerson, *Georgian London*, p. 29.

25 Hawksmoor, Letter to Dr George Clarke, 17 February 1714/15, in *All Souls: A College and its Buildings*, ed. Colvin and Simmons, p. 89.

26 McKellar, *The Birth of Modern London*, pp. 28–9, quoting a representation to the Privy Council of 24 July 1684, available at the National Archives (PC/2/70).

27 'Sir Christopher Wren's Letter of Recommendations to a Friend on the Commission for Building Fifty New Churches', in Du Prey, *Hawksmoor's London Churches*, pp. 133–7; 'Mr Van-Brugg's Proposals about Building ye New Churches', in Kerry Downes, *Vanbrugh* (London, 1977), pp. 257–8. For a discussion of the various recommendations to the Commission, see Du Prey, *Hawksmoor's London Churches*, pp. 57–60.

28 Du Prey, *Hawksmoor's London Churches*, p. 133.

29 Ibid., p. 134.

30 Downes has suggested that Vanbrugh's 'Proposals' might actually be a joint work undertaken with Hawksmoor. See Downes, *Vanbrugh*, pp. 354–5.

31 Vanbrugh, 'Proposals', p. 257; and Du Prey, *Hawksmoor's London Churches*, p. 134.

32 Revd George Hickes, 'Observations on Mr. Vanbruggs Proposals about Building the New Churches', in Du Prey, *Hawksmoor's London Churches*, pp. 139–42.

33 Du Prey, *Hawksmoor's London Churches*, p. 139.

34 Ibid., pp. 139–40.

35 Ibid., p. 139.

36 The 'Rules for the Fifty New Churches Set Down by the Commissioners and Their Subcommittee' as agreed at meetings on 11 and 16 July 1712 are reprinted ibid., pp. 143–4.

37 Ibid., p. 153.

38 Ibid., p. 144.

39 Ibid., p. 58, quoting from the records of the commissioners on 21
    November 1711 in Lambeth Palace Library (MS 2690, p. 16). Wren,
    in contrast, had suggested that the east–west orientation only be followed
    when it was convenient to do so.

40 A fuller description of how the ornament enriches the spatial experience
    can be found in Downes, *Hawksmoor*, pp. 187–9.

41 Soon after the church's completion the parishioners built a west gallery and
    in 1781 moved the altar. They clearly did not understand the building's
    spatial complexity and it seems in any case that the east–west orientation
    had become less important. See Downes, *Hawksmoor*, Appendix D, 'St
    George's, Bloomsbury', pp. 270–71.

42 For a full account, see Du Prey, *Hawksmoor's London Churches*, pp. 47–80.

43 For another mention of George Wheler, *An Account of the Churches, or
    Places of Assembly of the Primitive Christians* (London, 1689), see Hart,
    Rebuilding Ancient Wonders, p. 63.

44 A more detailed analysis of the drawing can be found in Du Prey,
    Hawksmoor's London Churches, pp. 61–6.

45 Ibid., p. 63.

46 Du Prey discusses Bingham in more detail: see ibid., pp. 66–70.

47 Ibid., pp. 78–9, quoting Joseph Bingham, *Origines Ecclesiasticae, or
    The Antiquities of the Christian Church* (London, 1708–22), vol. III,
    p. 146.

48 Alexandrina Buchanan, 'Interpretations of Medieval Architecture,
    c. 1550–*c.* 1750', in *Gothic Architecture and its Meanings, 1550–1830*, ed.
    Michael Hall (Reading, 2002), p. 28, n. 5, quoting Randle Cotgrave,
    A Dictionarie of the French and English Tongues (London, 1611). For an
    account on the evolution of the term, see E. S. de Beer, 'Gothic: Origin
    and Diffusion of the Term', *Journal of the Warburg and Courtauld Institutes*,
    XI (1948), p. 144.

49 Roger North, 'On Gothic Architecture' [*c.* 1696], in *British Architectural
    Theory, 1540–1750*, ed. Caroline van Eck (Aldershot, 2003), pp. 161–2.

50 John Evelyn, *An Account of Architects and Architecture together With an
    Historical, Etymological Explanation of certain Terms, particularly Affected
    by Architects* (London, 1706), p. 9.

51 For a general discussion of Wren and the Gothic, see Lydia M. Soo,
    Wren's 'Tracts' on Architecture and Other Writings (Cambridge, 1998),
    pp. 34–8.

52 Christopher Wren, 'Report on Salisbury Cathedral for Dr Seth Ward,
    Bishop (31 August 1668)', in Soo, *Wren's 'Tracts' on Architecture*, p. 62.

53 Ibid., p. 64.

54 Christopher Wren, 'Report on Westminster Abbey to Francis Atterbury, Dean (1713)', in Soo, *Wren's 'Tracts' on Architecture*, p. 90.

55 Regarding his work at Tom Tower at Christ Church, Oxford, Wren noted, for example, that he proceeded not 'soe busy as he [the medieval architect] began'. See Christopher Wren, 'Letter from Wren to Bishop of Oxford (26 May 1681)', *Wren Society*, vol. v, ed. A. T. Bolton and H. D. Hendry (London, 1928), p. 17.

56 Nairn's comment is regarding St Mary Aldermary. See Ian Nairn, *Nairn's London* (London, 1966), p. 21.

57 Howard Colvin, 'Hawksmoor and the North Quadrangle', in Colvin and Simmons, *All Souls*, p. 20. Downes, *Hawksmoor*, p. 101, notes that it is unknown how the two met but that Greenwich may have been the place on account of Dr Clarke's role in the Royal Navy.

58 Colvin, 'Hawksmoor and the North Quadrangle', pp. 22–3.

59 For a discussion of the other designs, see ibid., pp. 23–5.

60 Roger White notes that they are datable to 1708–9. See Roger White, *Nicholas Hawksmoor and the Replanning of Oxford* (London, 1997), p. 27.

61 Colvin, 'Hawksmoor and the North Quadrangle', pp. 29–30.

62 Ibid., p. 30.

63 Ibid., p. 31, quoted in H. E. Salter and Mary D. Lobel, eds, *The Victoria History of the County of Oxfordshire*, vol. III (Oxford, 1954), p. 191.

64 Hawksmoor, Letter to Dr George Clarke of 17 February 1714/15, p. 87.

65 For a brief description of all the drawings, see White, *Hawksmoor and the Replanning of Oxford*, pp. 38–40.

66 It was begun in 1712 and was habitable relatively soon after in 1713. For more on the Clarendon Building, see Downes, *Hawksmoor*, pp. 107–9.

67 He in fact produced three town plans for the area. The most notable and comprehensive plan is *Regio Prima Accademiae Oxoniēsis amplificatae et exornatae*. As the title suggests, this was to be a remaking of Oxford along Roman lines. A brief discussion of the plans can be found in Downes, *Hawksmoor*, p. 123.

68 The notable exception being a (now hidden) stone organ screen. See Downes, 'Westminster Abbey', p. 14.

69 Eighteen drawings and two adapted prints by Hawksmoor for the Abbey were only comparatively recently discovered, in 1992. See Kerry Downes, 'The Completion of Westminster Abbey: Newly Discovered Drawings by Nicholas Hawksmoor', *National Art Collections Fund Review* (1993), pp. 12–17; and Giles Worsley, 'Drawn to a Find', *Country Life*, CXCVII (20 May 1993), pp. 100–101. A plate by Paul Fourdrinier, made before 1737, shows Hawksmoor's west end towers as built but with a crossing

spire likely after a design by Wren. See Downes, *Hawksmoor*, pp. 215–16; see also Warwick Rodwell, *The Lantern Tower of Westminster Abbey, 1060–2010* (Oxford and Oakville, CT, 2010), pp. 39–70.

70 Nicholas Hawksmoor, Letter to the Dean of Westminster (1734–5), in Downes, *Hawksmoor*, pp. 255–8 (p. 255).

71 Ibid., pp. 255, 256.

72 Ibid., p. 256.

73 Wren rejected the Vasarian theory that medieval architecture was derived from the Goths, noting in his report to Atterbury that the Goths 'were rather Destroyers than Builders'. Instead, he suggested that the Gothic 'should with more Reason be called the *Saracen* Style'. See Wren, 'Report on Westminster Abbey (1713)', pp. 81–5. For a discussion on other more enlightened contemporary views on the evolution of Gothic architecture, see Howard Colvin, 'Aubrey's "Chronologia Architectonica"', in *Essays in English Architectural History*, ed. Howard Colvin (New Haven, CT, 1999), p. 209.

74 Hawksmoor, Letter to the Dean of Westminster (1734–5), pp. 256–7.

75 Downes, *Hawksmoor*, p. 167.

76 See Eric Fernie, *The Architecture of Norman England* (Oxford, 2000), p. 125.

77 The dormer windows were removed from the spire at Christ Church, Spitalfields, after a fire in the nineteenth century. An account of the various works at Christ Church during the nineteenth and twentieth centuries appears in chapter Seven.

78 In 1697 Hawksmoor was paid ten guineas 'for Coppy designes and Papers' for St Mary, Warwick, which are almost certainly those that survive among the collection of Wren office drawings at All Souls College, Oxford. In the end, Hawksmoor's designs were passed over in favour of those by William Wilson. See Downes, *Hawksmoor*, p. 55, quoting a document in the National Archives (c104/97). For the drawings, see Anthony Geraghty, *The Architectural Drawings of Sir Christopher Wren at All Souls College, Oxford: A Complete Catalogue* (London, 2007), pp. 111–16.

79 For an account of classicism of the period, see Barbara Arciszewska, 'Classicism: Constructing the Paradigm in Continental Europe and Britain', in *Articulating British Classicism: New Approaches to Eighteenth-century Architecture*, ed. Barbara Arciszewska and Elizabeth McKellar (Aldershot, 2004), pp. 1–33.

80 Peter Borsay, *The English Urban Renaissance: Culture and Society in the Provincial Town, 1660–1770* (Oxford, 1991), p. 305.

81 Hart, *Rebuilding Ancient Wonders*, p. 153.

82 Ibid., p. 151.

83 Ibid., pp. 167–85.

84 Buchanan, 'Interpretations', p. 28.

85 Nicholas Hawksmoor, Letter to the Dean of Westminster (1734–5), p. 257. Downes notes that two paintings from *c*. 1735 held by Westminster Abbey Library depict the spires (and a lantern) more or less as they appear in Hawksmoor's designs, indicating both the painter's access to the design process and also presumably just how close they came to being built. See Downes, 'Westminster Abbey', p. 17.

86 Downes, 'Westminster Abbey', p. 16.

87 The idea of an ogee dome to top the crossing tower also appears, as noted above, in his 1720s designs for the Abbey. Indeed, one drawing showing another variation of an ogee-domed octagonal crossing tower is simply re-dated from 1724. Downes, 'Westminster Abbey', p. 17.

88 Anna Keay and Roland B. Harris, 'The White Tower, 1485–1642', in *The White Tower*, ed. Edward Impey (New Haven, CT, and London, 2008), pp. 161–77.

89 Vanbrugh similarly, though more explicitly, sought to evoke architecture of the past for the perceived authority it held. See Giles Worsley, 'Sir John Vanbrugh and the Search for a National Style', pp. 114–16.

3   Falling into Shadow

1 Ptolemy Dean, *Imagining Hawksmoor*, Royal Academy Forum event, held on 27 February 2012.

2 Nicholas Hawksmoor, Letter to the Earl of Carlisle, 17 August 1734, in Geoffrey Webb, 'The Letters and Drawings of Nicholas Hawksmoor Relating to the Building of the Mausoleum at Castle Howard, 1726–1742', *Walpole Society*, XIX (1930–31), p. 153.

3 This was less of the case in the two university towns of Oxford and Cambridge, where Hawksmoor did produce overall town plans. Both, however, went unbuilt. For an in-depth discussion, see Vaughan Hart, *Nicholas Hawksmoor: Rebuilding Ancient Wonders* (New Haven, CT, and London, 2002), pp. 187–213.

4 Nicholas Hawksmoor, *Remarks on the Founding and Carrying on the Buildings of the Royal Hospital at Greenwich* (London, 1728), p. 7.

5 See Higgott's entry on 'Plan-proposal for a New Precinct around the Cathedral, with Arcaded Frontages on all Sides and a Rotunda or Mausoleum Adjoining Ludgate Hill at the West', in *Sir John Soane's Museum English Baroque Drawings Catalogue* (2009). A slightly earlier version is in Gordon Higgott, *St Paul's Cathedral Wren Office Drawings Catalogue* (2013), WRE/7/1/1 [221].

6 Kerry Downes, *Hawksmoor* (London, 1959), p. 51.

7 Hart describes how, on 25 June 1713, it was resolved that 'a statue of her majesty Queen Anne made by the best hands be set up in the most conspicuous & convenient parts of each of the 50 new Churches'. On 29 April 1714 it was 'Resolv'd that instead of the statues design'd to be put upon the 50 new Churches, a Steeple in Form of a pillar be built at the West End of the Church to be Erected near the Maypole in the Strand; wth the Queens Statue on top of it, with Bases capable of Inscriptions, to perpetuate the memory of the building 50 New Churches'. See Hart, *Rebuilding Ancient Wonders*, pp. 147–9.

8 Daniel Defoe, *A Tour thro' the Whole Island of Great Britain*, ed. G.D.H. Cole and D. C. Browning (London, 1962), p. 330; Alexander Pope, *Of Taste: An Epistle to the Right Honourable Richard Earl of Burlington* (London, 1731), p. 14. See also Hart, *Rebuilding Ancient Wonders*, pp. 227–9. The idea of the bridge was discussed widely, especially whether it should be wood or stone. An Act of Parliament was eventually passed in 1736. See Alison O'Byrne, 'Composing Westminster Bridge: Public Improvement and National Identity in Eighteenth-century London', in *The Age of Projects*, ed. Maximillian E. Novak (Toronto, 2008), pp. 243–70.

9 Nicholas Hawksmoor, *A Short Historical Account of London-Bridge with A Proposition for a New Stone-Bridge at Westminster* (London, 1736), p. 18.

10 Ibid., p. 6.

11 Ibid., p. 16.

12 Ibid., p. 21.

13 Nicholas Hawksmoor, Letter to the Earl of Carlisle, 17 February 1735, in Webb, 'Letters and Drawings of Nicholas Hawksmoor', p. 159.

14 Colen Campbell, *Vitruvius Britannicus, or the British Architect; containing The Plans, Elevations, and Sections of the Regular Buildings, both Publick and Private, in Great Britain*, I (London, 1715), introduction unpaginated.

15 Robert Morris, *An Essay in Defence of Ancient Architecture, Or, A Parallel of the Ancient Buildings with the Modern* (London, 1728), p. 14.

16 See Peter Borsay, *The English Urban Renaissance: Culture and Society in the Provincial Town, 1660–1770* (Oxford, 1991), pp. 305–7.

17 The *Critical Review* first appeared as a series of articles published between 20 October 1733 and 6 April 1734 as front-page features in the *Weekly Register*. See Matthew Craske, 'From Burlington to Billingsgate: James Ralph's Attempt to Impose Burlingtonian Classicism as a Canon of Public Taste', in *Articulating British Classicism: New Approaches to Eighteenth-century Architecture*, ed. Barbara Arciszewska and Elizabeth McKellar (Aldershot, 2004), p. 99, n. 4.

18 James Ralph, *A Critical Review of the Publick Buildings, Statues and Ornaments in, and about London and Westminster* (London, 1734), dedication unpaginated.

19 Ibid., pp. 5–6.

20 Mr Hiram [Batty Langley], *Grub Street Journal* (11 July 1734).

21 Mr Hiram [Batty Langley], *Grub Street Journal* (18 July 1734): 'In our last, pag. I, col. I. l. penult. for Nathaniel read Nicholas.'

22 Mr Hiram [Batty Langley], *Grub Street Journal* (11 July 1734).

23 Eileen Harris, *British Architectural Books and Writers, 1556–1785* (Cambridge, 1992), p. 383, quoting Anthony Ashley Cooper, 3rd Earl of Shaftesbury, *Characteristicks of Men, Manners, Opinions, Times*, III (London, 1737), p. 401.

24 Ralph, *Critical Review*, p. 14.

25 Mr Hiram [Batty Langley], *Grub Street Journal* (25 July 1734).

26 A few years later, in 1741, Langley began publishing his best-known work, *Ancient Architecture: Restored and Improved*, in which he made a pioneering attempt to reconcile the Gothic to the systems and orders of classical architecture, perhaps inspired by conversations with Hawksmoor.

27 Ralph, *Critical Review*, pp. 99–100.

28 The drawing was included in the so-called 'Heirloom' copy of *Parentalia*. Drawings now at All Souls show two further reconstructions of the Mausoleum, as well as two others in which it has been transformed into what is recognizably a church front, tower and spire. See Downes, *Hawksmoor*, pp. 21 and 187.

29 Downes, *Hawksmoor*, p. 186, quoting Lambeth Palace Library Minutes, II. 357.

30 We might see Hogarth's direct involvement at St Bartholomew's Hospital in Smithfield and, especially, in the establishment of the Foundling Hospital as examples of his ideal of morally enlightened concern for London's poor and needy.

31 Hart, *Rebuilding Ancient Wonders*, p. 2, quoting Downes, *Hawksmoor*, pp. 246–7.

32 Nicholas Hawksmoor, Letter to the Earl of Carlisle, 28 May 1726, in Downes, *Hawksmoor*, pp. 248–50.

33 Ibid., p. 249.

34 Hawksmoor, Letter to the Earl of Carlisle, 7 January 1724, in Downes, *Hawksmoor*, p. 243.

35 Downes, *Hawksmoor*, p. 219.

36 Hawksmoor, Letter to the Earl of Carlisle, 7 January 1724, p. 244.

37 The correspondence is in Webb, 'Letters and Drawings of Hawksmoor', pp. 111–64. For a full account of the design and construction history of the Mausoleum, see Downes, *Hawksmoor*, pp. 222–31.

38 The tomb of Porsenna had been discussed by Wren and Hooke, with Hooke drawing it in 1677. See Pierre de la Ruffinière du Prey, *Hawksmoor's London Churches: Architecture and Theology* (London, 2000), p. 15.

39 Nicholas Hawksmoor, Letter to the Earl of Carlisle, 3 September 1726, in Webb, 'Letters and Drawings of Hawksmoor', p. 117. The letter also contained the odd suggestion that nearby the Mausoleum be provided 'Six Small Rooms . . . for ye Accomodation of 6 old women (or 6 old men) . . . and these aged persons should be ye Curators, of ye Monument, to clean, sweep and Lock it up, and shew it to Strangers with many traditions, and accounts concerning it'.

40 Nicholas Hawksmoor, Letter to the Earl of Carlisle, 10 November 1727, in Webb, 'Letters and Drawings of Hawksmoor', p. 118.

41 Nicholas Hawksmoor, Letter to the Earl of Carlisle, 11 July 1728, in Webb, 'Letters and Drawings of Hawksmoor', pp. 119–20.

42 Hart, *Rebuilding Ancient Wonders*, pp. 236–7.

43 Wren had also produced a circular design for the library at Trinity College, Cambridge.

44 Nicholas Hawksmoor, Letter to the Earl of Carlisle, 29 March 1729, in Webb, 'Letters and Drawings of Hawksmoor', p. 120.

45 Nicholas Hawksmoor, Letter to the Earl of Carlisle, 4 January 1732, in Webb, 'Letters and Drawings of Hawksmoor', p. 129.

46 Nicholas Hawksmoor, Letter to the Earl of Carlisle, 3 October 1732, in Webb, 'Letters and Drawings of Hawksmoor', p. 133.

47 Noted by Webb, 'Letters and Drawings of Hawksmoor', p. 133.

48 Sir Thomas Robinson, Letter to the Earl of Carlisle, 18 November 1732, in Webb, 'Letters and Drawings of Hawksmoor', p. 133.

49 See Hart, *Rebuilding Ancient Wonders*, pp. 238–41.

50 Hawksmoor, Letter to the Earl of Carlisle, 3 October 1732, in Webb, 'Letters and Drawings of Hawksmoor', p. 136.

51 Endorsement by Lord Carlisle on Hawksmoor's letter to the Earl of Carlisle of 3 October 1732, in Webb, 'Letters and Drawings of Hawksmoor', p. 137.

52 Webb, 'Letters and Drawings of Hawksmoor', p. 141, quoting letters from Sir Thomas Robinson to the Earl of Carlisle of 23 December 1732 and 2 February 1733.

53 In a letter to Etty in June, Hawksmoor sends 'My spouses Love and Service to Mrs Etty Miss Nancy and the same from me to you'. Nicholas

Hawksmoor, Letter to William Etty, 25 June 1734, in Webb, 'Letters and Drawings of Hawksmoor', pp. 146–7.

54 Noted by Webb, 'Letters and Drawings of Hawksmoor', p. 148. Hawksmoor also recommended to Carlisle the qualifications of Etty's son, who was taken on: Letter to the Earl of Carlisle, 6 July 1734, in Webb, 'Letters and Drawings of Hawksmoor', p. 148.

55 Hawksmoor met Hodgeson in London in summer 1734, as noted in Hawksmoor's Letter to the Earl of Carlisle of 13 August 1734, in Webb, 'Letters and Drawings of Hawksmoor', p. 152.

56 Sir Thomas Robinson, Letter to the Earl of Carlisle, 20 July 1734, in Webb, 'Letters and Drawings of Hawksmoor', p. 149.

57 Nicholas Hawksmoor, Letter to the Earl of Carlisle, 1 August 1734, in Webb, 'Letters and Drawings of Hawksmoor', pp. 150–51.

58 Nicholas Hawksmoor, Letter to the Earl of Carlisle, 2 October 1734, in Webb, 'Letters and Drawings of Hawksmoor', p. 154.

59 Nicholas Hawksmoor, Letter to the Earl of Carlisle, 17 February 1736, in Webb, 'Letters and Drawings of Hawksmoor', p. 159. Rip-y was Sir Thomas Ripley.

60 The 'wooden-headed carpenter' was no doubt Thomas Ripley who, Hawksmoor noted, had usurped him at Greenwich. Ripley had apparently begun his career as a carpenter before turning to architecture and had in fact held the post of Master Carpenter in the Office of Works.

61 Nicholas Hawksmoor, Letter to the Earl of Carlisle, 2 March 1736, in Downes, *Hawksmoor*, pp. 260–61.

62 *Grub Street Journal*, 25 March 1736.

63 Hawksmoor's obituary is transcribed by Downes, *Hawksmoor*, pp. 7–8.

64 Suggested by Downes, *Hawksmoor*, p. 229.

65 See Webb, 'Letters and Drawings of Hawksmoor', pp. 159–62.

66 Downes, *Hawksmoor*, p. 230.

67 Nicholas Hawksmoor, Letter to the Earl of Carlisle, 3 June 1728, in Webb, 'Letters and Drawings of Hawksmoor', p. 119.

4 Neglect and Rehabilitation

1 For both quotations see Vaughan Hart, *Nicholas Hawksmoor: Rebuilding Ancient Wonders* (New Haven, CT, and London, 2002), p. 229.

2 Nicholas Hawksmoor, Letter to the Duchess of Marlborough, 17 April 1722, quoted in David Green, *Blenheim Palace* (London, 1951), pp. 309–10.

3 Duchess of Marlborough, Letter to Lord Chief Justice Parker, 23 December 1715, reprinted in Downes, *Hawksmoor*, p . 272.

4 Sir Thomas Robinson, Letter to the Earl of Carlisle, 20 July 1734, in Webb, 'Letters and Drawings of Hawksmoor', p. 149.

5 Arthur Maynwaring, Letter to the Duchess of Marlborough of late 1709, from an excerpt reprinted in Downes, *Hawksmoor*, p. 71. The full letter can be found in *Private Correspondence of the Duchess of Marlborough*, I (London, 1838), p. 266.

6 Sir John Vanbrugh, Letter to Brigadier-General William Watkins in 1721, in *The Complete Works of Sir John Vanbrugh*, vol. IV, *The Letters*, ed. Geoffrey Webb (London, 1927–8), pp. 137–8.

7 Nicholas Hawksmoor, Letter to the Bishop of London, 14 June 1721, quoted by Downes, *Hawksmoor*, p. 98, from the MS (Bodleian, MS. Rawl. B. 376, f. 261).

8 Vertue's transcription appears in his 'Notebooks', *Walpole Society*, XXII (1933–4), pp. 77–8.

9 Horace Walpole, *Anecdotes of Painting in England, with Some Account of the Principal Artists, and Notes on Other Arts; Collected by G. Vertue, Digested from his MSS. by the Honourable Horace Walpole; to Which is Added the History of the Modern Taste in Gardening, With Considerable Additions by the Rev. James Dallaway*, IV (London, 1827), pp. 71–2.

10 Horace Walpole, Letter to George Selwyn of 1772, in Horace Walpole, *The Letters of Horace Walpole: Fourth Earl of Orford, Chronologically Arranged and Edited with Notes and Indices by Mrs Paget Toynbee*, VIII (Oxford, 1904), p. 193. Walpole was less complimentary about Blenheim, describing it as 'execrable within, without & almost all round' and 'a quarry of stone that looked at a distance like a great house'. Letter to George Montagu, 20 May 1736, in *The Letters of Horace Walpole*, I, p. 6.

11 Walpole, *Anecdotes*, p. 73.

12 Ibid., p. 75.

13 Ibid., pp. 73–4.

14 Dallaway, for example, gave all of The Queen's College, Oxford, to Hawksmoor and actually cited it as his best work. This attribution was not to be overturned until well into the twentieth century. See Walpole, *Anecdotes*, p. 74.

15 'Hawksmoor universally mistook whim for genius, and love of ornament for taste'. See James Dallaway, *Observations on English Architecture, Military, Ecclesiastical, and Civil, Compared with Similar Buildings on the Continent: Including a Critical Itinerary of Oxford and Cambridge; and also Historical Notices of Stained Glass, Ornamental Gardening, &c. with Chronological Tables and Dimensions of Cathedral and Conventual Churches* (London, 1806), p. 151.

16   Walpole, *Anecdotes*, p. 74.

17   Not to be confused with his uncle, Sir Charles Lock Eastlake PRA, artist
     and also Keeper of National Gallery.

18   Charles L. Eastlake, *A History of the Gothic Revival edited with an
     Introduction by J. Mordaunt Crook* (Leicester, 1970), p. 34.

19   James Fergusson, *History of the Modern Styles of Architecture*, IV (New York,
     1891), p. 53. The book was first published in London in 1873. Interestingly,
     perhaps referring to the arguments and eventual riots that engulfed the
     church in 1859–60, Fergusson described St George-in-the-East as 'now
     celebrated'. To his eyes, however, it was 'vulgar', adding 'almost every trace of
     Classicality has disappeared, and where the effect is sought to be attained by
     grand massiveness of form and detail'. Fergusson, *History*, p. 54.

20   Eastlake, *Gothic Revival*, p. 54.

21   Joseph Gwilt, 'An Account of the Parish Church of St Mary Woolnoth',
     in *Illustrations of the Public Buildings of London*, ed. Augustus Pugin and
     John Britton, I (London, 1825), p. 90.

22   Ibid., p. 93.

23   H. A., 'Some Account of the Church of St George in the East, near
     Ratcliffe-Highway' in *Illustrations of the Public Buildings of London*, ed.
     Augustus Pugin and John Britton, II (London, 1825), p. 94.

24   Ibid., pp. 94–5.

25   At St George's, Bloomsbury, Malcolm wrote how 'the Attick baffles all
     description: it is the external wall of a prison, set thick with iron-barred
     windows, under one of the clumsiest, yet highly enriched, ceilings in
     Europe'. James Peller Malcolm, *Londinium Redivivum*, II (London,
     1802–7), p. 481.
           As the nineteenth century progressed, more positive remarks on
     Hawksmoor's architecture emerged. Writing in his *Curiosities of London*
     of 1855, John Timbs drew his readers' attention to St George's and its
     'magnificent portico of eight Corinthian columns, which Hawksmoor
     added to his design, influenced by Gibbs's portico at St Martin-in-the-
     Fields, then just completed; but St George's is the better, from its height
     above the level of the street. The church, altogether, is by some considered
     one of the most picturesque in the metropolis'. John Timbs, *The Curiosities
     of London* (London, 1855), p. 127.

26   Malcolm, *Londinium Redivivum*, III, pp. 477–8.

27   Ibid., p. 477.

28   Robert Adam and James Adam, *The Works in Architecture of Robert and
     James Adam edited with an Introduction by Robert Oresko* (London, 1975),
     p. 46, n. 1.

29 Quote from 'The Thirteenth Discourse Delivered to Students of the Royal
Academy on the Distribution of Prizes, December 11, 1786', in Sir Joshua
Reynolds, *The Discourses of Sir Joshua Reynolds*, P.R.A (London, 1924) p.
236. Reynolds also described Vanbrugh in terms of his own expertise as a
painter: 'To speak then of Vanbrugh in the language of a Painter, he had
originality and invention, he understood light and shadow, and had great
skill in composition' (p. 237).

30 Sir John Soane, 'Lecture v, delivered January 1810', in David Watkin, *Sir
John Soane: Enlightenment Thought and the Royal Academy Lectures of Sir
John Soane* (Cambridge, 1996), p. 563.

31 Soane described how the Mausoleum was an instance of the way Vanbrugh
'occasionally felt the force of the simplicity of the ancients'. Soane, 'Lecture
v', p. 563.

32 Sir John Soane, 'Lecture vi, first delivered in 1810', in Watkin, *Sir John
Soane*, p. 571. The statue is of course, George I.

33 Turner was elected Professor of Perspective at the General Assembly of
10 December 1807. See Andrea Fredericksen, 'Royal Academy Perspective
Lectures: Sketchbook, Diagrams and Related Material *c.* 1809–28' (June
2004), revised by David Blayney Brown, in *J.M.W. Turner: Sketchbooks,
Drawings and Watercolours*, ed. David Blayney Brown, at www.tate.org.uk,
accessed 18 March 2014.

34 Noted in Fredericksen, 'Royal Academy Perspective Lectures'.

35 The drawings of St George's, Bloomsbury, are from Turner's *Windmill and
Lock* sketchbook. For the Mausoleum at Halicarnassus drawing (D07973
Turner Bequest CXIV 10) see Matthew Imms, '*Inscription by Turner: Notes on
Ancient Art and Architecture c.* 1808–11 by Joseph Mallord William Turner',
catalogue entry (January 2012), in *J.M.W. Turner: Sketchbooks, Drawings
and Watercolours*, ed. Brown.

36 J.M.W. Turner, 'Royal Academy Lectures' (*c.* 1807–38), quoted by
Andrea Fredericksen, '*Lecture Diagram 6: St George's Church, Bloomsbury,
London c.* 1810 by Joseph Mallord William Turner', catalogue entry
(June 2004), in *J.M.W. Turner: Sketchbooks, Drawings and Watercolours*,
ed. Brown.

37 The catalogue entry quotes Maurice Davies's explanation of the range
of devices employed that 'enables Turner to evoke the feeling of vertigo
experienced when looking up at a high building.' Quoted from Andrea
Fredericksen, '*Lecture Diagram 7: St George's Church, Bloomsbury,
London c.* 1810 by Joseph Mallord William Turner', catalogue entry
(June 2004), in *J.M.W. Turner: Sketchbooks, Drawings and Watercolours*,
ed. Brown.

38 Andrew Wilton, '*Westminster Bridge and Abbey from the North East c.* 1796 by Joseph Mallord William Turner', catalogue entry (April 2012), in *J.M.W. Turner: Sketchbooks, Drawings and Watercolours*, ed. Brown.

39 David Watkin, *The Life and Work of C. R. Cockerell* (London, 1974), p. 144. In 1826 Cockerell produced a drawing of what was possibly an early model of St Anne, Limehouse. The model is lost but the drawing is in the collection of the Victoria & Albert Museum.

40 See ibid., p. 144.

41 Arthur Heygate Mackmurdo, *Wren's City Churches* (Orpington, 1883), p. 56.

42 Ibid., pp. 100–101.

43 Ibid., p. 104 (St Michael, Cornhill); p. 45 (St Vedast, Foster Lane).

44 Ibid., p. 56.

45 *The Builder*, I/19 (17 June 1843), p. 226.

46 For a discussion on Baker's Secretariat buildings, see Robert Grant Irving, *Indian Summer: Lutyens, Baker, and Imperial Delhi* (New Haven, CT, and London, 1981), pp. 282–7. For New Delhi, see Gavin Stamp, 'New Delhi', in *Lutyens: The Work of the English Architect Sir Edwin Lutyens (1869–1944)*, ed. Colin Amery, Margaret Richardson and Gavin Stamp, exh. cat. (London, 1981), pp. 33–43.

47 For a more detailed description of Castle Drogo, see Christopher Hussey, *The Life of Sir Edwin Lutyens* (London, 1950), pp. 217–20.

48 Laurence Whistler, *The Imagination of Vanbrugh and his Fellow Artists* (London, 1954), p. 54.

49 Alan Powers, ed., *H. S. Goodhart-Rendel, 1887–1959* (London, 1987), p. 7.

50 Summerson quote from ibid., p. 7.

51 The book was part of Ernest Benn's Masters of Architecture series, which also included works on Soane, Vanbrugh and Fischer von Erlach.

52 H. S. Goodhart-Rendel, *Nicholas Hawksmoor* (London, 1924), p. 7.

53 Ibid., p. 8.

54 Ibid., p. 12.

55 Ibid., pp. 17–18.

56 Ibid., p. 17.

57 H. S. Goodhart-Rendel, 'The Works of Hawksmoor' (Part One), *Architect & Building News*, CXLV (13 March 1936), p. 346. With Hawksmoor slowly emerging from Wren's shadow, Goodhart-Rendel was also anxious to ensure that he was not then obscured by Vanbrugh's: 'He had not Vanbrugh's scenic imagination, and this perhaps he would occasionally borrow. He had, however, what there is no evidence Vanbrugh had – an extreme sensitiveness to the emotional significance of forms delicately adjusted, and a very complete architectural technique.'

58 Ibid., p. 347.

59 Goodhart-Rendel, 'The Works of Hawksmoor' (Part Two), *Architect & Building News*, CXLV (20 March 1936), p. 373.

60 Goodhart-Rendel, 'The Works of Hawksmoor' (Part Four), *Architect & Building News*, CXLVI (3 April 1936), p. 19.

61 H. Avray Tipping and Christopher Hussey, *English Homes: Architecture from Medieval Times to the Early Part of the Nineteenth Century, Period IV*, vol. II: *The Work of Sir John Vanbrugh and his School, 1699–1736* (London, 1928), p. xxiii.

62 Then Architectural Editor at *Country Life*, Tipping was something of a mentor to the young Hussey. Later, Hussey would succeed Tipping in his role at *Country Life* and perhaps do more than anyone else to further the understanding of the English landscape garden, especially those of the Regency period. For the moment, however, in this field at least, it seems Hussey was largely happy to follow Tipping's lead. The section of Hawksmoor in *English Homes* is closely based on a lecture Tipping gave to the London Society in 1927, which was soon after printed in the RIBA Journal. H. Avray Tipping, 'Nicholas Hawksmoor', *RIBA Journal*, XXXIV/18 (13 August 1927), pp. 619–27; and also XXXIV/19 (17 September 1927), pp. 647–54.

63 Tipping and Hussey, *English Homes,* p. xxiii.

64 Tipping, 'Nicholas Hawksmoor', p. 622.

65 Arthur T. Bolton and H. Duncan Hendry, eds, 'The Royal Hospital for Seamen at Greenwich, 1694–1728', *Wren Society*, IV (Oxford, 1929), p. 12.

66 Arthur T. Bolton and H. Duncan Hendry, eds, 'The Royal Palaces of Winchester, Whitehall, Kensington, and St. James', *Wren Society*, VII (Oxford, 1930), p. 5.

67 Arthur T. Bolton and H. Duncan Hendry, eds, 'The Parochial Churches of Sir Christopher Wren, 1666–1718', *Wren Society*, IX (Oxford, 1932), unpaginated frontmatter.

68 See Arthur T. Bolton and H. Duncan Hendry, eds, 'Designs and Drawings Supplementary to Volume XII', *Wren Society*, XVII (Oxford, 1940), pp. 1–15.

69 The publication of the Wren Society volumes was reported in *The Spectator* (24 January 1925), p. 17.

70 John Betjeman, 'Obituary of H. S. Goodhart-Rendel', *RIBA Journal*, LXVI (1959), p. 406.

71 For more on Goodhart-Rendel's notion of style, see Powers, *Goodhart-Rendel*, p. 8.

72 H. S. Goodhart-Rendel, 'The Works of Hawksmoor' (Part Three), *Architect & Building News*, CXLV (27 March 1936), p. 408.

73 Goodhart-Rendel, 'The Works of Hawksmoor' (Part Three), p. 408.
    Several others remarked on St Mary Woolnoth around this time. For
    Herbert Reynolds, writing in 1922, 'The design of the church suggested
    a continuation of the scheme of his master in the building of St. Paul's.
    This is the only church in the City which presents the solid and substantial
    appearance of the cathedral . . . It is considered a building of great merit,
    both externally and internally, and possesses some handsome wood carving.'
    See Herbert Reynolds, *The Churches of the City of London* (London, 1922),
    p. 128. Referring surely to the church's interior, rather than its exterior,
    E. V. Lucas described it as 'light, almost gay. The black woodwork and
    the coloured walls have a pleasant effect'; see his *E. V. Lucas's London*
    (London, 1926), p. 201.

74 See Downes, *Hawksmoor*, pp. 189–94, especially p. 192.

75 John Timbs, *The Curiosities of London* (London, 1885), p. 189.

76 Mackmurdo, *Wren's City Churches*, pp. iii–iv.

77 David Lawrence, *Underground Architecture* (Harrow, 1994), p. 20.

78 House of Commons (HC) Debate (DEB), 24 April 1896, vol. XXIX, col. 1615.

79 House of Lords (HL) Debate, 6 August 1896, vol. XLIII, col. 1557.

80 Ibid., cols 1557–8.

81 HC DEB, 12 August 1896, vol XLIV, cols 578–83.

82 Ibid., cols 578–79

83 Ibid., col. 579.

84 Ibid., col. 580.

85 Ibid., col. 756.

86 Lawrence, *Underground Architecture*, p. 23.

87 Goodhart-Rendel, *Hawksmoor*, p. 24.

88 They remain visible on F. R. Yerbury's original photograph.

89 City of London Churches Commission, *Report of the City of London
    Churches Commission, 1919* (London, 1919), p. 6.

90 Ibid., p. 7.

91 Ibid., p. 8.

92 Ibid., pp. 10, 12.

93 Ibid., p. 14.

94 London County Council, *Proposed Demolition of Nineteen City Churches*
    (London, 1920), preface unpaginated.

95 Ibid., pp. 22, 23.

96 Ibid. p. 30.

97 *The Spectator* (11 October 1919), p. 13.

98 '"Save the Lot": City Club's Protest Against Demolition of Churches',
    The Times (15 June 1920), p. 13.

99 See 'Coverdale's Church: Appeal to the Bishop of London', *The Times* (15 September 1920), p. 13.

100 HL DEB, 15 July 1926, vol. LXIV, cols 1171–2.

101 Ibid., col. 1172.

102 Ibid., col. 1173.

103 Ibid., col. 1179.

104 Ibid., col. 1185.

105 'The Fate of the City Churches', *The Times* (25 November 1926), p. 15.

106 'The Threat to the City Churches: Today's Debate', *The Times* (25 November 1926), p. 18.

107 HC DEB, 25 November 1926, vol. CC, cols 673–708. Cecil's remark is at col. 681.

108 Christopher Hussey, 'The Menace to the City Churches', *Country Life* (13 November 1926), p. 742.

109 *The Builder*, XX/1018 (9 August 1862), p. 562.

110 Ibid., pp. 562–3.

111 RIBA *Journal*, XXVIII (27 June 1921), p. 485.

112 Ibid., p. 486.

5 INTO THE LIGHT

1 T. S. Eliot, 'The Waste Land', in *The Annotated Waste Land with Eliot's Contemporary Prose*, ed. Lawrence Rainey (New Haven, CT, and London, 2006), p. 59.

2 The 'Unreal City' passage, like the rest of the poem, is composed of fragments: from Eliot's own experience and also from literature, here, Dante's *Inferno*. See Rainey, ed., *Annotated Waste Land*, p. 84.

3 Ibid., p. 9.

4 These were most often of a vaguely neo-Baroque character, reflecting the general revival of interest in Wren's architecture. However, despite the relatively traditional Baroque styling, the white Portland stone frontages of these huge monoliths usually disguised their modern, rectilinear steel frame construction.

5 The autobiographical, even confessional, qualities of the poem are often noted. See Lyndall Gordon, *The Imperfect Life of T. S. Eliot* (London, 2012), pp. 144–5.

6 T. S. Eliot, 'Notes to "The Waste Land"', in Rainey, ed., *Annotated Waste Land*, p. 71.

7 Quoted in Barry Spurr, *Anglo-Catholic in Religion: T. S. Eliot and Christianity* (Cambridge, 2010), p. 36. Like St Mary Woolnoth, St Magnus was directly referred to in the House of Lords debates of July 1926. One

particularly fascinating mention, which included reference to *The Waste Land*, came from Sydney Olivier, 1st Baron Olivier, the former civil servant and leading Fabian, whose nephew, Laurence, would become famous as the greatest actor of his generation:

> I do not know whether your Lordships have read a recent poem called 'The Waste Land' by one of our modern poets, dealing with the ghastly aspect of our modern civilisation. One of the little oases of that civilisation is in Thames Street – 'Where the walls of Magnus Martyr hold Inexplicable splendour of Ionian white and gold.' The splendour and effect of these architectural works of art are inexplicable and cannot be reproduced. (HL DEB, 19 July 1926, vol. LXV, col. 39)

8 Harold P. Clunn, *The Face of London: The Record of a Century's Changes and Development* (London, 1932), p. 42.

9 Evelyn Waugh, *Scoop* (London, 2000), p. 5. *The Mystery of Dr Fu-Manchu* was first published in 1913 and was followed by a number of sequels that continued to appear well into the 1950s.

10 Christy Anderson, 'War Work: English Art and the Warburg Institute', *Common Knowledge*, XVIII/1 (2012), p. 149.

11 Ibid., p. 150. The exhibition was published as a book, *British Art and the Mediterranean* (1948).

12 John Summerson, *Georgian London* (London, 1945), p. v.

13 Ibid., pp. 1–2.

14 Ibid., p. 73.

15 Ibid., pp. 73–4.

16 Ibid., p. 74.

17 Ibid., p. 76.

18 See Sacheverell Sitwell, *British Architects and Craftsmen: A Survey of Taste, Design and Style during Three Centuries, 1600 to 1830* (London, 1960), pp. 15–16.

19 Ibid., p. 164.

20 Ibid, pp. 166–8.

21 H. M. Colvin, 'Fifty New Churches', *Architectural Review*, CVII (March 1950), pp. 189–96. Other notable articles were S. Lang, 'Cambridge and Oxford Replanned: Hawksmoor as a Town-Planner', *Architectural Review*, CIII/616 (April 1948), pp. 157–60; and S. Lang, 'By Hawksmoor out of Gibbs', *Architectural Review*, CV/628 (April 1949), pp. 183–90. Lang's article on Hawksmoor's town plans perhaps provided the inspiration for a small

book of very limited print run that appeared in 1955, which included eight drawings by Gordon Cullen of views of Cambridge as it was then and as it might have been if Hawksmoor's plan had been realized. Cullen was one of the leading lights around this time of the emerging 'townscape' movement that sought to integrate an appreciation of visual effects of the environments of towns and cities into thinking about planning. See David Roberts, *The Town of Cambridge as it ought to be Reformed: The Plan of Nicholas Hawksmoor interpreted in an Essay by David Roberts; and a Set of Eight Drawings by Gordon Cullen* (Cambridge, 1955).

22 See Howard Colvin, 'Writing a Biographical Dictionary of British Architects', in *Essays in English Architectural History*, ed. Howard Colvin (New Haven, CT, 1999), pp. 292–7.

23 H. M. Colvin, *A Biographical Dictionary of English Architects, 1660–1840* (London, 1954), p. 273.

24 H. M. Colvin, *A Biographical Dictionary of British Architects, 1600–1840*, 4th edn (New Haven, CT, and London, 2008), p. 497.

25 The following quotations from Kerry Downes are from two letters written to the author of 26 October and 8 November 2013.

26 Downes's account of discovering Christ Church appears in *Columns* (newsletter of the Friends of Christ Church Spitalfields), XXI (Autumn 2003), pp. 2–3.

27 Jonathan Glancey, 'Borromini: The First Architect', *The Guardian* (5 February 2011), www.theguardian.com, accessed 19 July 2014.

28 *English Art, 1625–1714* was published in 1957 as part of the Oxford History of English Art series. Margaret Whinney published an important book on Wren in 1971.

29 Kerry Downes, 'Introduction', in *The Architectural Outsiders*, ed. Roderick Brown (London, 1985), pp. ix–x.

30 For a more detailed account, see 'A History of the Courtauld', www.courtauld.ac.uk/about/history.shtml, accessed 19 July 2014.

31 Downes, 'Introduction', p. x.

32 Kerry Downes, *Hawksmoor* (London, 1959), pp. xv–xvi.

33 The following passage is indebted to 'Obituary: Desmond Zwemmer', *The Guardian* (21 September 2000), www.theguardian.com.

34 For a full history of Zwemmer, see Nigel Vaux Halliday, *More than a Bookshop: Zwemmer's and Art in the 20th Century* (London, 2001).

35 Downes, *Hawksmoor*, p. 233.

36 Elizabeth Young and Wayland Young, *Old London Churches* (London, 1956), p. 112.

37 Ibid., p. 284.

38 Ibid., p. 287.

39 Ibid., pp. 283–4.

40 Michael White, 'Obituary: Lord Kennet', *The Guardian* (12 May 2009), www.theguardian.com, accessed 19 July 2014.

41 Any subsequent quotations from Elizabeth Young which are unreferenced derive from an interview conducted with the author on 26 March 2013.

42 Elizabeth Young, 'The Campaigns for Christ Church, Spitalfields and Nicholas Hawksmoor, 1960–1995', *Journal of Architectural Conservation*, 11 (July 1996), p. 25.

43 Elizabeth Young, 'The Churches of Nicholas Hawksmoor', *The Guardian* (1 April 1961).

44 W. S. Allam, Letter to Elizabeth Young of 14 Feb 1961. This and subsequent correspondence involving Elizabeth Young is quoted from the uncatalogued personal archives of Elizabeth Young unless it is stated as coming from the Arts Council archive.

45 Elizabeth Young, Letter to W. S. Allam, 15 February 1961.

46 Elizabeth Young, Letter to W. S. Allam, 9 March 1961.

47 W. S. Allam, Letter to Elizabeth Young, 15 March 1961.

48 Elizabeth Young, Letter to William Emrys Williams, 4 October 1961.

49 Elizabeth Young, Letter to Gabriel White, 8 January 1962. The Royal Exchange and RIBA were also considered as possible venues, but neither was thought ideal. The Hawksmoor Committee was keen that the exhibition travel abroad, as David Thomas reported in a 'Note on Meeting of Hawksmore Committee' of 2 February 1962, which he sent to Gabriel White three days later: 'They want to do a U.S. tour after ours. I said we couldn't help' (Arts Council archive, ACGB/121/496, Hawksmoor Exhibition 1962).

50 David Thomas, Letter to Elizabeth Young, 5 March 1962.

51 The exhibition ended up costing £906, which was £45 less than was budgeted. Admissions raised £131 against £100 budgeted. See Arts Council report of 27 November 1962 (Arts Council archive ACGB/121/496, Hawksmoor Exhibition 1962).

52 David Thomas, Letter to Elizabeth Young, 18 June 1962; see also Gabriel White, Letter to Kerry Downes of 24 September 1962, in which he enclosed a cheque for £40 (Arts Council archive). Davies was paid the same amount. Kerry Downes had previously offered to put his fee towards the cost of the exhibition (see Kerry Downes, Letter to David Thomas, 9 July 1962, Arts Council archive).

53 The exhibition catalogue actually sold out. See Elizabeth Young, Letter to Sybil Fenn, 11 October 1962, in which she thanked her for sending a copy of the catalogue (Arts Council archive).

54 Young, 'The Campaigns', p. 25.

55 Kenneth Clark, Letter to Elizabeth Young, 21 July 1962, and Denys Lasdun, Letter to Elizabeth Young, 30 July 1962.

56 Lewis Mumford, Letter to Elizabeth Young, 5 August 1962.

57 T. S. Eliot, Letter to Elizabeth Young, 1 August 1962.

58 Letter to *The Times* (24 September 1962), p. 11. The letter was sent on 20 September. Elizabeth Young had written to J. M. Richards on 17 September enquiring whether he might be able to engineer a leader in *The Times*. He replied on 19 September to say 'I will then put in a word for it' but added 'the Times has been having so many letters appealing for funds to save old buildings that the Editor has become somewhat resistant to them'.

59 Elizabeth Young, Letter to David Thomas, 20 September 1962 (Arts Council archive).

60 Davies's talk was given on 15 May 1962. It also appeared in print: J.H.V. Davies, 'Nicholas Hawksmoor', RIBA Journal, LXIX (October 1962), pp. 368–75. John Betjeman article in the *Daily Express* (12 March 1962), quoted in Young, 'The Campaigns', p. 27.

61 *Vogue* (November 1962), pp. 63–9, quoted in Young, 'The Campaigns', p. 28.

62 *The Guardian* (7 September 1962), quoted in Young, 'The Campaigns', p. 28.

63 HC DEB, 1 August 1966, vol. DCCXXXIII, cols 7–8, quoted in Young, 'The Campaigns', pp. 28–9.

64 Report of the Archbishops' Commission on Redundant Churches (1960), p. 125.

65 Charles Dickens, *Our Mutual Friend* [1864–5] (Ware, 1997), p. 199.

66 Pamela Bennetts, Letter to Elizabeth Young, 27 November 1964.

67 The Ven. M. M. Hodgins, Letter to Elizabeth Young, 18 January 1965.

68 Elizabeth Young, Letter to Ivor Bulmer-Thomas, 9 November 1965.

69 Elizabeth Young, Letter to Pamela Bennetts, 8 June 1967, which included a cheque for £2,000.

70 Pamela Bennetts, Letter to Elizabeth Young, 28 March 1968.

71 See Gillian Darley and David McKie, *Ian Nairn: Words in Place* (Nottingham, 2013).

72 Ian Nairn, *Nairn's London* (London, 1966), pp. 25–6.

73 Ibid., p. 163.

74 Ibid., p. 168.

75 Ibid., pp. 161–2.

76 Ibid., pp. 112–13.

77 Alison and Peter Smithson, 'The Space Between', *Oppositions*, IV (1974), p. 77; Alison and Peter Smithson, 'House at Watford, Herts', *Architectural Review*, CXXII/728 (September 1957), p. 194.

78 Wölfflin's *Renaissance and Baroque* was first published in English in 1964. Several of his other works had appeared in English much earlier. Judith Hook, *The Baroque Age in England* (London, 1976) followed Downes's book of ten years previously and widened its scope.

79 Downes, *Hawksmoor* (1969), p. 7.

80 Promotional leaflet published by the The Hawksmoor Committee (1962), unpaginated.

81 The exhibition was organized by June Roberts. See Douglas Inger, (Bassetlaw District Council, Leisure Services Officer), Letter to the Arts Council, 10 April 1974 (Arts Council archive); also Paul Overy, 'Hawksmoor's Neglected Churches', *The Times* (29 March 1977).

82 See Gabriel White, Letter to Kerry Downes, 11 October 1962 (Arts Council archive).

83 Nicholas Serota, Letter to Kerry Downes, 16 November 1976 (Whitechapel Gallery archive, WAG /EXH/2/26/1; all subsequent references prefaced WAG are from the Whitechapel Gallery).

84 This and any subsequent quotations from Nicholas Serota which are unreferenced derive from a telephone interview with the author on 1 May 2014.

85 They did in fact try to get the models of Hawksmoor's designs for King's College, Cambridge, but they proved too delicate to travel as Professor Sir Edmund Leach, the Provost of King's, reported in a letter to Serota: 'I am afraid there is no possibility at all that you might be allowed to borrow the two wooden models for Hawksmoor's Fellows' buildings.' He had had a report from Professor Jaffé, who noted that they were 'extremely fragile. The glue has dried out. Quite a number of bits have fallen off them; and some are missing.' Edmund Leach, Letter to Nicholas Serota, 4 February 1977 (WAG/EXH/2/26/1).

86 The doorcase actually ended up at Castle Howard having been purchased by George Howard. See Joudy Sladden (secretary to George Howard), Letter to Susan Bolsom (exhibition co-ordinator), 19 August 1977 (WAG/EXH/2/261/31).

87 M. F. Levey (publicity officer for London Transport), Letter to Nicholas Serota, 7 February 1977 (WAG/EXH/2/261/31).

88 Hawksmoor was one of nine historical figures to be included. The others were Emma, Lady Hamilton; Albert, Prince Consort; Elizabeth Barrett Browning; Francis Bacon; Samuel Richardson; Daniel Defoe; Edward Boscawen; and Albert Chevalier.

89 Nicholas Serota, Letter to exhibition lenders, 23 May 1977 (WAG/EXH/2/26/1).

90 Marina Vaizey, 'And Landscape was Created', *Sunday Times* (17 March 1977).

91 Barbara Wright, 'London Reviews', *Arts Review* (15 April 1977), p. 246.

92 John Summerson, 'Review of the Nicholas Hawksmoor Exhibition', in *Kaleidoscope*, presented by Michael Oliver, broadcast on BBC Radio Four, 9.30 pm, 27 March 1977.

93 Trevor Dannatt, Letter to Nicholas Serota, 8 April 1977 (WAG/EXH/2/261/31): 'I am doing my best to get someone in Manchester [school of architecture] interested in the Hawksmoor exhibition. I hope I have success, but I probably won't owing to the holiday'. He also mentioned the security issue with having original drawings, so in the end they were shown in the exhibition as reproductions.

6 Rebirth

1 John Summerson, 'St. George's-in-the-East: An Obituary Note by John Summerson', *Architectural Review*, XC (November 1941), p. 135.

2 Ibid., p. 136.

3 Elizabeth Young and Wayland Young, *Old London Churches* (London, 1956), p. 287.

4 This was reported by J. M. Richards, 'New Structure within Burnt-out Shell', *The Times* (2 September 1959).

5 The following passage derives from my work cataloguing the St George-in-the-East drawings in the archive of Ansell & Bailey.

6 Maxwell Fry, *Autobiographical Sketches* (London, 1975), p. 153.

7 This point is made by Alan Powers, 'Conservative Attitudes: Walter Gropius in Cambridge and Maxwell Fry in Oxford', in *Oxford and Cambridge, Twentieth Century Architecture 11*, ed. Elain Harwood, Alan Powers and Otto Saumarez Smith (London, 2013), p. 74; see also Howard Colvin, *Unbuilt Oxford* (London, 1983).

8 This, of course, had intriguing parallels with Hawksmoor's own ideas, as noted by the present incumbent, Canon Michael Ainsworth, on the church's excellent website, www.stgite.org.uk, accessed 22 July 2014.

9 See Adrian Barrick, 'Hawksmoor Church to House Theatre in Revitalisation Plan', *Building Design* (2 February 1990), p. 5; and Jonathan Glancey, 'Reusing St George for Modern Times', *The Independent* (9 October 1991).

10 The following account derives from 'Christ Church: Historical Account', *Survey of London*, vol. XXVII: *Spitalfields and Mile End New Town* (1957), pp. 148–69, www.british-history.ac.uk, accessed 21 May 2014.

11 For more detail on the history of the latter, see Bridget Cherry, Charles O'Brien and Nikolaus Pevsner, *London 5: East – The Buildings of England* (New Haven, CT, and London, 2007), pp. 531–3.

12 Gordon Cullen was the early exception with his drawings that accompanied David Roberts's essay in *The Town of Cambridge as it Ought to be Reformed*, published in 1955, all about how Hawksmoor's interventions in Cambridge would have look and felt like in the urban environment.

13 Denys Lasdun, 'Royal Gold Medal Address', RIBA *Journal*, LXXXIV (September 1977), p. 366.

14 This idea derives from William J. R. Curtis, *Denys Lasdun: Architecture, City, Landscape* (London, 1994), p. 77.

15 Denys Lasdun, 'Notes for a Lecture on Hawksmoor' (1991), reprinted ibid., p. 223.

16 Robert Venturi, *Complexity and Contradiction in Architecture* (London, 2nd edn, 1977), p. 16.

17 Robert Venturi, 'Architecture as Sign rather than Space: New Mannerism Rather than Old Expressionism', in *Architecture as Signs and Symbols: For a Mannerist Time*, ed. Robert Venturi and Denise Scott Brown (Cambridge, MA, and London, 2004), p. 81.

18 Venturi, *Complexity and Contradiction*, p. 23.

19 Ibid., p. 25.

20 Ibid., p. 28.

21 Ibid., p. 30.

22 Ibid., p. 32.

23 Michael Graves, 'Life Class: Michael Graves', *Building Design* (14 April 2011), www.bdonline.co.uk. Graves also named the Swedish architect Gunnar Asplund.

24 Mark Girouard, *Big Jim: The Life and Work of James Stirling* (London, 1998), pp. 64–7; and *Columns* (newsletter of the Friends of Christ Church Spitalfields), 1 (Autumn 1994).

25 Sarah Menin and Stephen Kite, *An Architecture of Invitation: Colin St John Wilson* (London, 2005), p. 141. The idea actually dated back to the Royal Academy's Plan for London in 1942.

26 This and any subsequent quotations from Michael Wilford which are unreferenced are from a telephone interview with the author on 3 April 2014.

27 James Stirling, 'Acceptance of the Royal Gold Medal in Architecture 1980', *Stirling Gold AD Profile 144, Architectural Design*, L/7–8 (1980), p. 6.

28 Girouard, *Big Jim*, p. 295.

29 The exhibition, curated by Anthony Vidler, was entitled *Notes from the Archive: James Frazer Stirling*. As well as Tate Britain it was also shown at the Canadian Centre for Architecture.

30 Donations towards the church's restoration were asked in lieu of flowers at the memorial service. Stirling's ashes were cast in the churchyard. See *Columns*, 1 (Autumn 1994).

31 David Buckman, *From Bow to Biennale: Artists of the East London Group* (London, 2012).

32 The Gentle Author, 'Roland Collins, Artist', *Spitalfields Life* (11 June 2013), www.spitalfieldslife.com.

33 *Desert Island Discs: John Piper*, broadcast on Radio Four, 10 December 1983.

34 The Gentle Author, 'Anthony Eyton, Artist', *Spitalfields Life* (28 April 2011), www.spitalfieldslife.com.

35 Quotation from notes on Hawksmoor prepared by Anthony Eyton for the exhibition *Nicholas Hawksmoor: Architect of the Imagination*, Royal Academy of Arts, London (4 February–17 June 2012).

36 Quote from Stuart Jeffries, 'On the Road', *The Guardian* (24 April 2004), www.theguardian.com.

37 Iain Sinclair, video interview with Owen Hopkins for the exhibition *Nicholas Hawksmoor: Architect of the Imagination*, Royal Academy of Arts, London (4 February–17 June 2012).

38 A gruesome case in point can be found in a description by the historian James Peller Malcolm, from 1807, of how the burial ground to the north of St Anne's 'was violated very lately, in order to obtain a more convenient line for the new Commercial road to Blackwall'. As a consequence, the 'mouldering bones and decaying corpses . . . [were] raised from their graves and carried to the South church-yard, where they were reinterred'. 'How much more rational', Malcom asked, 'to suffer carts and waggons to pass over our relations four or five feet above them, than thus to disturb and mutilate the dead!'; see James Peller Malcolm, *Londinium Redivivum*, II (London, 1803), p. 84.

39 Quote from Jeffries, 'On the Road'.

40 Iain Sinclair, *Lud Heat: A Book of the Dead Hamlets, May 1974 to April 1975* (Cheltenham, 2012), p. 15.

41 For this and following quotations in the paragraph, see Sinclair, *Lud Heat*, pp. 23, 24.

42 Ibid., pp. 17, 28, 29.

43 Ibid., pp. 17, 22, 28.

44 Dickens, *Our Mutual Friend* [1864–5] (Ware, 1997), p. 330.

45 Sinclair, video interview for *Nicholas Hawksmoor: Architect of the Imagination*.

46 Sinclair, *Lud Heat*, pp. 16–17.

47 Quote from Jeffries, 'On the Road'.

48 Sinclair, video interview for *Nicholas Hawksmoor: Architect of the Imagination.*

49 Ibid.

50 Peter Ackroyd, *Hawksmoor* (London, 2010), Acknowledgements, unpaginated. In a BBC World Service interview Ackroyd has recalled how he 'first became acquainted with Hawksmoor's work and reputation when I read a very strange and powerful poem by a gentleman called Iain Sinclair entitled "Lud Heat".' This and subsequent unreferenced quotations from Ackroyd are from *Peter Ackroyd: Hawksmoor*, broadcast on BBC World Service, 6 May 2012.

51 Ackroyd, *Hawksmoor*, p. 9.

52 Pat Rogers, 'Street Wise', *London Review of Books*, VII/17 (3 October 1985).

53 John Summerson, Letter to Gavin Stamp, 2 October 1986, from the personal archive of Gavin Stamp.

54 Gavin Stamp, 'The Real Hawksmoor', *The Spectator* (29 March 1986), pp. 35–6.

55 John O'Mahony, 'London Calling: Peter Ackroyd', *The Guardian* (3 July 2004). It was perhaps for that reason that Ackroyd dedicated the book to Giles Gordon, his long-standing agent.

56 This and subsequent unreferenced quotations from McFadyen are from an interview conducted by the author on 27 March 2014.

57 The pub was the Five Bells & Blade Bone on Three Colt Street, which is now 5B Urban Bar. The bus stop was the same one that Iain Sinclair recalls seeing Francis Bacon standing at while he worked as a gardener in the 1970s. Bacon lived nearby and 'stood at this bus stop everyday and resolutely kept his back to St Anne's Limehouse, staring out at the road . . . I was waiting for him one day to start painting this building, but, no, it didn't register'.

58 Charlotte Higgins, 'Leon Kossoff's Love Affair with London', *The Guardian* (27 April 2013).

59 Quoted by Tom Overton, 'Leon Kossoff (1926)', *British Pavilion in Venice*, http://venicebiennale.britishcouncil.org, accessed 31 May 2014.

60 An observation made by Overton, 'Leon Kossoff (1926)'.

61 Jack London, *People of the Abyss* (New York, 1995; photo-offset of the original 1903 version), p. 64.

62 *Imagining Hawksmoor*, Royal Academy Forum event, held on 27 February 2012.

63 Evelyn Waugh, *Brideshead Revisited* (London, 1962), p. 79. The television series is remarkably close to Waugh's dialogue, at times using it verbatim.

Here, the only major change was swapping the book's reference to Inigo Jones for Vanbrugh to reflect the setting of Castle Howard.

64 This and subsequent unreferenced quotations from Amery are from an interview conducted by the author on 4 June 2014.

65 The Revd Eddy Stride, 'Postscript' to *Hawksmoor's Christ Church Spitalfields* AD *Profile 22, Architectural Design*, XLIX/7 (1980), p. 32.

66 Spitalfields resident Fay Catinni explains where the newspapers came from in the early 1970s: 'The church then seemed to be used as a storage place and I remember it was full of mattresses and things. When the bellringers asked if they could sell the old bells and replace them, they collected newspapers to sell and when the paper market prices slumped the piles of newspapers rose in the church.' Fay Catinni, 'Spitalfields: A Recollection', *Columns* (newsletter of the Friends of Christ Church Spitalfields), XII (Summer 1999), p. 7.

67 The Gentle Author, 'Irene Stride Remembers Spitalfields', *Spitalfields Life* (21 November 2013), www.spitalfieldslife.com.

68 Suzanne Lang and Alan Colquhoun, letter to *The Times* (11 June 1975).

69 Trevor Huddleston, Bishop of Stepney, letter to *The Times* (14 June 1975).

70 This was noted by Jonathan Balkind, letter to *The Times* (21 April 1977).

71 This and subsequent quotations from Mason are from an interview with the author conducted on 30 May 2014.

72 Another particularly important one was regarding the organ gallery and whether or not it was moved in the nineteenth century.

73 This episode naturally caught the imagination of the mainstream press. It is described in greater detail by Tim Ostler, 'Laying Bare the Bones', *Building Design Supplement*, DCCCXCIX (August 1988), pp. 16–19.

74 See Jeanette Winterson, 'Spitalfields', www.jeanettewinterson.com, accessed 22 July 2014; and Deyan Sudjic, 'Generation Gap Opens in Battle for Spitalfields', *The Observer* (2 December 2001), www.theguardian.com.

7 HAWKSMOOR TODAY

1 The sketches appeared in periodicals 1833–6, with the first book published in 1836 and the second in 1837. See Charles Dickens, *Sketches by Boz: Illustrative of Every-day life and Every-day People*, introduction by Thea Holme (Oxford, 1991).

2 'Care for St Anne's', www.stanneslimehouse.org, accessed 21 July 2014.

3 Interview with Biba Dow and Alun Jones conducted by the author on 15 May 2014.

4   Sam Jacob, 'Hawksmoor Undone', course outline, the School of
    Architecture at the University of Illinois at Chicago.

5   Interview with Alex Scott-Whitby conducted by the author on 2 July
    2014.

6   *Bunkers, Brutalism and Bloodymindedness: Concrete Poetry with Jonathan
    Meades*, episode one, first broadcast on BBC Four, 9 pm, 16 February 2014.

7   Richard MacCormac, *Columns* (newsletter of the Friends of Christ Church
    Spitalfields), XVI (Summer 2001).

8   Alan Moore and Eddie Campbell, *From Hell* [1999] (London, 2010).
    The graphic novel was made into a film of the same name, starring Johnny
    Depp, in 2001.

9   A confirmation of Hawksmoor's part in the architectural establishment is
    an episode in Alan Bennett's play *The History Boys*, when, during university
    interview practice, the teacher, Mrs Lintott, asks Akhtar about his interest
    in architecture. 'Who is your favourite architect?' she asks. Akhtar replies,
    'Richard Rogers.' 'I was thinking more along Wren–Hawksmoor lines.
    Richard Rogers? Doesn't he write musicals?' See Alan Bennett, *The History
    Boys* (London, 2004), p. 82.

10 *Imagining Hawksmoor*, Royal Academy Forum event, 27 February 2012.

11 Jo Noero, email to the author, 5 May 2014.

Select Bibliography

Ackroyd, Peter, *Hawksmoor* (London, 1985)

Bolton, Arthur T., and H. Duncan Henry, eds, *The Wren Society*, vols I–XX (Oxford, 1924–43)

Cast, David, 'Seeing Vanbrugh and Hawksmoor', *Journal of the Society of Architectural Historians*, XLIII (1984), pp. 310–27

Colvin, H. M., 'Fifty New Churches', *Architectural Review*, CVII (1950), pp. 189–96

—, *Unbuilt Oxford* (London, 1983)

Curtis, William J. R., *Denys Lasdun: Architecture, City, Landscape* (London, 1994)

Downes, Kerry, *Hawksmoor* (London, 1959, revd 1979)

—, *Hawksmoor*, World of Art series (London, 1969)

—, *Vanbrugh* (London, 1977)

Du Prey, Pierre de la Ruffinière, *Hawksmoor's London Churches: Architecture and Theology* (London, 2000)

Geraghty, Anthony, 'Nicholas Hawksmoor and the Wren City Church Steeples', *The Georgian Group Journal*, X (2000), pp. 1–14

—, 'Nicholas Hawksmoor's Drawing Technique of the 1690s and John Locke's "Essay Concerning Human Understanding"', in *Rethinking the Baroque*, ed. Helen Hills (Aldershot, 2011), pp. 125–41

Girouard, Mark, *Big Jim: The Life and Work of James Stirling* (London, 1998)

Goodhart-Rendel, H. S., *Nicholas Hawksmoor* (London, 1924)

—, 'The Works of Hawksmoor', *The Architect & Building News*, CXLV (13 March 1936), pp. 346–8; CXLV (20 March 1936), pp. 371–3; CXLV (27 March 1936), pp. 408–10; CXLVI (3 April 1936), pp. 18–19

Hawksmoor, Nicholas, *Remarks on the Founding and Carrying on the Building of the Royal Hospital Greenwich* (London, 1728)

—, *A Short Historical Account of London-Bridge with A Proposition for a New Stone-Bridge at Westminster* (London, 1736)

Higgott, Gordon, 'The Revised Design for St Paul's Cathedral, 1685–90: Wren, Hawksmoor and Les Invalides', *Burlington Magazine*, CXLVI (2004), pp. 534–47

—, *St Paul's Cathedral Wren Office Drawings Catalogue* (2013), www.stpauls.co.uk, accessed 6 July 2014

McKellar, Elizabeth, *The Birth of Modern London: The Development and Design of the City, 1660–1720* (Manchester and New York, 1999)

Nairn, Ian, *Nairn's London* (London, 1966)

Powers, Alan, ed., *H. S. Goodhart-Rendel, 1887–1959* (London, 1987)

Rainey, Lawrence, ed., *The Annotated 'Waste Land' with Eliot's Contemporary Prose* (New Haven, CT, and London, 2006)

Ralph, James, *A Critical Review of the Publick Buildings, Statues and Ornaments in, and about London and Westminster* (London, 1734)

Sinclair, Iain, *London Orbital* (London, 2003)

—, *Lud Heat: A Book of the Dead Hamlets – May 1974 to April 1975* [1975] (Cheltenham, 2012)

Soo, Lydia M., *Wren's 'Tracts' on Architecture and Other Writings* (Cambridge, 1998)

Summerson, John, *Georgian London* (London, 1945)

Tipping, H. Avray, and Christopher Hussey, *English Homes: Architecture from Medieval Times to the Early Part of the Nineteenth Century, Period* IV: vol. II: *The Work of Sir John Vanbrugh and his School, 1699–1736* (London, 1928)

Venturi, Robert, *Complexity and Contradiction in Architecture* (London, 1977)

Walpole, Horace, *Anecdotes of Painting in England, with Some Account of the Principal Artists, and Notes on Other Arts; Collected by G. Vertue, Digested from his* MSS *by the Honourable Horace Walpole; to which is added the History of the Modern Taste in Gardening. With Considerable Additions by the Rev. James Dallaway*, IV (London, 1827)

Watkin, David, *The Life and Work of C. R. Cockerell* (London, 1974)

—, *Sir John Soane: Enlightenment Thought and the Royal Academy Lectures of Sir John Soane* (Cambridge, 1996)

Webb, Geoffrey, 'The Letters and Drawings of Nicholas Hawksmoor Relating to the Building of the Mausoleum at Castle Howard 1726–1742', *Walpole Society*, XIX (1930–31), pp. 111–64

White, Roger, *Nicholas Hawksmoor and the Replanning of Oxford* (London, 1997)

Wren, Christopher, *Parentalia: or Memoirs of the Family of the Wrens viz. of Mathew Bishop of Ely, Christopher Dean of Windsor, &c. but chiefly of Sir Christopher Wren, Late Surveyor-General of the Royal Buildings, President of the Royal Society, &c.* (London, 1750)

Young, Elizabeth, 'The Campaigns for Christ Church, Spitalfields and Nicholas Hawksmoor, 1960–1995', *Journal of Architectural Conservation*, II (July 1996), pp. 21–38
—, and Wayland Young, *Old London Churches* (London, 1956)

ACKNOWLEDGEMENTS

This is not the first book about the architect Nicholas Hawksmoor and it will certainly not be the last. It is, however, the only book that gives equal measure to both the creation of Hawksmoor's architecture in the late seventeenth and early eighteenth centuries and the ways he and his buildings have been evaluated since, right up to the present day. The existing scholarly literature on Hawksmoor, when and how it has arisen, is, therefore, part of this book's story and to which it is greatly in debt.

For those readers pursuing further detail, especially as to the basic chronology of Hawksmoor's key works, Kerry Downes's pioneering monograph of 1959 and also his second, smaller book for Thames & Hudson's World of Art series, should be the starting points. Further analysis, particularly of Hawksmoor's sources and of the contemporary theological context, can be found in Pierre de la Ruffinière du Prey's *Hawksmoor's London Churches* (2000) and Vaughan Hart's *Nicholas Hawksmoor: Rebuilding Ancient Wonders* (2002).

In light of the existing literature, the present book's concern in its first half is principally to offer several new interpretations of Hawksmoor's architecture. In this, it draws from two previous articles of mine: 'Hawksmoor and the Gothic', in *Gothic Legacies: Four Centuries of Tradition and Innovation in Art and Architecture* (2012) edited by Laura Cleaver and Ayla Lepine, and '"Mere Gothique heaps of stone"? Uses and Abuses of the "Gothic" in James Ralph's "Critical Review" (1734)' in the journal *Immediations* in 2010. My thanks to the editors of those two publications for their help in refining and offering greater clarity to my ideas.

The research for the second half of the book began in the preparation of a small exhibition, 'Nicholas Hawksmoor: Architect of the Imagination', which was shown at London's Royal Academy of Arts in 2012. My thanks are due to my colleagues, present and former, at the RA – MaryAnne Stevens, Kate Goodwin,

Jeremy Melvin – for giving me the opportunity to realize the exhibition that, in turn, has fed into *From the Shadows*.

I am also very grateful for those who agreed to allow me to interview them for this book: Colin Amery, Biba Dow and Alun Jones, Gordon Higgott, the late Lady Kennet, Red Mason, Jock McFadyen, Nicholas Serota, Alex Scott-Whitby, Gavin Stamp and Michael Wilford. The book has also benefited from the advice and assistance of Patricia Brown, Kerry Downes, Sam Jacob, Andrea Klettner, Alex Link, Alan Powers, Charles Saumarez Smith, Otto Saumarez Smith and Adam Waterton. My thanks are also due to Christine Stevenson, who first introduced me to Hawksmoor at the Courtauld, and, along with MaryAnne Stevens, very kindly wrote references for several funding applications related to *From the Shadows*. Financial support for illustrations was kindly provided by The Paul Mellon Centre for Studies in British Art and the Society of Architectural Historians of Great Britain.

Vivian Constantinopoulos at Reaktion saw the potential of the project at an early stage, and has expertly guided its progression from inception to completion. Gordon Higgott and Anthony Geraghty kindly read the initial typescript. The finished version is immeasurably better for their generous insights and expertise. Naturally, all remaining errors are wholly my own. My father, David Hopkins, read the book in, I think, every draft it went through. His advice and enthusiasm for the project (not to mention historical expertise) have been invaluable. Finally, I would like to thank Johanna Harding for her patience and constant support during the writing of this book and for being such wonderful company on many an architectural pilgrimage. This book is for her.

Photo
Acknowledgements

The author and publishers wish to express their thanks to the below sources of illustrative material and/or permission to reproduce it:

© The Architectural Association / F. R. Yerbury: p. 185; © the artist (Jock McFadyen): 270; © Hélène Binet: p. 16; The Bodleian Library, University of Oxford (ms.Top. Oxon.a.37* fol.ll): p. 42; © The British Library Board: p. 84 (k.Top.28.11.d), 98 (left) (k.Top.23.11.0); from the Castle Howard Archive, reproduced by kind permission of the Howard family: pp. 128, 131; reproduced by permission of the Chapter of St Paul's Cathedral (London Metropolitan Archives): pp. 36, 37; The Courtauld Institute of Art, London (Conway Library): pp. 48, 92, 95, 218 (photograph by A. F. Kersting); © Dean and Chapter of Westminster: pp. 98 (right), 103; © Dow Jones Architects: p. 286; © Electric Egg/Roland Collins: p. 257; reproduced by permission of English Heritage: pp. 76, 109; © English Heritage (Aerofilms Collection): p. 201; reproduced by permission of English Heritage and the Howard family: p. 129; © Nigel Green: pp. 70–71; © Guardian News & Media Ltd, 1961: p. 213; Guildhall Art Gallery, City of London: p. 167; Guildhall Library, City of London: pp. 117, 244; © Owen Hopkins: pp. 8, 40, 44, 45, 46, 50, 67, 74, 75, 78–9, 80, 83, 85, 86, 96, 97, 106, 138–9, 145, 148, 149, 150, 151, 152, 169, 177, 184, 234, 246, 254, 271, 287; © Imperial War Museum (D 1511): p. 242; Don Kalant, uic School of Architecture Advanced Studio, 2013: p. 289; Lambeth Palace Library: p. 82; London Metropolitan Archives, City of London: p. 105; Herbert Mason/Daily Mail/Solo Syndication: p. 199; © Museum of London: p. 243; riba Library Photographs Collection: pp. 28, 53 (photo Edwin Smith), 113, 116, 146 (right), 162, 164, 168, 277; the Provost and Fellows of Worcester College, Oxford: p. 90; © Royal Academy of Arts, London: pp. 6, 119, 126; © The Samuel Courtauld Trust, The Courtauld Gallery, London: pp. 43; © David Secombe: 147 (left), 183 (right); © Tate, London 2015: pp. 147

(right) (© The Piper Estate/DACS 2015), 160, 161, 272 (the artist, Leon Kossoff); courtesy of and © Transport for London: p. 183 (left); © Transport for London, from the London Transport Museum collection: pp. 146 (left), 200; by courtesy of the Trustees of Sir John Soane's Museum, London: pp. 114, 158; © UK Government Art Collection/Anthony Eyton: p. 259; © Victoria & Albert Museum, London: p. 163; The Warden and Fellows of All Souls College, Oxford: pp. 33 (AS II.13), 35 (AS II.29), 38 (AS IV.84), 39 (AS IV.33), 91, 99 (AS IV.46), 110–11 (AS I.7), 240; courtesy of Whitechapel Gallery, Whitechapel Gallery Archive: p. 228.

INDEX